THE RISE OF THE
FRENCH NOVEL

MARIVAUX   CRÈBILLON *FILS*   ROUSSEAU
STENDHAL   FLAUBERT   ALAIN–FOURNIER
RAYMOND RADIGUET

BY
MARTIN TURNELL

A NEW DIRECTIONS BOOK

First published clothbound and as New Directions Paperbook 474 in 1978

Library of Congress Cataloging in Publication Data

Turnell, Martin.
   The rise of the French novel.
   (A New Directions Book)
   Bibliography: p. 297
   Includes index.
   1. French fiction—History and criticism.
I. Title.
PQ631.T83   843'.03   77–26792
ISBN 0–8112–0688–2
ISBN 0-8112-0716-1 pbk.

New Directions Books are published for James Laughlin
by New Directions Publishing Corporation,
333 Sixth Avenue, New York 10014

CONTENTS

FOREWORD

THERE ARE few great writers who have escaped serious criticism at one time or another and have lost their popularity for periods either during their lives or after their deaths. This applies particularly to eighteenth-century French novelists. Marivaux's popularity as a novelist and dramatist fell in his later years. Crébillon *fils* was popular during his lifetime, but fell badly in the next century. The same or much the same has happened to Rousseau, whom I regard with Choderlos de Laclos as one of the two greatest French novelists of the eighteenth century.

Able French critics have been busy during recent years restoring all three writers, but those writers have never had their full due in the English speaking world. This applies particularly to Crébillon *fils* and Rousseau. In his own country Crébillon had to wait until 1959 for *Les Egarements du coeur et de l'esprit,* his one undoubtedly great novel, to be republished for the first time since his death in 1777 and there was no translation at all of it in English until 1963. Although Rousseau's *Julie ou La Nouvelle Héloise* is his greatest imaginative work, it has been obscured by the preference for his *Confessions* and even for his works of social and political criticism. What I have tried to emphasize is that the work of all three novelists, including some of the lesser works of Crébillon *fils,* deserve to be a good deal more widely read and enjoyed.

Although the seven novelists dealt with in this study are divided between the eighteenth, nineteenth and twentieth centuries, they all deal in their different ways with the same principal subjects. The two main subjects are love and social criticism. With the sole exception of an apparently short marriage between an elderly lady (who was soon to die) and a youth thirty years her junior in Marivaux's *Le Paysan parvenu,* all the love affairs end unhappily with no marriage between the couples who are really in love with one another. The kind of love belongs to all the known ways. Some of the lovers are highly chaste and others the reverse. In Rousseau there is lovemaking followed by the lovers being prevented from marriage by the girl's father and a return to chastity which ends in tragedy. There is no real chastity in Flaubert's heroine any more than in the couple in Radiguet's *Le Diable au corps,* which also ends in tragedy, and in *Le Bal du comte d'Orgel* chastity leads only to unhappiness.

What needs to be emphasized is that in spite of a lack of chastity on the part of the protagonists in most of the novels, there is nothing obscene about them and no attempt to approve of illicit love-making on the part of novelists.

With the exception of Alain-Fournier's *Le Grand Meaulnes*, all the novelists are concerned in varying degrees with criticism of contemporary society. Marivaux confines his criticism to sections of society which oppose the proposed marriages of his protagonists and his strong feeling against what he regards as spurious religious devotion. One of the severest and furthest reaching criticisms is Crébillon *fils's Les Egarements du coeur et de l'esprit*. There is considerable variation in Rousseau, who comes down heavily on smart society in Paris and produces, as we shall see, a utopia in the second half of the novel which makes him the most positive student of society among all these novelists. Stendhal is naturally a good deal less impressive in *Lamiel* than in his three major novels, but it is clear that in this work, as in the others, the society which he sees is rejected completely. Flaubert is naturally concerned with provincial society, but somehow his criticism gives the impression of an exposure of all contemporary society. Radiguet deals with the middle and lower middle class in *Le Diable au corps* and something like high society in *Le Bal du comte d'Orgel* and none of them comes out well.

What deserves special emphasis is that, in spite of the important technical developments which have taken place since the eighteenth century, none of the novels discussed here are out of date, that none of the faults of individuals and society have disappeared in our deplorable world, and that many of the faults are treated with more indulgence than they were in the past.

With the exception of Crébillon *fils* and Rousseau, the studies of all the other novelists in the present work contain some of the material which has been used in contributions to *The Times Literary Supplement, Cornhill Magazine, Scrutiny, Southern Review, Sewanee Review, Commonweal* and *Twentieth Century Views* and I am indebted to the publishers for allowing the material to be used here.

M.T.

FROM MARIVAUX TO RAYMOND RADIGUET

FROM MARIVAUX TO RAYMOND RADIGUET

1

ALTHOUGH the seventeenth century produced a large number of works of fiction and though they appear to have been widely read and apparently enjoyed, it is clear that in many respects the French novel could not yet be regarded as a true literary form. The writers were not without talent but their works, as we can see from the practice of Honoré d'Urfé and Madeleine de Scudéry, often consisted of lengthy collections of adventure and love stories which today are found unreadable and a serious burden for literary historians. The plot was used to introduce them and link them together, but there were no compelling relations between them or with the main plot, which meant that the novel was usually lacking in a unified experience.

The main problem was that instead of being a collection of miscellaneous entertainments, the novel had to become the vehicle for a compelling imaginative experience and the novelists had to find an effective method of expressing it, which meant that it had in a prosaic sense to be convincing.

In spite of the fact that the novel as a whole did not achieve its complete supremacy until the nineteenth century and though it is only in our own time that the eighteenth-century novel has been appreciated to the full, this should not blind us to the fact of one of the major events of the eighteenth century, which was the rise of the French novel, which came to replace drama and poetry as the outstanding literary achievement of the period, or that though full recognition was not without difficulties and complications the century produced a number of great works in the form of the novel.

There is a distinction to be drawn between invention and development. It would naturally be a complete error to assume that all the different periods of the novel are completely separate and have nothing to do with one another. It is clear that whatever its shortcomings, every literary period has some influence on the periods which follow. This leads to a definition of the concept of influence.

The term is complex and has three principal meanings. A creative writer usually begins by borrowing the techniques of his predecessors even if it produces something like a caricature, as we shall see presently. When he grows to maturity, he tends to modify the techniques that he has borrowed from his predecessors and to adapt them to his own originality. The third meaning is less precise, but in its way is easier to follow. The success of the masters of one period is a matter of inspiration. It awakens the creative instinct of prospective writers and fills them with the ambition to match or even to exceed the success of their predecessors by inventing new methods of communication, with the result that they often react strongly against the methods of their predecessors and finally reject them almost completely.

This prompts us to take a look at the seventeenth and eighteenth centuries. We have seen that one of the commonest seventeenth-century practices was to incorporate a collection of side stories in the main work. It had of course been greatly used by Cervantes in *Don Quixote* and was a major influence on his seventeenth-century successors in France. It turns up in the early novels of Marivaux. In *Pharsamon* (significantly subtitled *ou Les Nouvelles Folies romanesques*), the sight of the protagonist and his servant riding round the area in which they live and in which they have adventures, is deliberately something like a caricature of the practice of Cervantes. What is much more important is the use that Diderot made of it in *Jacques le fataliste*. It is a comic novel, but not a caricature. The captain and his servant, Jacques, ride round the country; most of the work is a dialogue between the two of them and others, but the novel is used very effectively as a picture of contemporary society. Diderot's handling of form in this and his other novels prompted Henri Coulet, one of the great authorities on the history of the French novel, to describe him as 'the first of our modern novelists because he has an intuition of true life and the feeling of the relations which link every event to the whole world and each of man's existence to human society'.[1]

[1] *Le Roman jusqu'à la Révolution*, Tome I, 1967, p. 517.

Although the view that the modern novel was born in the eighteenth century is largely true, it is right to emphasize that *La Princesse de Clèves* provides something like an exception, that it is not merely the greatest French novel of its century, but has some grounds for being described as the first modern novel. It is at once an example of what I have called a compelling imaginative experience, a remarkably penetrating exposure of court life under Louis XIV and a considerable technical triumph. In short, *La Princesse de Clèves* is a brilliant example of the blending of experience and the technique which conveys it. What needs emphasis is that though there are several stories about characters other than the protagonists in the novel, they are not in any way mere additions, as they are in most seventeenth-century novels: they have a direct bearing on the main experience, which is that in life love is pure tragedy, and in this way they have an important bearing on the heroine's experience. We should also anticipate by saying that Mme de La Fayette's disguising of the reign of Louis XIV as sixteenth-century court life and the mixing of imaginary and real characters was to have an important influence on the novels to come.

The inference which emerges is that in the work of major novelists, technique is part of the creative experience and that in various ways it makes the experience more convincing—a word that needs emphasis, as we shall see, in view of the situation in France in the eighteenth century, when novelists were faced with the highbrow refusal to recognise that their work was a genuine art form.[1]

2

The way in which the novelists tackled the problem was an important contribution to their work's development. They had

---

[1] It is important to observe that the hostility was largely confined to critics and officials. The novels of Marivaux, Prévost, Rousseau and plenty of other novelists were decidedly popular with the reading public. Marivaux's *Le Paysan parvenu*, for example, had more than twenty editions in the eighteenth century besides being translated into Dutch, English, German and Italian. We also know that the hostility of officials led to a delay of three years before *La Vie de Marianne* began publication and that parts of it like the work of other novelists had to be published in Holland.

to break with the heroic style which had dominated the seventeenth-century novel, bring it down to earth and make use of a contemporary, or near contemporary setting in order to make it more convincing to the reader. This led not exactly to three technical innovations, but to three important developments. They were the epistolary novel, the novel in the form of memoirs and the use of the autobiographical novel.

Although there are important variations in the methods used by the novelists, the principal merit of the epistolary novel is its *immediacy*. The letters are written, or purport to be written, for the most part at critical stages in the development of the experience of the novel. This means that the letter writers in the novels take a direct look at their feelings and the situation in which they find themselves at the moment of writing: their feelings for the correspondent to whom the letter is addressed, their hopes and fears based on other people's feelings, or the turn which events are taking or appear to be taking. The strength of the feelings expressed in this way naturally has a considerable effect on the reader, makes the work seem more moving and more convincing.

The main variations or differences to which I referred are the novels which only contain the letters written by a single character and those which contain letters, or rather exchanges of letters, between a number of different correspondents. It is apparent that in most of the novels of the first kind the writer receives replies from the person to whom the letters are addressed—it is usually in these cases a woman writing to a male lover—and though we never see them we are told what line they are taking. The Chevalier de Guilleragues' *Lettres portugaises,* published anonymously in 1669, is a good example. It is rightly regarded as one of the great epistolary novels. It consists of only five letters written by the Portuguese nun to her lover—a soldier who has deserted her and moved to a distant part of the country. Although it seems that there are responses to some of her five letters, the author not only avoids reproducing them, but we are told nothing about their content. The reason is evident from the wording of the nun's own letters. She realises from the first that she has been deserted and though she reproaches the lover, she knows that there is no possibility of his repentance. What emerges is that the aims of the letters are not to change events, but simply to give vent to the nun's own feelings:

> I felt that you were less dear to me than my passion ... I write more for me than for you ... it seems to me that I speak to you when I write to you, and that you are a little closer to me.

We can see from this that the letter writing is something like a subjective process, that it gives vent to the unhappy writer's feelings without making any serious attempt to deal in a practical way with life: she knows from the start that she is lost and simply meditates on it.

Lettres portugaises should be compared to Crébillon *fils's Les Lettres de la Marquise de M * * * au Comte de R * * *,* which has been rightly applauded as one of the outstanding epistolary novels of the eighteenth century. Once again the marquise's letters are the only ones we see. Yet in their way they are not only longer, but cover a much wider experience. The marquise is married to an unfaithful husband to whom her marriage was probably no more than a marriage of convenience without much in the way of love on either side. The count lays siege to her. Although she knows that her husband is unfaithful, she is determined to remain virtuous and to be no more than a friend to the count. The letters reveal that in spite of herself she falls in love with him and becomes his mistress. Her references to his letters show that he turns out to be no more than a *libertin,* and that once she has fallen, he begins characteristically to lose interest in her and to look round for other women as replacements because the novelty of sexual experience is the *libertin's* main interest in life. The tragedy is revealed in the later letters: the count ceases to reply and when the marquise learns that she has got to depart to a distant country where her husband has been made ambassador, she dies of a broken heart. The great merit of the work is that with the use of a single writer it gives a brilliant picture of the noble woman's tragedy.

There is one other difference between these two novels. Although the main theme in both, or rather the only theme in the *Lettres portugaises,* is the tragedy of an abandoned woman, Crébillon manages to add to the colour by giving us some

glimpses of the society in which the marquise is living and re-
counts the affairs not only of her husband, but of one or two
others in a way which fits in well with the main theme. It looks
forward to an important change of method. Samuel Richardson
was the inventor of the epistolary novel with a number of correspondents and thanks to Prévost's translations they had a
decisive influence, which enabled Rousseau and Laclos to produce *La Nouvelle Héloïse* and the *Liaisons dangereuses,* which
are undoubtedly the two greatest epistolary novels of the century. Rousseau's novel, as we shall see, discusses or rather ex-
plores at much greater length and much more widely than
Laclos' the short-comings of contemporary society and even
tries to picture a sort of miniature utopia in the second half of
the work. Perhaps the most remarkable thing about the *Liaisons dangereuses,* which distinguishes it from any other epistolary novel, is the extraordinary varieties of style that we find
in the letters of the different correspondents. It is not simply
what they say that counts, but the *tone* in which they say it.
The result is that we have the impression that we are continually listening to a number of different voices, and it is this more
than anything else which makes it one of the most compelling
novels of the century. One feels inclined to add that it is a sign
of Laclos' exceptional originality because in some respects the
device is even more effective than conversations in novels with
an omniscient narrator.

The suggestion has been made that the 'memoir-novel cannot
be distinguished, in the manner of presentation, from an authentic autobiography'.[1] This calls for certain reservations.
We know that there were plenty of autobiographical novels in
the eighteenth century. They include Lesage's *Gil Blas* and all
Prévost's works of fiction except his two historical novels. Nor
should we overlook the fact that in many of the earlier novels
from Cervantes onwards and including *Gil Blas* the inserted
stories by lesser characters are nearly all pieces of autobiography. Although on the surface the difference between the autobiographical and the memoir-novel appears slender enough,
it was not for nothing that Marivaux went out of his way to
emphasize that *La Vie de Marianne* was a work of memoirs.

[1] Vivienne Mylne, *The Eighteenth-century Novel,* 1969, p. 133.

One of the most important things about the memoir-novel has been well defined by Jean Rousset, who attributes it to what he calls the *double registre*.[1] It means that the novelist places special emphasis on something like a twofold view of experience. The vivid description of what happened to the principal character and the feelings that it provoked when he or she was young is subjected to a critical commentary by the mature person when the time comes to write the memoirs, which is a little different from the attitude adopted in the autobiographical novel. The double view is naturally brought out with particular strength in Marivaux's *La Vie de Marianne* and Crébillon's *Egarements du coeur et de l'esprit*. It is, indeed, the critical view of the protagonists' early experience and the part it played in the development of life that explains the emphasis placed on 'memoirs' as distinct from autobiography where we do not find the same striking difference between the two periods of the protagonist.

I suggested earlier that one of the problems which faced the eighteenth-century novelists was to make their work convincing in a way in which most of the seventeenth-century novels were not. We can go further than this and say that the aim of the three major techniques discussed was to encourage the reader's 'willing suspension of disbelief'.

This invites us to take another look at Mme de La Fayette. In a letter to Lescheraine she said of *La Princesse de Clèves*:

> There is nothing romantic or ambitious about it. Therefore it is not a novel. It is properly speaking memoirs and from what I am told this was the original title of the book, but it has been changed . . .

Roger Francillon, author of one of the most penetrating of recent studies of Mme de La Fayette, takes a different, but equally illuminating view of her work as a whole:

> *La Vie de la Princesse d'Angleterre* is not only a precious document for historians: it is the novel of the loves of Henriette and it is with the romantic vision that it was conceived.[2]

---

[1] *Forme et signification*, 1962, pp. 45–64.
[2] *L'Oeuvre romanesque de Madame de La Fayette*, 1974, p. 45.

The novelist's description of her greatest novel as 'memoirs' and the critic's suggestion that the method which she used in her biography of Henriette d'Angleterre is the method of the novelist bring out an important connection between works of fiction and other forms of writing. The successful novel is essentially an imaginative experience. In many cases, which include Constant's *Adolphe* or, in our own time, Alain-Fournier's *Le Grand Meaulnes* and Radiguet's *Le Diable au corps,* this does not exclude genuine autobiographical elements in the author's life. In the same way, it is frequently a picture or a critical view of the society in which the novelist is living. This explains the eighteenth-century novelists' use of their different methods. They presented their works in the form of documents, 'letters', 'memoirs' and 'autobiographies' not only to make them appear more convincing, but to overcome the widespread prejudice against the novel on the part of critics and officials, to which I have drawn attention, and to capture the reading public, which they did. The novels, as we shall see, were usually vigorous social criticism. This explains the setting. The novelists were determined to have their say about society, but in order to avoid trouble they concentrated on the method of presentation. I have spoken of the way in which Mme de La Fayette disguised the age of Louis XIV as the sixteenth century. Lesage adopted a similar device in *Gil Blas,* but went further. The change of period was accompanied by a change of country. The setting is supposedly Spain in the first quarter or rather beyond of the seventeenth century. Although he had never actually been to Spain, the setting strikes one as convincing. Like Mme de La Fayette he actually introduces people who lived in his own age and who include not only public figures, but writers. His pungent criticisms of society may well have applied to Spain, but we know that his real target was French society. We find that under pretended Spanish names Mme de Lambert and Mme de Tencin, who were famous for their salons, turn up in the novel as they were to do again in Marivaux's *Vie de Marianne,* though in comparison with Marivaux, we see very little of them and there were plenty of other French people who are much less easy to recognise today. This explains one other device. We observe that *La Vie de Marianne* was supposed to be memoirs written when the heroine was an old lady and to deal therefore with the past. The main reason was to avoid accusations of something like libels about living people. The safeguard did not always work as we shall see when we come to Crébillon *fils's L'Ecumoire,* in which not even an imaginary foreign country as the setting saved the novelist from a brief imprisonment.

There was, as we know, one other device or rather trick to make the novels more convincing and probably to protect the writer from prosecution. It was the pretence that the letters and memoirs were genuine documents which had turned up unexpectedly after the deaths of the narrators in a drawer or something of that sort. On a number of occasions it was heavily emphasised in a foreword by an imaginary editor of a novel which made its first appearance anonymously. Examples which at once come to mind are Crébillon *fils,* Rousseau and Laclos. Crébillon and Rousseau were categoric. 'This book', each of them said, 'is not a novel'. What is of particular interest is that many readers took Rousseau at his word and were apparently convinced that *La Nouvelle Héloïse* was a collection of genuine letters written by real people to one another!

We can see from this that one of the novelists' most important aims was to make the novel convincing and that it emphasised the realistic side of life. It was one of the main differences between the appeal of the novel and classical drama, or rather classical tragedy, in which the overwhelming appeal was the result of poetry and vision. We can also see that in spite of their many virtues, the novels were not without limitations and even improbabilities. For this reason the expression 'willing suspension of disbelief' is preferable in the present context to 'convincing'. It means that in order to enjoy the novel readers were ready enough to avoid noticing what might be described as reasonable limitations and improbabilities. This applies equally to the epistolary, memoir and autobiographical novel, which are all restricted to a single narrator. It means that however acute he is, the narrator can only see his own feelings from within. Marivaux went to some lengths to enable the narrator to read the minds of his or her fellow characters in his two great novels, which clearly shows that the novelist himself is taking care to help the supposed narrator to do his job. Two of the most obvious examples of this particular limitation are provided by Prévost.

We know that *Manon Lescaut* was a late addition to the *Mémoires et aventures d'un homme de qualité* and that the entire story purports to be the autobiography of Des Grieux, which he relates in full to the 'homme de qualité', who seems to meet him by chance at the most important or most convenient times in the adventure. What strikes us most about the account of the love affair is that Manon herself remains something of a mystery to us simply because we never have an inside view of her even at the moment of her least defensible actions. The mystery is still more striking in the heroine of *Histoire d'une Grecque moderne*. It seems clear that she does not respond to the love of her admirer, but we never have any idea of her real feelings, nor do we know any more than himself—the examination of her empty bed is the outstanding example—whether she has fallen for a different lover.

I have mentioned the great impressiveness of the insight into the letter writer's feelings in Crébillon's *Les Lettres de la Marquise de M*, but though it is clear from her references to her lover's unseen letters that he is one of those male and basically uninteresting *libertins* of the age, the absence of his letters is clearly a limitation on the work. It is brought out when we compare it with *La Nouvelle Héloïse,* in which not only the protagonists, but all the letter writers give full scope to their thoughts and feelings. This does not blind us to the improbability of two young people writing letters of great length to one another at a time when they are still living in the same house. The fact that more readers seem to have believed that the letters were genuine in this rather than in any other novel of the period underlines what I have said about the 'willing suspension of disbelief'. We should also observe that in the *Liaisons dangereuses* the two ruthless protagonists manage characteristically to see virtually all the letters of the other correspondents, which adds considerably to the dramatic force of this superb novel.

One of the most obvious improbabilities in the memoir and autobiographical novels is the prodigious power of memory attributed to many of the characters. It applies particularly to the numerous incorporated stories or *récits* in Lesage's *Gil Blas,* which was admittedly an early eighteenth-century novel and began publication in 1715. We find that the different narrators tell the stories of their lives in completely formal and correct style; that they have no difficulty in repeating word for word dialogues that they are supposed to have had with other people and on occasion can even quote word for word a letter written a long time earlier without having the text in their possession. This is clearly the way in which the novelist, as I said of Marivaux, plays his anonymous part in all the different styles of the novel.

There are two other novels which invite attention. Robert Chasles' *Les Illustres Françoises* was first published anonymously in Holland in 1713. It became a decidedly popular work in the eighteenth century and it is believed that it went into a total of twenty editions which were all anonymous. The last of them appeared in 1780, but in spite of its early popularity it was not republished again until 1959 except for a volume containing two of its parts in 1927, while translations appear to have been limited to one in English and one in German in 1727 and 1728. After the long period of neglect it is now being praised by critics as one of the most important novels of the eighteenth century.

Les Illustres Françoises is a collection of seven stories. Four of them are autobiographical and five of them are related to a group of people. They all deal with marriages and love affairs. There are happy marriages, unfortunate marriages, marriages opposed by hostile parents, leading in one case to the death of a daughter on the day of the birth of her only child, unfaithfulness on the part of one wife who commits suicide, and on the part of husbands and fiancés.

The relation of the stories may remind us of the method of the seventeenth-century works which continued in some cases, as we have seen, in the eighteenth century, but there are important changes in spite of the fact that the last two stories both run to well over a hundred pages and each of them is related to the group at a single meeting. All the speakers appear as characters in the novel as a whole. Some of them are personal friends and occasionally add information to one another's love stories. The members of the listening group, in which there are only a few small changes, know one another and a considerable portion of them can equally be regarded as characters in the novel, which is underlined by the fact that after each story they give their verdict and assess the penalties in so far as they have the power. The result of all this is that the novel possesses the unity which was lacking in the works of many of Chasles' predecessors as well as in *Gil Blas,* mentioned above. The other important qualities are the way in which the love affairs are clearly related in a personal way to society and the skill with which the characters of women are drawn and which is emphasised in the novel's title. It follows from this that Chasles is believed to have influenced not only Prévost and Marivaux, but even Samuel Richardson, and that his novel has been described as 'one of the most original novels of the eighteenth century' and as 'deliberately opening the way to the modern novel'.[1]

The second novel which invites attention is Diderot's *La Religieuse.* It has been said that in it he combined the epistolary, memoir and autobiographical novel in a single work. This is clearly true. The novel, as we know, takes the form of an appeal by the runaway nun to the Marquis de Croismare in a single letter of prodigious length which occupies the entire work and in which she relates the history of her whole life in detail. More than almost any other single work it looks forward to what was to come, the widespread use of the omniscient narrator in the nineteenth century.

We can see that in spite of a good deal of the contemporary unpopularity of the novel and in spite of the slowness with which some of the leading eighteenth-century novelists have achieved full recognition, the period really did mark the rise of the French novel and that the outstanding eighteenth-century novelists were in most ways superior to their seventeenth-century predecessors. It was in a strict sense an age of development. The novelists, as I have pointed out, concentrated largely on three techniques in order to make their work more convincing and to promote a 'willing suspension of disbelief'. Although they were widely successful, there remain in many of them the improbabilities and the failure to achieve full insight into some of their leading characters. This means that in spite of their

---

[1] English Showalter, *The Evolution of the French Novel* 1641–1782, 1972, p. 212; *Les Illustres Françoises,* edited by Frédéric Deloffre, 3rd ed., 1973, p. xxxvi.

success, there were certain limitations which had to be overcome. This brings us to the nineteenth century.

3

Although the three forms of influence described earlier are visible in the eighteenth century, they are a good deal more striking in the nineteenth century.

The main ambition of the nineteenth-century novelists was to make their work more convincing than the work of their predecessors appeared to them and to enlarge the field of the novel enormously. Their reaction against the past therefore led to five major changes: the adoption of the omniscient narrator; the introduction of characters belonging to all classes of society; an emphasis on 'realism' or, more accurately, as we shall see, on what they took for 'realism'; and changes in language and technique.

Although it was in no sense a nineteenth-century invention and had been used by seventeenth-century novelists, with Mme de La Fayette as the outstanding example, the omniscient narrator was the most widespread general change. It was adopted for two main reasons: to make the novel more convincing and, most important of all, to carry to the fullest possible extent the scope of the novel. With regard to the first, it was no longer necessary to disguise fiction as memoirs, letters or autobiography in order to make it convincing to sceptical readers; the new generation of readers accepted the novel as a work of imagination and found a straight story by an omniscient narrator a good deal more convincing than the methods of the predecessors. It was clearly a reaction against the practice of the seventeenth- and to some extent of the eighteenth-century writers of filling their novels with a collection of *récits* by other characters which were only loosely related to the experience of the protagonists compared with the far tighter relations between the omniscient narrator and the characters generally. It is still more evident that the novelists themselves must have been aware that one of the most effective changes introduced by the omniscient narrator was to escape the limitations imposed on the three kinds of narrator generally employed by the eighteenth century. We have seen that two of Prévost's novels give the impression that the use of a single narrator in the person of the protagonist prevents a genuine insight into the mind and feelings of the heroine. Whatever the novelists' conscious views, they tried various ways of extending their insight by conversations between the narrator and other characters, which clearly looks forward to the future. It is illustrated, for example, by the dialogues in *Manon Lescaut* between Des Grieux and Tiberge, which reveal with great clarity the narrator's moral problems. For he is, so to speak, faced with a choice between two ways of life, represented by Manon, who is a woman of dubious morality, and his clerical friend. We shall find in due course that Crébillon *fils* made a far more extensive use of dialogue in his most important novel and did so in order to reveal the problems of the narrator, an immature young man who is trying to fit himself into society. The problems are well summarised by the novel's title: *Les Egarements du coeur et de l'esprit*.

I have said on various occasions that all major imaginative works contain something of a personal portrait of the creator even if it is divided among several of his characters and that this applies to French classical drama as well as to novels. For reasons which will presently be explained, it became decidedly marked in the eighteenth-century novels. It has been said with truth that in *La Vie de Marianne* there are times when we are aware that the memoir writer becomes something like a dual personality in revealing the novelist's own views and observations. A still more obvious example is to be found in Diderot's *La Religieuse*. In spite of the novelist's antireligious views, there is nothing which can be fairly described as antireligious in the novel, which explains why the Vatican never put it on the Index. It does, however, contain come perfectly legitimate criticisms of convent life in the eighteenth century, but when they are put into the mouth of the nun we are conscious at moments that it is Diderot's voice that we are hearing, that the critical views as distinct from her actual experience in her three convents were something that only the novelist could have made. We can go on to point out that in *La Nouvelle Héloïse* Rousseau put a good deal of himself in Saint-Preux and Wolmar and that there is even something of himself in Julie as well.

What emerges from this is that the novelists were in fact trying to extend their range and to do so without relying on conversations between the protagonists and others. It points to the way in which the nineteenth century was to develop in its own fashion. We can see that the cult of the omniscient narrator was not only designed to lead to a far greater range in the novel, which depended for success on the breadth of the novelist's experience, but enabled him to deal with the principal characters as fully as the first person narrator deals with himself. The nature of the development is illustrated by a comparison between Rousseau and Stendhal. The eighteenth-century protagonists were individualists who were often engaged in a battle with society in order to obtain what they felt was their due. It is clear, however, that they were essentially a product of the society in which they were living, that in spite of the clash between the protagonists and the father in the first part of *La Nouvelle Héloïse,* they were not trying to change society any more than Marivaux's Marianne or his Jacob: they were simply trying to win a happy life for themselves by overcoming what they simply regarded as unfair obstacles, which was the result of failings that were common to their society. It is significant that in spite of their obviously unfair treatment, an innate respectability leads to defeat, to a not entirely unsuccessful attempt to overcome their own objections, and for a time to a respectable life in a tiny section of society which is held up to the reader as a form of utopia.

Stendhal's attitude is as far removed from this as it could well be. I have insisted in other places that the protagonists of the three greatest novels are essentially 'outsiders'. They feel from the first that they are in an alien world to which they can never belong in the conventional sense, which explains why even in *Armance,* the first of his novels, the hero, who is not of the status of the heroes of the three great novels, is continually looking back to an earlier period into which he is convinced that he would have been able to fit himself perfectly happily. In *Le Rouge et le noir, Lucien Leuwen* and *La Chartreuse de Parme* the heroes are each born into different social classes— working, bourgeois and the nobility—and belong to different periods politically. Although the protagonists would like to transform society, the very fact that they all look back to what they regard as something like the great ages of civilisation shows that from the first they realise that they have no hope of doing so. This explains Stendhal's insistence on 'the happy few'. It may be the way in which he addresses himself to his readers, but it shows a desire for the formation of a small and favourable community. What is most striking of all is that, in its own way, his 'happy few' clearly remind us of Rousseau's picture of an imaginary utopia.

The characters' psychology naturally explains their attitude to their world and their ambitions. The result, as we can see from the tragic ending of the two finished novels, is something like a double failure from the protagonists' point of view: failure to find a right world for themselves or to achieve their ambitions in the world in which they are born. This does not alter the fact that it is precisely the originality of their psychology and the novelist's power of penetration that give the novels their immense appeal, at any rate to those of us who belong to 'the happy few'. It is this that makes him a unique novelist for us and at the same time reveals his relations between the novelists of the past and the future.

We can see from the development of the novel in the nineteenth and twentieth centuries that the influence clearly works, as I have already said, in two ways. There is the rejection of certain practices and the retention and improvement of others. It is illustrated not merely by the retention of the autobiographical novel and the virtual disappearance of both the memoir and epistolary novels, but by the way in which novelists nearly always continued to put something of themselves in varying degrees into their work. It is apparent in a comparison between Stendhal and Proust. In *La Chartreuse de Parme* we find that Fabrice and Mosca are both partial portraits of the novelist: one is a young man who will come to grief by the death of his lover (who has married or rather been married to another man), which drives him into abandoning his bishopric and becoming a monk, and the other an elderly man enjoying the equivalent of what Stendhal himself would like to have won. Proust's handling of narrator is naturally the most elaborate and the most complex technique of all. Although the novel is related in the first person and the narrator called 'Marcel', Proust went out of his way to emphasise that there was a difference between the narrator and himself, which is clearly a reference to the perspective of which we are conscious. This does not prevent a detailed account of Swann's disastrous love affair containing many scenes which the narrator could never have witnessed in spite of Swann's friendship with the family. The conclusion that we reach is that though there is a deliberate linking of Swann's affair with Odette and Marcel's with Albertine, they are not both partial portraits of the novelist, which is confined to Marcel. It follows that in spite of the death of Albertine, the downfall of Swann was used to emphasise the superiority of Marcel and, indeed, of the novelist himself, by drawing attention to Swann's failure to achieve his ambition as a writer. What we see therefore is the sort of modification of technique to which I have referred. Proust's novel is, in spite of his denial, partly autobiographical and partly the work of an omniscient narrator.

It is clear from what I have said that though the leading eighteenth-century novelists are extremely acute social critics, their criticism was confined, whatever the disguise used from Mme de La Fayette to Lesage and Marivaux, to contemporary society. Stendhal's choice of different political periods, the longing of the protagonists for a return to an earlier age, or something like its equivalent, and the different classes to which in the three novels they belong show already that the novelists wanted a wider range in which to operate. The change, when it came to the full, was very different and in spite of his remarkable ingenuities its source cannot be attributed to Stendhal.

What I have in mind is naturally the work of Balzac and Zola. We know that with occasional exceptions the eighteenth-century novels were confined to the upper classes. It is clearly true of the novels of Crébillon *fils,* but does not apply to anything like the same extent, for example, to Marivaux's. We shall see that there is a strong contrast between *La Vie de Marianne,* in which the principal characters are all upper class, and *Le Paysan parvenu,* which is the story, as the title indicates, of the success of a working-class youth who makes his way into the middle class. The particular achievement of Balzac and Zola in this respect is to have dealt with all the different social classes.

It was Walter Scott's historical novels which inspired Balzac with his conception of the *Comédie humaine.* It is an example of the way in which the influence of one writer prompts another writer to react against him and to produce a much more original work. In spite of the differences between their work, Balzac clearly had a decisive and direct influence on Zola. It is, indeed, impossible to believe that without the *Comédie humaine* we should ever have had *Les Rougon-Macquart.* Balzac's influence was not confined to his own compatriots. Although Pérez Galdós is the greatest Spanish novelist after Cervantes, the forty-six volumes of the *Episodios nacionales* are not among his finest works, but as with Zola it is impossible to believe that they would ever have been written without the example of the *Comédie humaine.*[1]

Although Balzac and Zola both deal with substantial periods of history, their works are not 'historical novels' in a conventional sense. This brings us to an important difference between the eighteenth and nineteenth centuries. The eighteenth-century novelists give little space to descriptions of landscapes, buildings and environment generally while their descriptions of the physical appearance of people are limited to general terms which do little more than record the characters' attraction or repulsion for one another. The nineteenth century went in the opposite direction. We know that its novelists give an enormous amount of space to detailed descriptions of environment and people. This explains the critics' insistence on 'realism' as one of the most important and convincing characteristics of the novel. Its aim was to avoid not only what they regarded as the improbabilities of the eighteenth-century novels, but to make the works far more convincing by situating them to a world which was, or at any rate would appear, familiar to the majority of readers.

Whether they realised it or not, it was not the only reason or the sole aim. The nineteenth century was an age of the decline of religious belief. It had begun on a large scale with the French Revolution, but was not in any way confined to France. The absence of belief in the supernatural inevitably prompted a belief in realism and naturalism which led the writers to concentrate on what can only be called materialism. It is evident in a pronouncement of Zola's. 'In spite of contradictions', he said in *Une Campagne,* 'the positivist Diderot is the true master of

---

[1] When he visited Paris for the first time in 1867 he came across Balzac's novels, and is believed to have read them all; the first volume of the *Episodios nacionales* was published in 1873.

Naturalism; he was the first to insist on exact truth in the theatre and the novel'. Although Zola also described Balzac as 'the
father of Naturalism', we find that a good many years before
his pronouncement, Baudelaire had taken a very different and
much more impressive view. 'I have often been astonished', he
said in his essay on Théophile Gautier, 'to find that Balzac owes
his great fame to the fact that he was taken for a realist; it has
always seemed to me that his chief merit was to be a visionary,
and a passionate visionary'.

Although Balzac was not an unbeliever and describes imaginary supernatural events in some of his novels, like *Ursule
Mirouët,* in which the heroine's dead godfather appears to her
in several dreams to expose the family's attempt to rob her of
the money that he has left her, it must be emphasised strongly
that there is nothing supernatural about 'vision' as it is being
discussed here. Baudelaire went on to suggest a right view by
saying of Balzac 'All his characters are endowed with the vital
ardour with which he himself was animated. All his novels are
as profoundly coloured as dreams'. Proust went a good deal
further in discussing 'vision' in general. 'Style for writers', he
said, 'as much as colour for painters, is a question not of technique, but of vision'. 'By man's art alone', he went on, 'we can
get outside ourselves, discover what another person sees of this
world which is not the same as ours . . . Thanks to art, instead
of seeing a single world, which is our own, we see it multiply
itself, and, as many original artists as there are, we have the
same number of worlds at our disposition, more different from
one another than those which roll in the infinite . . .' [1] What
this really means is that different writers give different views of
the same world, or in other words display different 'visions' of
this world. It follows from this that so far as novelists are concerned, 'realism' and 'vision' are not contradictions, but are
very effective supporters of one another. 'Vision' is the means of
achieving a true view of the variety of life and is responsible for
the particular attraction of both Balzac and Zola. Instead of
simply encouraging realism, the decline in religious belief led
to an attempt to plunge more deeply into human nature in the
hope of reaching the ultimate truth about life without relying

[1] *A la Recherche du temps perdu,* Pléiade, III, pp. 895–96.

on the supernatural. It is reflected even more obviously in the poets than in the novelists. It is apparent in the emphasis of the Symbolists, who naturally had no interest in realism, on vision, leading in our own time to Valéry, who claimed that his aim was to achieve the union of a number of different selves which were supposed to exist in him and to reach what he called 'the universal Self', which was his nonreligious conception of the ultimate truth of life. The extreme was reached in the invention of Surrealism, which for one critic was anticipated by a poem of Tristan Corbière's called 'Litanies du sommeil'.[1]

What emerges from what has already been said is that we find in the work of Balzac and Zola more clearly than in any other nineteenth-century novelists the combination of realism and vision which played a major role in their achievement. It is easily assumed that Balzac's discovery of the 'reappearing character' (which incidentally was to have a valuable influence on Galdós's major novels) was something like a lucky find. He himself took a somewhat different view. It was this discovery that in the spring of 1833 sent him bursting into his sister's home and saying breathlessly: 'Saluez-moi, car je suis tout bonnement en train de devenir un génie'.[2] In short, without using the term, he regarded his discovery as an element of vision which was to prove a vast help in the presentation of French life and led to an immediate revision of parts of novels already published. It was later endorsed by Proust, who described it as an 'admirable invention . . . un rayon détaché du fond de l'oeuvre, passant sur toute une vie',[3] which is an excellent description of what I regard as *secular* vision. For it was precisely this discovery which was a major addition to the concept of vision and gives his work a unity which would otherwise have been lacking.

The nature of vision becomes still clearer if we take a look at the three divisions of the *Comédie humaine*: 'Studies of Manners', 'Philosophical Studies' and 'Analytical Studies'. The 'Analytical Studies' contain his only two treatises (as distinct from novels) on marriage; the 'Philosophical Studies' consist mainly

---

1 André Breton: *Anthologie de l'humour noir*, 1940, pp. 121–23.

2 'Salute me, for I am simply in the process of becoming a genius'.

3 'admirable invention . . . a beam detached from the bottom of the work, passing over the whole of a life'.

of occult works of fiction which though not among his greatest achievements are an important indication of the way in which vision was developed. 'Studies in Manners' is naturally by far the largest and most important of the three groups. It deals with scenes from private life, provincial life, Parisian life, political life and country life, while the sixth section called, 'Scenes from Military Life', was planned, but never written. These divisions naturally recall Proust's views on the true way of seeing life and the function of the artist. We can see in fact that Balzac's divisions of his work not only show the wide scope of his view of human life, but emphasise the nature of his personal vision. For it is only by looking at all or nearly all the different sides of life—summed up in the use of *La Comédie humaine* as the general title of his work—that the novelist achieves a vision of life as a whole and manages to combine 'realism' and 'vision' in the way suggested.[1]

Although Balzac is naturally the greater novelist, Zola is in some ways the earlier of the two novelists to illustrate the effects of 'vision'. In spite of his pretence that 'naturalism' was a purely scientific approach which presented an even more exact picture of life than 'realism', his greatness really depends on the way in which imagination transcended the scientific approach and produced 'vision'. His vision appears in many scenes which might almost appear incidental, like the remarkable vision of the great store in *Au Bonheur des dames,* the machines in *Germinal* or the more striking examples in which he deliberately set out to present a naturalist view of some of the principal Christian dogmas in novels like *La Fortune des Rougon, La Faute de l'abbé Mouret* and *Le Docteur Pascal.* Yet as with Balzac, vision is most impressive in the picture of life as a whole. It is, as I have already observed elsewhere, 'his picture of a doomed world going down to destruction in flame, smoke and ashes which gives his most memorable pages their sulphurous visionary quality'.[2]

It is important to emphasize the special originality of nineteenth-century vision, which is most apparent in the way that Balzac and Zola deal with the whole of life in a substan-

---

[1] Balzac no doubt chose his general title in contrast to Dante's *Divina Commedia.*

[2] *The Art of French Fiction,* p. 94.

tial period of the history of their country. It means that though in some ways they are not such impressive creators of character as the greatest eighteenth-century novelists their vision goes deeper and is more far-reaching than either the insight or the imagination of their predecessors. The way in which it absorbed them is illustrated by two incidents in Balzac's life. After commiserating in a decidedly perfunctory manner with a friend who had just lost his father, the novelist said: 'Let us return to reality. Whom will Eugénie Grandet [the heroine of the novel of that name] marry?' When Balzac himself was on his deathbed, he constantly cried out: 'Send for Bianchon [the famous doctor of the *Comédie humaine*]. He can save me'. This shows that the novelist was completely absorbed by his most important literary gift, which had become part of his everyday life.

Although the omniscient narrator was not a nineteenth-century invention, it was clearly the century's most widespread single change, but there are many other technical changes of varying importance. I do not propose to discuss them in detail here, but a word must be said about one of the most striking, which is to be found in Flaubert. I once described him as a 'great literary engineer rather than a great novelist'.[1] It was admittedly a controversial statement, but its aim was not to depreciate the writer so much as to insist on his immense technical accomplishment. It is clear, as I have insisted here, that technique and vision must be seen as a combination in novelists of real standing. With this in mind I came to describe Flaubert later as 'the greatest virtuoso who ever practised prose fiction'.[2] What is most striking, as we shall see in the chapter on Flaubert and the cinema, is his use of symbolism, which provides his particular kind of fiction with the tightest form of internal unity, distinguishing it from Balzac's aim, which was to give a special form of unity to his vision of an age. This again does not mean that symbolism in the novel was a complete nineteenth-century discovery any more than the omniscient narrator. We shall see that Rousseau's use of the 'veil' in *La Nouvelle Héloïse* is an important example of it and that it plays a valuable part in the novel, but in Flaubert it is used

[1] *The Novel in France*, p. 216.   [2] *The Art of French Fiction*, p. 7.

like other nineteenth-century changes much more widely and much more systematically. The result is that it becomes the absolute basis of the unity of his novels through the combined relations between the various symbols, which will naturally be related to 'montage' in film.

In spite of the fact that I once described Flaubert as 'the greatest virtuoso who ever practiced prose fiction', it must be admitted that this not only applies to the nineteenth-century novelists. The one French novelist to whom it applies absolutely is naturally Proust. I have described *A la Recherche du temps perdu* as a novel which was completely unlike anything anyone had ever dreamed of before him: a singular combination of memoirs, autobiography, fiction and criticism. For what we find in the novel is a combination and development of virtually all the techniques which had been used by his predecessors. It is reflected by his own description of the novel in different places as 'the memoirs of Saint-Simon of another period' and 'the story of an invisible vocation'. The expression 'invisible vocation' naturally underlines the originality of his conception of the novel and the experience that he sets out to communicate to the reader. One of the most striking qualities of his novel is his particular use of 'vision'. He was like the Symbolist poets determined to reach what both Rimbaud and he himself described as *la vraie vie*. It is apparent in the incidents of the *madeleine,* the uneven paving stones, the three spires and the starched tower. What is remarkable is that 'vision' has times of failure and success, but that in the end it can be seen, as we know from the astonishing incident of the *madeleine,* to have played the most important part of all in the communication of his highly original experience, which is too complicated to summarise in a few lines and can only be fully brought out by a detailed study of every aspect of what must be called his supreme novel.

The many technical changes which took place in the nineteenth century are naturally closely associated with the changes or rather the expansion of language. I have discussed the expansion of language in some detail in another place and it is only necessary in considering the rise of the French novel to give a brief summary here.[1]

[1] *The Art of French Fiction,* pp. 15–29.

The language used in the eighteenth-century novel was an admirable instrument for the analysis of the emotional states of the characters, but the field in which it could operate was necessarily a narrow one which reflects the restrictions imposed by the classical period primarily in its drama. The nature of the change is well explained by a pronouncement of Proust's which I quoted in discussing 'vision'. It was 'thanks to art', he said, that 'instead of seeing a single world, which is our own, we see it multiply itself, and, as many original artists as there are, we have the same number of worlds at our disposition'. This means that at times there are different languages for each of the worlds which Proust attributes to the different writers.

We know that the upheaval caused by the French Revolution and the Romantic movement created conditions which were a prerequirement for expansion: they removed the restrictions which had been remorselessly imposed by the seventeenth century but with few exceptions lasted all through the eighteenth century and, as we shall see presently, even into the first part of the nineteenth century. The machine age, the Industrial Revolution and the growth of science led to the invention of new words in all languages because they pointed to an expansion of the world. The changes in France went much deeper than in other countries because it had been more restricted than they, as we can see by a comparison between the languages used by the English and French novelists of the previous century. In the nineteenth century the French language underwent the same process of expansion as other languages in the seventeenth century, but it naturally had much further to go in order to keep up with them. The classic search for *le mot juste* was replaced by the search for *le mot propre,* for the word which would convey not only sights, sounds and smells, which are one of the signs of 'realism', but the very aura in which the novelists' characters were situated. The process began among the novelists with Balzac and Hugo, continued with still more different effects in Flaubert, Zola, the Goncourts and Huysmans, and culminated with Proust. Stendhal has been described by a French critic as 'un prince du langage', but when we compare the sober, colourless, unemphatic prose in which he presents a 'case' in *Armance* with the botanical imagery used by Proust to introduce the theme of homosexuality in *Sodome et Gomorrhe,* we realise what a vast change, an immense increase in subtlety and power of expression, had taken place and something like the gulf which separates modern French prose style from the style of the seventeenth and eighteenth centuries. The changes are a clear indication of the growth of sensibility, a reaching out to new realms of experience.

It is appropriate to conclude this general survey with a glance at the last two novelists of the seven discussed in this study. They are a good illustration of the double nature of influence that I have emphasized in comparing Stendhal and Proust. We shall see that in *Le Grand Meaulnes* François and Meaulnes are once again two partial portraits of the novelist and that it is precisely the close relationship between them which to a greater extent than in almost any other work is responsible for the extraordinary effectiveness of this great novel. We should also observe that it is not merely the direct contact between the two, but the discovery by François of Meaulnes's diaries compiled after their separation that are an essential part of the novel and that without them, as much as without Meaulnes's first-person relation of his visit to the *domaine merveilleux,* it could never have been achieved. On the face of it we may have the feeling that the method of communication is less satisfactory than the use of the omniscient narrator would have been. In a sense this is true, but what has to be emphasised is that the novel was inspired by Alain-Fournier's experience as a young man, that the strong personal feeling as well as the discovery of something like a 'vision' in real life and its tragic fading away—an interesting contrast with the 'vision' writers that I have been discussing—could only have been effectively expressed by the method that he used.

Finally, there is Radiguet. What makes *Le Diable au corps* an exceptional novel is that a youthful novelist produced a decidedly autobiographical novel in which he displays an amazingly penetrating insight not merely into his own, but into the characters of his heroine and the people with whom they are associated. Although I shall argue that *Le Bal du comte d'Orgel* is less impressive than the first novel, what is important is that the omniscient narrator shows an almost deeper insight into the characters, who are inevitably more complex than those of *Le Diable au corps*. What is also of particular interest is that *Le Bal du comte d'Orgel*, as we shall see, was influenced by Mme de La Fayette, but was used to produce a very different picture of society than *La Princesse de Clèves*.

MARIVAUX

I. THE MAN AND THE WRITER

ON FEBRUARY 4, 1743, Pierre Carlet de Chamblain de Marivaux, the celebrated novelist and dramatist, took his seat in the French Academy in place of the Abbé de Houtteville, the learned author of *De la Religion prouvée par les faits* to whom the new academician paid a generous tribute in his *discours de réception*.

The election was a curious one in several ways. Marivaux's defeated rival was none other than Voltaire. The two men never got on well and the literary history of the period records a number of amusing exchanges between them. 'He's a man who spends his life weighing flies' eggs in the scales of a spider's web', said Voltaire contemptuously of Marivaux's plays. 'M. de Voltaire', retorted Marivaux, 'is the first man in the world for writing down what other people have thought'.

Their rivalry on this occasion, however, was not purely personal. When they stood for the Academy, Marivaux was the candidate of the *bien pensants* and Voltaire of the anticlerical party. It was not one of the 'cleanest' elections and skilled manoeuvring led to the unanimous election of Marivaux.

There have been speculations about Marivaux's religious views. There is no particular reason for doubting his orthodoxy, but we shall find that he held very strong views about the *dévots* and was by no means impressed by the clergy. He must therefore have felt that it was too much of a good thing when he learnt that he was not merely to succeed to the chair of one priest, but was to be welcomed by another. For the reply to the *discours de réception* was pronounced by Languet de Gergy, Archbishop of Sens. The Academy could hardly have made a worse choice. When Marivaux's candidature was first put forward, the archbishop was one of the signatories of a document which opposed it significantly on the grounds that while the Academy was working at the 'composition' of the language, Marivaux was working on its 'decomposition'.

The archbishop evidently did not relish the task of welcoming a supposedly 'profane' writer.

> Although you have won the place which you have just occupied among us by a large number of works which the public has read with avidity [he said], it is not so much to them that you owe your selection as to the esteem in which we hold your conduct, your kind-heartedness, the pleasure of your company and, if I may say so, your amiability.

It must have been strange for a celebrated writer to be told that he owed his election to being a 'good mixer' rather than a good writer, but worse was to come.

The archbishop could not avoid all mention of the works of the man he was welcoming. He admitted to 'glancing at a few of them', but saw at once that 'the reading of these agreeable novels little became the austere dignity of his calling'. He had therefore been 'reduced to informing himself about them from other people'.

> They tell me [he went on] that in the course of these works you often describe tender and passionate adventures; that while you attempt to combat licence, you depict it with tender and naïve colours so that the impression on the reader must be very different from the one you intended.

Marivaux was a very good-natured man, but this was almost too much for him. It is said that it was only with the greatest difficulty that he refrained from protesting on the spot against the archbishop's innuendoes. The archbishop, however, was not allowed to escape altogether. In the eighteenth century it was customary for the police to be represented at meetings of the Academy. The representative who attended on this occasion observed, in the course of his report, that members were overwhelmed by the archbishop's speech, but that 'the long bursts of laughter which greeted his onslaught against M. de Marivaux on account of his *Paysan parvenu* should have made him understand what they thought of him'. 'Nothing so strange', the report concluded, 'has ever occurred at the Academy'.

One feels inclined to add that the strange reception boded ill for the future of the new member of the Academy. Marivaux was only fifty-five at the time of his election, but far from being an apotheosis it marked in a sense the end of his career as a popular writer.

If we are well informed about the career of the writer and about the events like his election to the Academy, our information about his private life is decidedly meagre. It will be seen from what follows that even the dates of a number of important happenings are only approximate.

Marivaux was born on February 4, 1688. We know that he came of a Norman family, that his father was a banker and that some time between 1699 and 1702 he was appointed Director of the Mint at Riom, a post that he held until his death in 1719. We do not know whether Marivaux was an only child or where he went to school. He reappears in Paris in 1710 and registers at the Faculty of Law. He does not seem to have been a particuvlarly ardent student and it has been suggested that his registrations at the faculty over the next three years were used to pacify his family while he worked at his career as a writer.

In 1717 he married Colombe Ballogne, who was some five years older than himself and the possessor of a handsome dowry of 40,000 livres. They had a daughter named Colombe Prospère who was probably born in 1719. The mother died four years later. It is thought that her death occurred towards the end of 1723 or the beginning of 1724, but the actual date like the cause remains unknown.

Marivaux was never interested in money as such, but friends of his father are thought to have persuaded him and his wife to invest part of their capital in Law's India Company. The immediate result was a steep rise in their income. It was followed in 1720 by the notorious Law bankruptcy, which led to the partial ruin of Marivaux. He remained a poor man for the rest of his life. His inability to provide his daughter with a dowry may have been one of the reasons why in 1745 she became a nun and why, when she took her final vows a year later, the monies due to the convent were paid by the Duke of Orléans. He himself was probably only saved from bankruptcy by a mysterious financial arrangement in 1753 with Mlle Angélique Gabrielle Anquetin de la Chapelle Saint-Jean. His fame vanished and his death on February 12, 1765, at the age of seventy-seven, went almost unnoticed.

Marivaux's first known work was a comedy in one act in verse called *Le Père prudent et équitable* which was written between 1708 and 1712, but was never performed except possibly by an amateur cast. It was followed by four works of fiction known as the 'oeuvres de jeunesse': *Les Aventures de *** ou Les Effets sur-prenants de la sympathie* in 1713-14; *La Voiture embourbée* and *Le Bilboquet* in 1714; and *L'Homère travesti,* a skit on Homer in verse, in 1717. *Le Télémaque travesti* was completed in 1714, but not published until 1736, while *Pharsamon ou Les Nouvel-les folies romanesques* was completed a year earlier and not published until 1737. His first success in the theatre came in 1720 with *Arlequin poli par l'amour,* a one-act comedy in prose which was given twelve performances. The year 1720 also saw the failure of *Annibal,* a tragedy in five acts in verse, which was no more than a feeble imitation of Racine and only had one per-formance. The next year he began publication of *Le Spectateur français,* the first of his one-man journals, which are a mixture of meditations on Life and fragments of fiction. *La Surprise de l'amour* was the first of his full-length major comedies and was given the same number of public performances as *Arlequin poli par l'amour.*

It was thought at one time that the loss caused by the Law bankruptcy turned Marivaux from an amateur man of letters into a professional writer, but there is no evidence that this was so, particularly as the earnings of eighteenth-century writers were usually insufficient to keep a writer without help from other sources.

The alternation of plays and prose fiction in this early period is not without importance. It shows clearly the direction in which he was moving. Marivaux was not a novelist who became a dramatist or a dramatist who wrote novels on the side. He was essentially a dramatist and a novelist. *La Vie de Marianne* began publication in 1731, the year after the production of *Le Jeu de l'amour du hasard* and the year before the production of *Le Triomphe de l'amour* and *Les Serments indiscrets.* It went on, in desultory fashion, until 1741, while the publication of *Le Paysan parvenu,* his other major novel, took place in 1735-36 and was followed by *Les Fausses confidences* in 1737.

II. THE NOVELIST

1 *The Early Works*

MARIVAUX has never been given his due in England either as a
dramatist or a novelist. Productions of his plays in English
seem to have been confined to sound broadcasting and there
have been no translations of his novels since the eighteenth century. We may suspect that one of the main reasons for the pau-
city of translations is that his two major novels were never
completed or rather that their final sequences were the work of
minor writers instead of their creator, who did not even attempt
to complete *La Vie de Marianne*. This is something that the
general reader, particularly in England, finds exasperating.
The result has naturally been the total neglect of the minor
novels, which are at present receiving belated, but very capable
treatment in the hands of French scholars. I do not intend to
discuss them in detail here, but I must mention them briefly in
order to show their place in the novelist's later development.

They are works of apprenticeship in the clearest sense. They
reveal, as I indicated earlier, the continuing influence of those
seventeenth-century novelists against whom the eighteenth-century novelists later reacted as part of their plan to find new and
more convincing techniques. At the same time they provide a
glimpse of the direction in which Marivaux was to move. In
his preface to *Les Aventures de *** ou Les Effets surprenants
de la sympathie* he insists on the importance of the novel not
merely as an experience, but as a moving experience. The most
important factor in a novel is not 'reason', but the 'heart'. His
description of it as 'un ouvrage dont le sujet est le coeur' looks
forward to the remarkably acute and decidedly original forms
of insight that his characters were to display in both the plays
and the novels of his maturity.

*Les Aventures de *** ou Les Effets surprenants de la sym-
pathie* was Marivaux's first full-length novel. Its main theme is

35

amour-passion, which is related with all the violence and brutality associated with the work of the novelists of the past. It is right to argue, as one scholar has done, that the method is slightly archaic. One should, however, go even further than that. The story is related in the form of memoirs, but it is done in the seventeenth-century style and is very different from the method of *La Vie de Marianne* and *Le Paysan parvenu,* for the simple reason that they are what might be described as indirect memoirs. The memoir writer in the work is really a narrator who has simply recorded a series of stories by the different characters. There are no less than five decidedly long stories about the protagonists and their relatives. They are not always easy to follow, which prompted Frédéric Deloffre to remark that 'this cascade of *récits à tiroirs* presents an almost insoluble problem at the first reading'.[1]

The chief influence on Marivaux's first full-length novel was Cervantes' *Trabajos de Persíles y Sigismunda,* which was published posthumously in 1617. It has been described by a recent biographer of Cervantes as 'the fantastic romance of adventure written in imitation of the fourth-century Greek author Heliodorus'.[2] It is, indeed, a long uneven novel of adventure with a considerable number of what the French call *récits à tiroirs.* They are easier to follow at the first reading than Marivaux's, though not only the reader but the other characters grow tired at the length of Persíles's own *récit.* It is interesting to find that Périandre, the name of one of Marivaux's two villains, is borrowed from Cervantes' Periandro, which is the pseudonym of Persíles, whose real name is only revealed in the last chapter but two of the novel.

In *La Voiture embourbée* Marivaux uses the same method. We may think it more convincing since the stories are told as a way of passing the time by a group of people who are stranded in the country owing to the breakdown of their carriage. This short work, however, hardly compares with the three full-length *romans de jeunesse.* The most interesting of them is *Pharsamon ou les Nouvelles folies romanesques.* In two of its later eighteenth-century editions the title was changed to *Le Don Quichotte moderne.* What Cervantes did once again was to provide

---

[1] *Oeuvres de jeunesse,* Pléiade, p. 1095.
[2] R. L. Predmore, *Cervantes,* 1973, p. 205.

the framework. Pharsamon, as the hero chose to call himself, has been encouraged by his uncle to read the same early romances as Don Quixote. He decides to become a knight-errant with Cliton as his squire. He is, however, much more concerned with amusing himself and trying to find a wife than in rescuing unfortunate, or supposedly unfortunate beings from their tormentors by force of arms. At a late stage in the novel he comes to realise that like Don Quixote he is suffering from some form of mental disorder. It is a good deal milder, but his 'enchanté' is clearly an echo of Don Quixote's 'encantado'. He is cured like his squire by a Seigneur Géronimo, who appears to be an early version of the psychiatrist, loses interest in Cidalise, the heroine who also comes to her senses and is no longer in love with him, and is about to marry the sensible widow Félonde. The most interesting part of the novel is the narration of Clorinne, the charming girl whose lover has lost his life and whom Pharsamon rejects because he is still committed at the time of his meeting with her to Cidalise. Clorinne's importance lies in the fact that she clearly looks forward to Marianne, or rather to Marivaux's handling of her.

Le Télémaque travesti, as the title shows, is a skit on Fénelon's Télémaque. There is a tendency at present to treat it as the most important of the three full-length early novels. I must confess, however, to finding it almost unreadable. What I wish to emphasise is that in spite of the difficulties which have been mentioned, Les Aventures de *** ou Les Efforts surprenants de la sympathie and Pharsamon ou Les Nouvelles folies romanesques strike me as two enjoyable and readable novels which deserve to be much better known than they are.

2 La Vie de Marianne
ou Les Aventures de Madame la Comtesse de ***

'Racine by moonlight', said Lytton Strachey of Marivaux's plays. The words described very well the strangely intangible world of the comedies, the 'caprices' and the intricate 'sentiers du coeur' of its inhabitants. The world of the novels is very different as we can see from the early novels of adventure, but the difference is much more pronounced and much more important in the two major novels. In La Vie de Marianne and

Le Paysan parvenu Marivaux gives a vivid, racy picture of life
in eighteenth-century Paris with a few of its street brawls, its
murders or attempted murders. The ghostly Dorantes, Silvias,
marquises and comtesses of the plays are replaced by characters
who are as carefully observed as those by English novelists of
the same period and whose feelings and insights are much
subtler. Marivaux does not confine himself to the emotional
complexities of the upper classes. His picture of society includes
the nobility, the clergy, the bourgeoisie, merchants and servants
who are very unlike the witty *suivantes* of the plays. We shall
also find that there is one section of the community in which he
displays a special interest. His *dévots* are comparable to Molière's in *Tartuffe*. His irony may seem less fierce, but we shall
find that it is not less effective and that with his smug ecclesias-
tic, M. Doucin, who must have embarrassed the Archbishop of
Sens if ever he got as far as 'glancing at' *Le Paysan parvenu,* he
ventures into places where Molière feared to tread.

Highwaymen have attacked and robbed a coach. All the occu-
pants, masters and servants, have been killed with the exception
of a priest, who runs away and is never heard of again, and a
two-year-old child, who is orphaned by the murder of her
parents and is rescued and brought up by a village priest and
his sister. The sister, who has taken the child to Paris in the
hope of finding her a job, suddenly falls ill and dies. The
brother collapses and becomes senile. It is one of the peculiarities of this world that it has proved impossible to identify the
members of Marianne's family. Her protectors manage to discover the names of the parents, or supposed parents, but it does
not help. The names are thought to be either assumed or those
of foreigners who were travelling through France. The clothing
and appearance of the dead suggest that they belonged to the
nobility. It is something, however, which cannot be proved.
And that is the crux of the matter.

The eighteenth century displayed a considerable interest in
orphans, foundlings, abandoned children and social beginners.
In his two major novels, as in the early novels, Marivaux is very
much a product of his century. Marianne is clearly an orphan.
Jacob, the protagonist of *Le Paysan parvenu,* has a father, but
we never see him. He lives far away on a farm in Champagne

while his son, starting like Marianne from nothing, wins himself a place in society.

The appearance of the orphan and his like is a recurrence of the Cinderella myth: the story of the person who starting from nothing achieves success through the good offices of a fairy godmother, combined with his or her personal qualities and good looks. Marivaux keeps close to the myth. In *La Vie de Marianne*, Mme de Miran is 'the fairy godmother' and Mme de Fare 'the wicked fairy'; in *Le Paysan parvenu* the parts are played by Mlle Habert (whom Jacob marries) and her sister.

This brings us to the main theme, which is really the same in both novels. Marianne is striving to gain a position in society to which she is convinced that she has a right; Jacob to win a higher place in society which he may deserve, but to which he has no automatic right. They both face the same obstacle. It is the snobbery which for Marivaux is one of the most serious failings of the society that he is depicting: the attempt for 'social reasons' to keep the newcomers out and wreck their hopes of a happy marriage. The result is a series of conflicts between the individual and society. 'The fairy godmothers' and their supporters represent a minority with the right views; 'three wicked fairies' and their allies, the majority with the wrong ones.

On the face of it, the orphans look like outsiders who are trying to make their way into society. There is, however, an important difference between the Cinderella myth and the 'outsider' myth of the nineteenth century which begins with Stendhal. It is partly due to the changes in the structure of society, but the most important factor is the psychology of the 'outsider' himself. The background of Marivaux's novels, as of his plays, is a stable society. In spite of assassins, rogues, unworthy ecclesiastics, *faux dévots* and social snobs, society is regarded as reasonably good in itself and Marivaux like Molière confines himself to flaws in an otherwise tolerable order, looking forward incidentally to Rousseau's *La Nouvelle Héloïse*. The 'outsider' of the next century is the man of superior abilities who cannot accept the conventions and subterfuges of a disintegrating society and tries, unsuccessfully, to remould it. The Cinderella story ends with the integration of the orphan in society; the 'outsider' myth—represented by Stendhal in fiction and Rimbaud in life—closes with the voluntary exile or the death of the man who cannot fit in.

When she realises that the village priest's sister is on the point of death during their stay in Paris, Marianne is overcome with horror:

> It seemed to me that the whole world was a desert where I was going to remain alone.

'Desert' is a key word. It shows the path that the heroine will have to take, suggests that she will sometimes be inside and sometimes outside society, sometimes on the map and sometimes off it, or in the 'desert'.

The first major encounter occurs when the priest, who takes charge of her after the sister's death, hands her over to M. de Climal, a supposedly religious man who is to help her financially and find her a job. He begins by suggesting that she should become a housemaid at his sister-in-law's. The reply is instant and crystal clear:

> I feel that I would rather die than live with someone as a domestic servant; if I had my father and mother, there is every reason to think that I should have servants myself instead of serving anybody.

It is clear from the second half of the sentence that, in spite of her youth, Marianne is absolutely convinced of her noble birth and makes no bones about it.

M. de Climal's reply is equally forthright:

> Whatever the conjectures that can be made about your birth, it gives you no status, and you will have to accept the position.

Marianne's conviction is dismissed as mere 'conjecture', which has no validity in M. de Climal's world.

There is a compromise. Marianne is lodged at Climal's expense at the home of a milliner with the idea of training her as a shop assistant. We are given a view of a social class in which Marianne feels decidedly out of place. Mme Dutour is a good-hearted woman, but her language, particularly in the famous dispute with the coachman, and her conversation stamp her as lower middle-class.

We are also shown the way in which Marianne's mind works and the tactics she adopts. In one of the reflections in which she indulges for the friend to whom the memoirs are supposed to be addressed, she observes:

> I think myself that feeling is the only thing which can give us information about ourselves which is at all reliable, and that we must not put too much trust in the information that our mind chooses to produce in its own manner because it seems to me that it is a great visionary.

It is a good illustration of what was said earlier about the differing importance that Marivaux attached to 'reason' and 'heart'. In the novels, as in the plays, problems are solved or dangers avoided by sudden insights into one's own mind and the minds of other people which are the result of 'feeling'. Marianne constantly has a sense of the way things are going and the attitude of people who are dangerous or hostile to her. The supposedly pious M. de Climal will turn out to be a potential seducer. There is a hint of it at her first sight of him when she speaks of a 'gentle and serious expression' and 'an air of mortification which prevented you from noticing the extent of his plumpness'.

She soon becomes much more explicit:

> Cependant, malgré l'anéantissement où je me sentais, j'étais étonnée des choses dont il m'entretenait; je trouvais sa conversation singulière; il me semblait que mon homme se mitigeait, qu'il était plus flatteur que zélé, plus généreux que charitable; il me paraissait tout changé.

> [In spite, however, of the state of prostration in which I felt myself, I was astonished at the things that he talked to me about; I found his conversation strange; it seemed that my man was relaxing, that he was more flattering than zealous, more generous than charitable; he appeared to me to be completely changed.]

The passage is a good example of the skill with which Marivaux reveals Marianne's penetrating insights. 'Etonnée' shows

that there has been a change in the man's behaviour; 'singulière'
suggests that there is something odd or even startling about it.
The use of 'mitigeait' as a reflexive verb is a sign that he has
deliberately changed himself. The nature of the change is apparent in the contrasts between 'flatteur' and 'zélé', 'généreux'
and 'charitable', meaning that there has been a move from the
religious to the profane in the supposed *dévot*. 'Tout changé',
brings the pronouncement to a neatly logical conclusion and
looks forward to worse things to come.

Climal's behaviour does, indeed, gradually give him away:

> Car M. de Climal, tête à tête avec moi, ne ressemblait point du
> tout au M. de Climal parlant aux autres: à la lettre, c'était deux
> hommes différents; et quand je lui voyais son visage dévot, je ne
> pouvais pas comprendre comment ce visage-là ferait pour devenir
> profane, et tel qu'il était avec moi.

> [For in private with me, M. de Climal was nothing like the M.
> de Climal in conversation with other people; it was literally two
> different men; and when I was looking at his pious face, I could
> not understand what this face did in order to become profane,
> and such as he was with me.]

The change of expression is a sign of danger for Marianne.
It also looks forward to a later change of expression which will
be much more painful.

As soon as he has completed the arrangements to lodge Marianne at the milliner's, M. de Climal decides to buy her some
new clothes. He does so at shops whose wares are very much
superior to those sold by Mme Dutour. The reasons are obvious.
He is determined not to place her in a class to which she does
not belong officially and to avoid criticism by his fellow snobs.
It is equally his snobbery which prevents him from taking as
his mistress a girl in lower-class dress. What he sets out to do
therefore is to dress her temporarily as a 'gentle-woman' when
she is with him, which means that he is attempting to get what
he wants without letting her 'in'. Fortunately, Marianne and
her perceptiveness save her, but it is a good example of the particular complications of the heroine's path and the traps which
await her.

Marianne is embarrassed by the procedure, which rouses the

indignation of Mme Dutour, but it will not prevent her from making good use of the garments on one important occasion.

Although Marianne is something like a model of virtue, it does not prevent her from applauding coquetry as one of the methods of winning a place in society. 'If one knew what goes on in the head of a coquette', she says amusingly, 'it would have a humiliating effect on the strongest minds and Aristotle would appear to be nothing more than a little boy'.[1]

She then proceeds to describe her own techniques:

> Quand je voulais avoir un air fripon, j'avais un maintient et une parure qui faisaient mon affaire; le lendemain on me trouvait avec des grâces tendres; ensuite j'étais une beauté modeste, sérieuse, nonchalante. Je fixais l'homme le plus volage; je dupais son inconstance, parce que tous les jours je lui renouvelais sa maîtresse; et c'était comme s'il en avait changé.

> [When I wanted to put on a mischievous air, I adopted a bearing and dress which did my job; the next day one found me with tender graces; after that I was a modest beauty, serious, unconcerned. I fixed the ficklest of men; I foiled his inconstancy because every day I renewed his mistress for him; and it was as though he had made a change.]

I must confess that these personal observations strike me as decidedly odd. In spite of what she says of herself, Marianne never goes in for flirting or trying to make a series of conquests, at any rate as we know her, which makes us regard the reference to 'mistress' in her personal observations as incredible. She confines herself in the novel to a single case of genuine love, which is wrecked by the fiancé's abandonment of her.[2]

---

[1] A typical example of the novelist's personal intervention referred to in the opening chapter of the present work.

[2] In spite of Marianne's virtue, as we know her, and our doubts about these personal observations, one cannot help suspecting that this passage may have influenced Laclos, possibly unconsciously, when he described a performance by Mme de Merteuil in very different circumstances:

'Après le souper, tour à tour enfant et raisonnable, folâtre et sensible, quelquefois même libertine, je me plaisais à le considérer comme un sultan au milieu de son sérail, dont j'étais tour à tour les favorites différentes. En effet ses hommages réitérés, quoique toujours reçus par la même femme, les furent par une maîtresse nouvelle'.

['After supper I was in turn childish and reasonable, playful and respon-

Whatever we think of them, these observations are a prelude
to Marianne's appearance in church on a feast day when she
gives something like a demonstration of her methods. She is
dressed up to the nines in the garments provided by Climal in
order to impress the congregation. She succeeds, but it is interesting to find that she places more emphasis on her personality
than her good looks:

> I brought as much pleasure to the heart as to the eyes, and the
> least of my advantages was to look beautiful.

During the Mass, Marianne and Valville see one another for
the first time. It points to a major change in the situation. She
is accidentally run down by Valville's carriage and slightly in-
jured. She is taken to his house. He is a susceptible young man.
He falls for her and she for him. M. de Climal, who turns out
to be Valville's uncle, arrives unexpectedly and finds his nephew
at Marianne's feet. She is too proud to tell Valville where she
is living; he manages to find out and the incident is reversed
when he turns up and finds his uncle at the girl's feet.

Climal denounces his nephew as a 'libertine'. In order to try
to keep Marianne for himself, he invites her to move to the
home of a dubious acquaintance who sounds like a procurer.
She realises that he is trying to turn her into a 'kept woman'
and refuses. This produces a breach. He stops paying for her
board. Mme Dutour cannot afford to keep her for nothing. She
returns M. de Climal's gifts and finds herself once more in the
'desert':

> But how was I to get out of the desert in which I found myself?
> The whole world was one for me because I had no relations in it
> with anyone.

An appeal to the prioress of the convent leads to a meeting
with Mme de Miran, whom I have described as 'the fairy godmother' and who will play something like the part of the adop-

sive, and sometimes even licentious; it amused me to treat him as a Sultan
in his seraglio where I was in turn his different favourites. In fact, his
repeated homage, though always received by the same woman, was always
accepted by a fresh mistress'.]

tive mother. She turns out by one of the coincidences which are typical of Marivaux to be the mother of Valville and the sister of Climal.[1]

Mme de Miran lodges Marianne at the convent while she considers what arrangements she can make for her future. The move is important. A convent is a neutral zone in the sense that it is outside the world in which Marianne is seeking to establish herself and a refuge from the 'desert', which is a symbol of a continual threat of disaster. Mme de Miran certainly intends the convent to be a temporary refuge and at the same time a sort of transit camp which will enable her to introduce Marianne into the world, or rather the class of society, in which she hopes to live. We should observe, however, that though the convent is a refuge, it is at the same time a threat of a different sort to Marianne's worldly ambitions. There are moments of extreme depression when, in spite of the absence of any vocation, she thinks seriously of becoming a nun and making the temporary refuge a permanent one. It also looks forward to the time when her enemies will use a convent as a temporary prison and threaten to make it a permanent one, as well as to the fate which, as we shall see later, overtook one of the sisters at the convent who had battled unsuccessfully with a problem that was not unlike Marianne's.

This prompts the observation that the image of the 'desert' which haunts Marianne and the different possible functions of a convent—refuge, prison, permanent exile in a form of no-man's land—are an important contribution to the unity of the work.

The plan for what might be described as Marianne's change of camps, is a prelude to the main crisis or, better, a series of crises. M. de Climal told her that she had no status and no place in polite society. When Mme de Miran learns that her son and Marianne are in love and want to marry, she is more explicit and much more sympathetic. Marianne, she says, possesses all the gifts which should lead to a very happy marriage—beauty, grace, virtue, *bel esprit* and an excellent heart—but she

---

[1] Somewhat oddly Mme de Miran is originally referred to as Mme de Valville. We are not told whether there had been a second marriage to a M. de Miran. One suspects that the change of name was a rather careless device by the novelist to surprise the heroine and the reader.

is without a dowry of 20,000 livres and nobody knows her
parents:

> Reason would choose you; the stupidity of practice rejects you.

The concluding sentence of her reflexions is a very neat summary of the position. Mme de Miran dismisses the ban on *déclassement* (which is a social and not a legal ban) as 'the stupidity of practice', but feels bound to conform. So does Marianne.
She tells Valville, in the presence of his mother, that they cannot marry. He is prepared to conform, but says that it will
make him unhappy, with the result that his mother gives in.
She begins to think of some way of avoiding the ban, possibly
by means of a secret marriage. Their opponents would be
faced with a *fait accompli*. It would cause temporary wrath,
but would quickly be forgotten when they came to appreciate
the qualities of the bride, or so she thinks.

In view of what we know of Marivaux's psychological perception, his taste for portraits in both the plays and the novels,
and his impressive use of language, it is worth pausing for a
moment to look at what Marianne says about Mme de Miran
and Mme Dorsin. The orphan is deeply devoted to both of
them. When Valville proves inconstant, she does not hesitate to
tell his mother that she is fonder of her than of him and that
she would sooner lose the son than 'ma mère'. Yet her insights
are so acute that she cannot fail to notice Mme de Miran's
limitations or the ways in which she is inferior to Mme Dorsin.
'With all her goodness of heart', Mme de Miran only possessed 'an ordinary mind' and a 'reasonably moderate amount
of good sense and understanding'. She 'only did for you what
you asked her to do, or provided the exact service for which you
ventured to ask'. 'She saw nothing except what you actually
mentioned' which was, so to speak, in front of her eyes. It was
responsible for 'the mediocrity of her understanding' and 'an
obstacle to her goodness of heart'. Mme Dorsin was very different. She was 'un esprit supérieur' who possessed precisely those
qualities which were lacking in Mme de Miran. She 'perceived
all the things which you did not venture to say to her'. Her
mind 'informed her heart, warmed it with its perceptiveness,

and provided her on your behalf with every degree of goodness that you needed'.

There is nothing unkind or uncharitable about the comparison. Marianne simply feels that she must give the right rating to two kindhearted women to whom she is equally devoted. Mme de Miran is a prosaic, down-to-earth person who is only capable of seeing the obvious. Mme Dorsin's superior intelligence means that she is far-seeing and possesses exactly the same kind of insight or intuition as Marianne herself.[1]

His relations suddenly learn that M. de Climal is dying and go to see him. Marianne accompanies Mme de Miran and Valville. M. de Climal remains something of a puzzle. His deathbed confession to his relations and to Marianne leaves us wondering whether he was a righteous man who was carried away by the sight of a well-favoured girl, a combination of 'inclination and opportunity', or whether he really was a *faux dévot* in the full sense who consistently used religion to conceal a licentious career. Marianne's description of him, in a passage quoted earlier, as 'deux hommes différents' whose expression changed from 'dévot' to 'profane' when he found himself in her presence, and his plan for sending her to live with a man who sounded like a procurer, show that even if he were genuinely pious, he certainly played a dual role which can hardly have been confined to Marianne. She rightly came to describe him in his lifetime as 'mon tartufe', but withdrew after the confession and mourned his death.

Ironically, the meeting at which the first of Marianne's opponents makes a confession, is given something like a lay absolution by friends and relations, and dies, is also the occasion on which Marianne comes into contact for the first time with Mme de Fare, 'the wicked fairy'.

It triggers off the main crisis. Marianne and Valville go to spend a night with Mme de Fare and her daughter, who will turn out to be an amiable friend. The crisis is thrown into relief, as one critic points out, by a 'pastoral interlude' with the

---

[1] As already suggested, there are good reasons for thinking that the portraits of Mme de Miran and Mme Dorsin were based on Mme de Lambert and Mme de Tencin, owners of two of the best known eighteenth-century salons.

three young people larking in the garden.[1] Valville's 'tenderness' continually interrupts talks between the two girls. They
make up their minds, as a 'gesture of gaiety', to run away from
him, push him out of their way and throw leaves at him which
they tear off bushes—an ironic picture of what is to come:

> Valville pursued us; we ran; he seized me, she came to my
> rescue; and my spirit gave itself up to a joy which was not to last.

The novel switches at once, with something like a cinematic
cut, to the next morning with a chambermaid helping Marianne to dress:

> However unaccustomed the service that she was about to under-
> take was for me, I accepted it, I think, with as much good grace as
> if it had been familiar to me. It was very necessary to maintain
> my rank, and it was one of those things on which I fastened with
> all the speed in the world. I had a natural taste or, if you prefer,
> a sort of delicate vanity which suddenly taught me such things,
> and the chambermaid did not take me for a novice.

It looks straight back to the earlier passage in which Marianne declares that she 'would rather die than find herself in the
position of a domestic servant'. It is echoed by the words, 'Il
fallait bien soutenir mon rang'. Marianne has a glimpse of
what life will in fact turn out to be for her later on. It is no
more than a tantalising glimpse which is followed by an appalling shock: the sudden appearance in the room of Mme
Dutour, who has called at the house on business:

> 'Eh! que Dieu nous soit en aide! Aurais-je la berlue? N'est-ce
> pas vous, Marianne?'... Et tout de suite, elle se jeta à mon col.
> 'Quelle bonne fortune avez-vous donc eue?' ajouta-t-elle tout de
> suite. 'Comme la voilà belle et bien mise! Ah! que je suis aise de
> vous voir brave! que cela vous sied bien!'

> [Oh! Heaven help us! Could I be mistaken? Isn't it you, Mari-
> anne?' . . . And she promptly flung herself on to my neck. 'What
> good fortune have you had then?' she added immediately after-
> wards. 'How beautiful and nicely dressed she is! Ah! I'm relieved
> to find you looking so smart! How well it suits you!']

1 Peter Brooks: *The Novel of Worldliness*, 1969, p. 121.

It is a brilliant device: something like black, or rather pale black comedy. Mme Dutour's totally unexpected appearance, her cheery lower-middle-class language and decidedly informal behaviour bring out the precariousness of Marianne's position and are a very uncomfortable reminder of the way in which life in Paris began for her.

The three young people are appalled, particularly Marianne:

> A ce discours, pas un mot de ma part; j'étais anéanti.

> [At this discourse, not a word from me; I was annihilated.]

When the chambermaid finds that she has been dressing a girl from the milliner's, she 'laughs behind her hand and leaves the room'. Mlle de Fare's attempt to prevent a leak is too late. The mother appears. Her treatment of her guest bodes ill:

> Mme de Fare looked at me, and did not greet me.

She no longer addresses her as 'Mademoiselle'. Marianne feigns indisposition and retreats to the convent, 'renvoyée, pour ainsi dire, d'une maison où l'on m'avait reçue la veille avec tant d'accueil'.[1]

We soon find that Mme de Fare has set to work to organise resistance to the marriage. Although there is no violence, Marianne is virtually kidnapped and planted in a different convent. She learns that she is to be brought before a minister of the crown whose aid has been sought by the enemy, and given the choice of marriage to a lower-class youth, which would doom her attempt to establish herself in polite society forever, becoming a nun or being kept prisoner in some distant house belonging to the enemy. It is clearly a choice between abandoning her claims forever or being condemned for life to one kind of 'desert' or another.

The meeting between Marianne and the compulsory candidate for her hand enables Marivaux to bring out the difference between the noble heroine and the ignoble youth who is com-

---

[1] 'Sent back, so to speak, from a house where one had received me the day before with such welcome'.

pletely crushed by her. The appearance before the minister
turns out to be her greatest, or rather her only real triumph.
She refuses to marry the youth or to become a nun, but announces that she will not marry Valville. Mme de Miran and
her son have discovered the plot and arrive belatedly, but in
time to speak for the defence. The minister (for whom Cardinal
Fleury is believed to have served as a model) turns out to be
wise, just and benevolent:

> C'était comme un père de famille qui veille au bien, au repos
> et à la considération de ses enfants.[1]

He is converted to the view of Marianne's friends. The meeting, he announces, should be treated as though it had never
taken place, which releases Marianne from her promise not to
marry Valville. The enemy retire in disorder.

'Je nageais dans la joie', says Marianne, 'et me disais: Tous
mes malheurs sont donc finis'.[2] She is wrong. We remember
that when he found that his nephew was a rival for Marianne,
M. de Climal denounced him as a 'libertine' and declared that
he would prove unfaithful. His words were prophetic.

There has been some speculation about the reasons for Valville's inconstancy.[3] One or two points deserve notice. When
we look back, we find that there is nothing very impressive
about him, that in spite of his reluctance to accept the ban on
déclassement, there is nothing to suggest that he is a strong
man. Although the minister came out in favour of Marianne,
it seems that her fiancé had been given a rough time by members of the family and friends. What is more important is that
he fell for Marianne after her accident and does exactly the
same when the next girl is taken ill and faints on arrival at
Marianne's convent, which suggests susceptibility, sentimentality and weakness.

---

1 It was like a family father who keeps his eye on the comfort, repose
and consideration of his children.

2 I was swimming in joy, and said to myself: All my misfortunes are
therefore over and done with'.

3 See R. Mercier. 'Le Héros inconstant: Roman et réflexions morales
(1730–1750), *Revue des Sciences Humaines,* Fasc. 143, 1971, pp. 333–355.

The best declaration comes from Marianne herself:

> ... les âmes tendres et délicates ont volontiers le défaut de se relâcher dans leur tendresse, quand elles ont obtenu toute la vôtre; l'envie de vous plaire leur fournit des grâces infinies, leur fait faire des efforts qui sont délicieux pour elles, mais dès qu'elles ont plu, les voilà désoeuvrées.

> [... tender and delicate souls are willingly guilty of the mistake of relaxing in their tenderness, when they have obtained the whole of yours; the desire to please you provides them with infinite grace, drives them into making efforts which are a delight to them, but as soon as they have given pleasure, we find them no longer concerned.]

It is a kindly as well as a perceptive explanation. There are plenty of male characters in the eighteenth-century French novel, as we shall see when we come to Crébillon *fils*, whose aim is conquest and not love or, in other words, sex without emotion. Valville is not a 'libertine' in Climal's sense of the word. He does not think consciously in terms of conquest; he is to all appearances a chaste lover and there is no lack of feeling in his relations with Marianne. Yet the basic principle applies. His principal weakness lies in the fact that there is not much to him, that he is a poor instead of a rich and generous personality. He is not seeking physical change; he simply needs in spite of himself an emotional change, a fresh girl who will stimulate the emotions which are beginning to flag.

Marianne elaborates on her explanation in terms which recall the importance that she attaches to the technique of the coquette, which is permissible for the woman of integrity and even necessary in her relations with a wayward man:

> Mais le goût lui en reviendra; c'est pour se reposer qu'il s'écarte; il reprend haleine, il court après une nouveauté, et j'en redeviendrai une pour lui, plus piquante que jamais: il me reverra, pour ainsi dire, sous une figure qu'il ne connaît pas encore ... Ce ne sera plus la même Marianne ...

> [But the attraction will come back to him from it; it is in order to rest himself that he is moving away; he is taking back his breath, running after something new, and I shall become one for

him again, more compelling than ever; he will see me afresh, so
to speak, with a face that he does not yet know...It will no
longer be the same Marianne...]

It is evident that the passage is almost an echo of Marianne's
earlier description of the coquette's methods, which I suggested was a trifle odd in so far as she applied it to herself
(page 43).

Marivaux's style is seen at its most impressive in these singularly lucid, simple, closely observed and decidedly penetrating
pronouncements. We should look, finally, at the description
of the change that has taken place in Valville which follows
the optimistic statement about his expected return to her:

> En un mot, je ne le reconnus plus; ce n'était plus le même
> homme; il n'y avait plus de franchise, plus de naïveté, plus de
> joie de me voir dans cette physionomie autrefois si pénétrée et
> si attendrie quand j'étais présente. Tout l'amour en était effacé;
> je n'y vis plus qu'embarras et qu'imposture; je ne trouvai plus
> qu'un visage froid et contraint, qu'il tâchait d'animer, pour m'en
> cacher l'ennui, l'indifférence et la sécheresse.

> [In short, I no longer recognised him; it was no longer the same
> man; there was no longer any frankness, any simplicity, any joy
> in seeing me in this face previously so moved and so filled with
> tenderness when I was present. The whole of love had disappeared
> from it; I saw only embarrassment and imposture; I only saw a
> face which was cold and still, to which he tried to give some live-
> liness in order to hide his boredom from me, his indifference and
> his dryness.]

It is evident from this passage that whatever Marianne's
conscious views, the optimism expressed in the previous statement about Valville's eventual return to her is beginning to
fade away. The ternary phrases, which in the present context
show a preference for substantives, produce a strong contrast
between 'franchise', 'naïveté,' and 'joie' on the one hand, and
'ennui', 'indifférence' and 'sécheresse' on the other. The first
three substantives, which are strengthened by the association
with the adjectives, 'pénétrée' and 'attendrie', stand for positive
qualities which are effectively obliterated by the last three.

The ternary phrases form a framework and are made still more
effective by the process which goes on, as it were, inside it, and
is expressed by 'amour' and 'effacé', which demolish 'pénétrée'
and 'attendrie', and becomes still more specific with 'embarras'
and 'imposture', 'froid' and 'contraint'.

Since Marianne has tried to convince herself that Valville
will return to her and that she will take him back, she behaves
generously and makes no attempt to force the issue. She releases
him from his promise of marriage and tells him that he is free
to marry the new girl if he wishes. She describes the effect very
impressively:

> Ma générosité le terrassa.

> [My generosity overwhelmed him.]

We can see now that Climal's change of expression when he
was with Marianne looked forward to Valville's as Valville's
looks back to Climal's. Climal's was a sign of male craftiness;
Valville's a sign of male weakness. The inference is that men
are so wayward that women have to resort to every imaginable
device to bring them to heel, which is the justification for the
questionable practices of coquetry. Marianne is evidently convinced that women are superior to men; that they are stronger,
wiser and more generous. We may suspect that in this instance
her generosity and her youthfulness obscured her normally
acute insight. Whatever her views, it seems obvious that an inconstant man like Valville would never make a satisfactory
husband. The fact that Marianne became the Comtesse de
* * * must be proof that Valville never did return, or try to
return to her, or if he did that she did not take him back.

It seems strange that Marivaux's two finest novels should
have remained unfinished. It seems stranger still that the last
three parts of *La Vie de Marianne*, amounting to more than
a quarter of the work, should have been devoted to the friendly
nun's account of her own youthful misfortunes in an attempt
to console Marianne for Valville's betrayal and to dissuade her
from following her example by becoming a nun—something
that she was contemplating in spite of her alleged expectation
that Valville would eventually return to her and in spite of

his evident unsuitability as a husband. The nun's story, belonging to a more modest section of society, has certain resemblances to Marianne's and like hers remains unfinished. She, too, falls in love with a young man, but unlike the initial opposition of Valville's mother, the opposition of the nun's fiancé effectively broke off the engagement and sent the girl into a convent.

Leo Spitzer maintained that if Marivaux had finished his novel, the two stories would have fitted perfectly into the work as a whole and given it complete unity.[1] I find this view almost impossible to accept. In spite of resemblances between the two stories—particularly the nun's evident failure and Marianne's presumed success in another direction—the nun's memoirs are much less impressive than Marianne's, are in fact largely an account of the sort of trickery which was rampant in the less impressive eighteenth-century novels and are without the brilliant insights and the subtlety of style of Marianne's.

A very different view has been advanced by John Heckman. 'Everything in the novel', he writes, 'dictates that Marianne can never, either socially or imaginatively, bridge the gap that separates her from the world of Mme de Miran—and neither could Marivaux. Yet the donnée of the novel, that Marianne is "Mme la Comtesse de * * *" contradicts the only feasible interpretation of it. The control of its very structure renders the novel unfinishable'.[2]

It is an interesting view, but I myself remain unconvinced by it. Its weakness is that it does not give sufficient credit to Marianne's abilities or take sufficient account of the minister's judgement in her favour. Nevertheless, Marivaux's failure to finish his novel remains something of a mystery. Even if he could have told the story of Marianne's supposed success, it is possible that by the time he reached the end of Part VIII he had said all that he really wanted to say about Marianne. This would mean that he switched to the nun's story through lack of any further inspiration and simply felt that he had to go on writing—reminding us oddly of Valville's change of girls. It may well be that nothing of great value or great interest was

---

[1] *Romanische Literaturstudien* 1936–1956, 1959, pp. 248–276.
[2] '*Marianne:* The Making of an Author' in *Modern Language Notes,* May 1971, Vol. 86, No. 4, p. 522.

lost by what he did, but no admirer can help feeling that it is decidedly tantalising to be left in the dark without knowing what happened to Valville or what exactly became of Marianne.

3 *Le Paysan parvenu*

There have been differences of opinion about the merits of Marivaux's two major novels. 'We can compare *La Vie de Marianne* to a peaceful river', wrote Henri Clouard, 'in order to give ourselves the right to say that *Le Paysan parvenu* eats away the ground from its bank because the story of a boy who arrives through women contains some touches of satire which are absent from the story of Marianne. The second novel is more solid and more powerful than the first, but so much less airy, so much less rich in enjoyment! We no longer find in it the delicious novelties of the heart, the subtle embroideries of narration that in future Marivaux will reserve for his plays'.[1]

It is a matter of taste. There is substance in what Henri Clouard says of the differences between the two novels, but though I admire Marianne, who is a much more engaging figure than Jacob, I must confess to a preference for the power of the second and the special interest of the way in which Jacob reaches his goal.

We have already seen that there are marked resemblances as well as marked differences between the two novels which call for further discussion. The main resemblances are the goals at which the protagonists aim and the obstacles which they face. The main difference is that one is a girl and the other is a boy. Yet it is precisely this that makes me feel that the two novels should be regarded as a diptych: different approaches to a similar goal by two people of different sexes and different social standing.

Marianne and Jacob are both eighteen years old at the time of their 'adventures'.[2] They are both decidedly mature for

[1] *Petite histoire de la littérature française*, 1965, p. 177.

[2] There are inconsistencies in *La Vie de Marianne*. In Part I we are told that at the time of her arrival in Paris she was fifteen and a half. In Part III we are suddenly told that she was eighteen. There are no inconsistencies about Jacob's age. We are told at the start that he was eighteen when he came to Paris.

their years; they possess the same talents; they display the same
frankness and are both greatly helped by their good looks.
They are both equally conscious of their origins, but in different ways and for different reasons. Marianne would rather
die, she says, than become a domestic servant. Jacob, the peasant youth, naturally has no such reservations. When he comes
to Paris on a business errand for his father, he does not hesitate
to accept a job as a servant in the home of the man who owns
the property where his father works. The acceptance of a
second post of the same kind makes his fortune; it starts as an
engagement as a servant and turns into marriage with his employer. His comments on his origins and his abilities underline
the differences and the resemblances between Marianne and
himself:

> ... I have ability and no money, which doesn't work out well.

> I was without learning and had no other occupation except that
> of a peasant; I knew perfectly well how to sow, plough, dress a
> vine, and that was all.

Next comes one of the most important resemblances:

> ... the art of reading other peoples' minds and unravelling their
> secret feelings is a gift which I have always had and which has
> sometimes been very useful.

The resemblances are not confined to the narrators' talents
and their tactics; they extend to the pattern of the novels.
Jacob's engagement to Mlle Habert like Marianne's to Valville
divides the circle in which they move into two hostile parties.
Marianne is brought before a minister; Jacob before the president of a magistrate's court. The verdict is the same. In both
cases the objections to the marriages are seen to be without
genuine foundation and the magistrate like the minister finds
for the victim of persecution.[1]
Although in a sense Jacob travels further than Marianne,

---

[1] The difference between a minister and magistrate is clearly a reflection of the difference between those sections of society in which the
protagonists were trying to establish themselves.

his passage (except for his temporary arrest when he is quite wrongly suspected of murder) is much smoother and his victory much more rapid, taking apparently only twelve days. Marianne owes her success, in so far as it can be called success, to the maternal fondness of elderly women. Jacob's ascent is also due largely to the assistance of elderly women, but their fondness for him is not exactly maternal, which brings us to one of the most important points of all and is responsible for the particular novelty of the work.

I observed earlier that Marivaux had strong feelings about the *dévots*. In *La Vie de Marianne* he confined himself to .a portrait of M. de Climal, who remains, as we saw, something of a mystery. In *Le Paysan parvenu* he probes much more deeply. He begins by drawing a broad distinction between the 'pious' and the 'devout'. The pious are the true, the *dévots* the false 'servants of God'. Although he does not draw a hard and fast distinction, it becomes clear that for him there are two kinds of *dévot*. The *faux dévots* are complete hypocrites, are people without any genuine religious feeling who pretend to be 'devout' in order to curry favour with their fellows and to use religion as a mask for evil-doing. The ordinary *dévots* are people who have genuine religious feeling, which for Marivaux is nevertheless tainted by an element of hypocrisy.

This leads to a further distinction. If hypocrisy appears to be Marivaux's main charge against the *dévots,* it is not the only one. What he is always on his guard against is passion of any kind and that is one of the problems of the *dévots*. Passion is a blind force and the form it takes is determined by the character of the individual. If the *dévots* succeed in deluding their fellows, there are a good many who delude themselves. The pre-Freudian age naturally had no word for it, but with the kind of *dévot* that I am discussing religion is a defence mechanism. An apparently intense love of God is a substitute for repressed sexual feeling as well as for other forms of sensuality. We shall find that what is most original about *Le Paysan parvenu,* what has not been sufficiently remarked—in some cases on account of squeamishness—is that it is a study of the relations between religiosity and sexuality revealed primarily in the person of the younger Mlle Habert.

Jacob's first sight of the elderly spinster's home produces a

brilliantly ironical account of the way in which the *dévots*
delude themselves as well as other people:

> On eût dit que chaque chambre était un oratoire; l'envie d'y
> faire oraison y prenait en y entrant; tout y était modeste et luisant,
> tout y invitait à goûter la douceur d'un saint recueillement.
>
> L'autre soeur était dans son cabinet, qui, les deux mains sur les
> bras d'un fauteuil, s'y reposait de la fatigue d'un déjeuner qu'elle
> venait de faire, et en attendant la digestion en paix.

> [One would have said that each room was an oratory; the de-
> sire to pray seized you as you entered; everything there was modest
> and shiny, everything there invited you to enjoy the gentleness of
> a holy meditation.
>
> The other sister was in her small room and, with both her hands
> on the arms of an armchair, was resting from the fatigue of a
> lunch that she had just finished, and waiting for digestion in
> peace.]

The irony emerges in the contrast between 'oratory' and the
evident cosiness of the rooms, between prayer and the way in
which a supposedly ascetic character installs herself in an
armchair in order to digest a sumptuous lunch.

The description of meals which follows demonstrates the way
in which religion is used to conceal other forms of sensuality
on the part of the two pretended or imaginary ascetics:

> Jamais elles n'avaient d'appétit; du moins on ne voyait point
> celui qu'elles avaient; il escamotait les morceaux; ils disparais-
> saient sans qu'il parût presque y toucher.
>
> On voyait ces dames se servir négligemment de leurs four-
> chettes; à peine avaient-elles la force d'ouvrir la bouche; elles
> jetaient des regards indifférents sur ce bon vivre: 'Je n'ai point de
> goût aujourd'hui'. 'Ni moi non plus. Je trouve tout fade'. 'Et moi
> trop salé'.
>
> Ces discours me jetaient de la poudre aux yeux, de manière que
> je croyais voir les créatures les plus dégoûtées du monde, et cepen-
> dant le résultat de tout cela était que les plats se trouvaient si
> considérablement diminués quand on desservait, que je ne savais
> les premiers jours comment ajuster tout cela.
>
> Mais je vis à la fin de quoi j'avais été les premiers jours dupe.
> C'était de ces airs de dégoût, que marquaient nos maîtresses, et qui
> m'avaient caché la sourde activité de leurs dents.

Le plus plaisant, c'est qu'elles s'imaginaient elles-mêmes être de très petites et de très sobres mangeuses. Et comme il n'était pas décent que les dévotes fussen gourmandes; qu'il faut se nourrir pour vivre, et non pas vivre pour manger; que, malgré cette maxime raisonnable et chrétienne, leur appétit ne voulait rien perdre, elles avaient trouvé le secret de le laisser faire, sans tremper dans la gloutonnerie; et c'était par le moyen de ces apparences de dédain pour les viandes, c'était par l'indolence avec laquelle elles y touchaient, qu'elles se persuadaient être sobres en se conservant le plaisir de ne pas l'être; c'était à la faveur de cette singerie que leur dévotion laissait innocemment le champ libre à l'intempérance.

[They never had any appetite; at least one never saw the appetite that they had; it made bits of food vanish; they disappeared almost without the appearance of being touched.

You saw these ladies serving themselves carelessly with their forks; they hardly had the strength to open the mouth; they cast glances of indifference on this good living: 'I have no appetite today'. 'Nor me either. I find everything tasteless'. 'And I all too salty'.

These conversations threw powder into my eyes, in the way in which I thought that I was seeing the most disgusted creatures in the world, and yet the result of it all was that the dishes found themselves so considerably reduced when the table was cleared, that in the first days I did not know how to explain things.

But I saw in the end of what I had been a dupe during the first days. It was these airs of disgust, which marked out our mistresses, and which concealed from me the muffled activity of their teeth.

The most amusing thing is that they themselves imagined that they were very small and very modest eaters. And as it was not decent that the devout should be gluttons, that one must nourish oneself in order to live, and not to live in order to eat; that, in spite of this reasonable and Christian maxim, they had found the secret which let them do it without being absorbed by gluttony; and it was by this appearance of disdain for food, by the indolence with which they handled it that they persuaded themselves that they were temperate in retaining the pleasure of not being it; it was the result of this apish antic that their devotion innocently left the field free to intemperance.]

It is a brilliantly comic scene with the ironical 'sourde activité de leurs dents' and 'l'indolence avec laquelle elles y

touchaient'.[1] At the same time, it is a fair criticism of the mixture of deception and self-deception which is characteristic of
the milder type of *dévotes* and it is well brought out by 'c'était
à la faveur de cette singerie, que leur dévotion laissait innocent
le champ libre à l'intempérance'. In spite of the reference to
them as 'gourmandes' and the appearance of the word 'intempérance', there is naturally nothing wrong in having a
hearty appetite. The real issue is the way in which they consistently deceive themselves 'innocently' into believing that
they are only modest eaters.

When we remember that every room in the house looked like
an 'oratory', the ending of the meal becomes something like
a caricature of religious practice. In order to convince themselves of their devotion and innocence, the two well-fed sisters
engage together in prayers of thanksgiving. They then sink into
soft, deep, comfortable chairs and speak complacently of the
good that some sermon might have done to people who in their
opinion were a good deal less devout than themselves.

The most important event in the novel is naturally the marriage of the fifty-year-old *dévote* to the peasant boy who is more
than thirty years her junior, the problems that it creates and
the particular nature of the relations between them.

Jacob is a sympathetic character, very definitely a 'paysan
parvenu' and in no sense a 'paysan perverti', but he is not
exactly a model of virtue like the sister-figure of Marianne. He
is a highly susceptible young man whose susceptibilities are
greatly stimulated by the variety of women whom he meets in
Paris and who are very different from the women whom he
may have met in the country. Although we shall find—it is
simply a psychological fact—that elderly and experienced
women have a special attraction for the young man and he
for them, no woman, whether young or old, fails to interest
him.

He begins by being attracted by the wife of his first employer
in Paris, especially by the 'freshness' of her complexion and her

[1] The two references to 'les premiers jours' appear to be an example of
Marivaux's carelessness. The breach between the two sisters occurred and
they parted on the evening of Jacob's arrival. He could not therefore have
seen them have more than one meal together.

'plumpness'. It looks forward to what is to come and produces
an amusing incident:

> There then took place between us a short, silent scene which is
> the pleasantest thing in the world.

It is not without significance that he fixes on the same physical traits at his first meeting with the woman whom he will
marry:

> I examined her appearance for a bit while she was speaking to
> me. I saw a round face [*face ronde*] which gave the impression of
> being succulently nourished [*succulemment*] . . . As for the per-
> son's age, the roundness of her face, her paleness and her plump-
> ness [*embonpoint*] made it difficult to decide.

'Succulemment nourrie', which is a foretaste of the sisters' performance at table, 'face ronde' and 'embonpoint' are a clear
indication of the countryman's taste for plumpness of face and
body. Still another reference to 'freshness' and 'round face' on
the next page shows that Jacob has begun to react with his
customary promptness:

> Since this person had a fresh and appetising appearance and a
> round face—the sort of face that I have always liked—I felt some
> concern for her.

Although Jacob is not a model of virtue, it is greatly to his
credit that he abandoned the marriage that he was planning
with a servant of his own age at his first employer's on moral
grounds. Although they are in love with one another (according to him), the discovery that she is prostituting herself to her
employer in order to provide money for the marriage filled him
with a 'disgust which could only have affected a decent and
honourable person'.

Jacob's use of the word 'aimer' invites comment. In a passage describing the approach of the moment when the declaration of love, which comes significantly from the woman and
not the man, will be made, he says of Mlle Habert:

> . . . son coeur s'épancha, j'en tirai tout ce qu'il méditait pour

moi; et peut-être qu'à son tour elle tira du mien plus de tendresse
qu'il n'en avait à lui rendre; car je me trouvai moi-même étonné de
l'aimer tant . . .

[. . . her heart overflowed; I drew from it all that it was contemplating for me; and perhaps she in turn drew from mine more
tenderness than it had to offer her because I myself was astonished that I loved her so much . . .]

Although Jacob describes himself as 'étonné de l'aimer tant',
the important words are those suggesting the limitation of his
feelings: 'elle tira du mien plus de tendresse qu'il n'en avait à
lui rendre'. He is completely free from the cynicism that we find
in many male characters in eighteenth-century novels. Except
in a rather special context in the last stages of the novel, he
never uses the verb 'aimer' in the sense of physical desire without feeling, but one has the impression that his use of the word
here only means something like 'fondness' or even 'like'. Mlle
Habert is amiable, kindly, helpful and very much in love with
Jacob. Their marriage will be a complete success, but there is
no question of his being 'in love' in the traditional sense with
her or any other woman. He is genuinely fond of her and
strongly attracted by an elderly woman who retains a high
degree of sex appeal, which produces still another luscious
reference to her face—'car elle était encore aimable et d'une
figure appétissante'.

Although opposition to Jacob's marriage like the opposition
to Marianne's is based primarily on social grounds, there is
even less reason for it. Mlle Habert's father like Jacob's was a
farmer, but she has managed somehow to establish herself as
a prosperous member of the Paris bourgeoisie. What is important is that the opposition is organised by the sister and her unworthy confessor, who is M. Douchin. It means that they are
trying to use religion for a thoroughly uncharitable purpose.
It provides Marivaux with a sitting target for his attack on the
dévots and dubious clergy.

It does not mean, however, that the younger sister escapes
entirely. Jacob's fondness for her and the strong attraction that
she exercises over his feelings do not prevent him from taking
a detached and decidedly objective view of her weaknesses in

the same way that Marianne did of Mme de Miran in admittedly different circumstances. We saw that she was included in the criticism of the 'gluttony' of the 'devout'. There is an element of youthful brutality in the comment that he makes at a comparatively early stage in their relations:

> I took advantage of her hypocritical way of listening to me. I opened my eyes to my good fortune, and I decided on the spot that she had an inclination for me since she did nothing to put a stop to talk which was as tender as mine.

The most revealing passages from every point of view are naturally those describing their marital relations:

> J'ai bien vu des amours en ma vie . . . mais je n'ai jamais rien vu d'égal à l'amour de ma femme . . .
> Pour aimer comme elle, il faut avoir été trente ans dévote, et pendant trente ans avoir eu besoin de courage pour l'être; il faut pendant trente ans avoir résisté à la tentation de songer à l'amour, et trente ans s'être fait un scrupule d'écouter ou même de regarder les hommes qu'on ne haïssait pas.

> [I have seen plenty of love affairs in my life . . . but I have never seen anything equal to the love of my wife . . .
> In order to love like her, it was necessary to have been devout for thirty years, and for thirty years to have had the courage which was needed to be it; it is necessary during thirty years to have resisted the temptation to think of love, and thirty years to have developed a scruple for oneself against listening or even looking at men whom one did not hate.]

The passage was inspired by Jacob's experience on the wedding night. It is an illuminating account not merely of the way in which religion is used as a defence mechanism to curb an innate sexual passion, but the exceptional violence of the passion of a sexually starved middle-aged woman the moment that she finds herself in the happy position of being able to discard it, to indulge in love without any feeling of guilt. We should also observe that Jacob's language is considerably more sympathetic than that used in the earlier passage, that instead of a word like 'hypocrite', he dwells on 'courage', 'resistance to

temptation' and 'scruple', which are very effectively emphasised
by the four uses of 'trente ans'.

In another passage we find that Mme de la Vallée, as she
now is, is so anxious for her husband to join her in bed that
she cannot wait to listen to his account of the help that he is
being given by Mme de Fervel to find a job:[1]

> ... c'est que jamais femme dévote n'usa avec tant de passion du
> privilège de marquer son chaste amour; je vis le moment qu'elle
> s'écrierait: Quel plaisir de frustrer les droits du diable, et de pou-
> voir sans péché être aussi aise que les pécheurs!

> [. . . it means that a devout woman never used with so much
> passion the privilege to make her chaste love; I saw the moment
> that she would say to herself: What a pleasure to frustrate the
> rights of the devil, and without sin to be as much at ease as the
> sinners!]

There is still another passage which completes the picture of
the relations between devotion and sexual pleasure. It is inspired by the sight of Mme de la Vallée at prayer:

> Et jugez combien de pareilles prières étaient ferventes; les dé-
> vots n'aiment jamais tant Dieu que lorsqu'ils en ont obtenu leurs
> petites satisfactions temporelles, et jamais ne prient mieux que
> quand l'esprit et la chair sont contents, et prient ensemble; il n'y
> a lorsque la chair languit, souffre, et n'a pas son compte, et qu'il
> faut que l'esprit soit dévot tout seul, qu'on a de la peine.

> [And judge how fervent such prayers were; the devout never
> love God so much as when they have obtained their little temporal
> satisfactions, and they never pray better than when the mind and
> the body are content, and they pray together; it is only when the
> flesh languishes and has no count of itself, and that the mind has
> to be devout all alone, that one has pain.]

We see that there is another change of tone, that there is
clearly an amusingly ironical element in the slightly patronis-
ing reference to 'leurs petites satisfactions temporelles' and

---

[1] It should be observed that Jacob's family name was simply 'La Vallée'
and that the introduction of 'de' was obviously used in order to improve
his social standing.

'jamais on ne prie mieux que quand l'esprit et la chair sont
contents, et prient ensemble'. There is nothing harsh or unkind
about it, but it is a clear demonstration that Jacob never abandons his critical attitude toward the 'devout'.

It is also very far from detracting in any way from the psychological acumen with which Marivaux invests his protagonists. What the completed picture demonstrates convincingly
is that genuinely religious people are often very highly sexed
and that they are only truly happy when the sexual inclination
can be satisfied without sin. When sexual feeling is repressed or
frustrated, there is a lack of balance and harmony. The in-
tensive religious practice, which is characteristic of *dévots,* acts
as a palliative. It helps to maintain some degree of calm by providing an outlet for strong feelings whose origin is not religious. We can also see that when a devout person makes a be-
lately happy marriage, religion itself does a great deal to increase the intensity of the sexual passion. Nor should we overlook what might be called the moral paradox. Mme de la
Vallée's sexual satisfaction in marriage, as we are expressly
told, was heightened by the knowledge that she was enjoying
chastely something which she had come to associate essentially
with sin. Finally, in order to complete Marivaux's admirable
picture of the *dévots,* we should remind ourselves that the concealed 'gluttony' described earlier, was used— probably unconsciously—by them when unmarried as a substitute for
sexual sensuality.

I have already said that Jacob is not in love with anybody in
the orthodox sense. His marriage to Mlle Habert and his un-
doubted fondness for her do nothing to curb his susceptibility
or the attraction that he feels for other women, which in the
last part of the novel verges on promiscuity. He is frank about
the reasons:

> As for love, even if you are already completely bound to one
> person, the vanity of giving pleasure in other places turns you into
> an unfaithful character, and on such occasions makes you yield in
> the cowardliest fashion.

At his first meeting with Mme de Ferval, which takes place
immediately after his success with the magistrate, we are aware

of a mutual attraction. 'I left', he remarks, 'filled with an agreeable feeling'.

Although this hints at promiscuity, there is no feeling of guilt, religious or otherwise:

> Never for a moment did I have any sense that my feelings were doing wrong to those I owed to Mlle Habert; there had not been the slightest change in my attitude towards her . . . I was delighted to marry the one and give pleasure to the other and was very conscious of both forms of pleasure at the same time.[1]

When he pays his first solo visit to Mme de Ferval to hear her suggestion for a job, he finds her lying on a sofa in a very correct, but 'rather carelessly arranged' *déshabillé*:

> Imagine a skirt which is not completely pulled down to the feet and even provides a glimpse of the loveliest leg in the world; (and with a woman, a lovely leg is a source of great beauty).
>
> The slipper had fallen off one of those two attractive feet to which this form of nakedness gave great charm.
>
> Nothing about her touching posture escaped me; for the first time in my life, I became very conscious of the attraction of a woman's feet and legs; until then, they simply hadn't counted for me. I had only noticed women's faces and waists; I now realised that they were women all over.

We can see from the description of Mme de Ferval's appearance that Jacob is becoming quite sophisticated and his language not perhaps erotic, but decidedly suggestive. It is most evident in something like a change of direction: a downward movement from 'une face ronde', 'une figure appétissante' and even 'embonpoint' to skirts, lovely arms, naked legs and feet. It is obvious that marriage—he was a virgin when it took place —has increased his sexual appetite considerably. What is still more significant is that though he is not an eighteenth-century cynic, his failure really to fall in love with his amorous wife has encouraged a taste for variety and is turning him into something like an all-rounder who could enjoy two people as different as Mlle Habert and Mme de Ferval.

---

[1] Compare with the behaviour of the protagonists of Crébillon and Radiguet on pp. 100 and 276.

It is evident from the way that she behaves that Mme de Ferval is out to seduce the young man. The next meeting takes place, at her invitation, in a room in a house off the beaten track which is managed by a woman of humble origin. It is what the eighteenth-century called *une petite maison,* meaning that whether it belonged to a man or a woman it was something like a private brothel.[1] (Paradoxically, sexual intercourse by Jacob would be the 'fee' for helping him to find a job!) Adultery within two days of marriage is only avoided by the unexpected appearance of a distinctly aggressive rival, which leads to Jacob's retreat.

Jacob has given a lively description of Mme de Ferval's physical attractions. His account of the psychological appeals, which adds considerably to their power, is another impressive example of the novelist's insight:

> Elle avait des grâces naturelles. Par-dessus cela, elle était fausse dévote, et ces femmes-là, en fait d'amour, ont quelque chose de plus piquant que les autres; il y a dans leurs façons je ne sais quel mélange indéfinissable de mystère, de fourberie, d'avidité libertine et solitaire, et en même temps de retenue, qui tente extrêmement: vous sentez qu'elles voudraient jouir furtivement du plaisir de vous aimer et d'être aimée, sans que vous y prissiez garde, ou qu'elles voudraient du moins vous persuader que, dans tout ce qui passe, elles sont vos dupes et non pas vos complices.

> [She had some natural graces. On top of that she was falsely devout, and those women, in the case of love, have something more piquant than the rest; in their behaviour and indefinable mixture of mystery, deceit, libertine and solitary greed, and at the same time restraint, which is an extreme temptation: you feel that they would like to enjoy furtively the pleasure of loving you and to be loved without your taking guard, or that they would at least like to persuade you that, in all that passes, they are your dupes and not your accomplices.]

What he says here is clearly related to the theme of religiosity and sexuality, and should be compared to the description of Mlle Habert's performance on the wedding night. We know

---

[1] We find in *Les Liaisons dangereuses* that Mme de Merteuil has a *petite maison* and uses it for the same purpose. See also E. and J. Goncourts, *La Femme au dix-huitième siècle,* Nouv. Ed., 1901, p. 173.

that in the case of the genuine or, for Jacob, the comparatively
genuine *dévote,* abstention on religious grounds greatly intensifies legitimate passion. In the case of the *fausse dévote,* the
pretence of religion engenders every kind of sexual ruse and
adds enormously to the woman's skill as a seductress while
enabling her to give the impression, at any rate to people less
acute than Jacob, that the man is the guilty party and that she
herself is not an 'accomplice'.

We also notice that in discussing the tactics of the *fausse
dévote,* Jacob has begun to use the word 'aimer' in the
eighteenth-century sense of desire without emotion. The fact is
that he has no illusions about the kind of life to which he is
now exposing himself or its moral implications:

> . . . voyez quelle école de mollesse, de volupté, de corruption, et
> par conséquent de sentiment; car l'âme se raffine à mesure qu'elle
> se gâte.
>
> [. . . see what a school of softness, of voluptuousness, of corrup-
> tion, and in consequence of feeling; for the spirit refines itself in
> the measure in which it spoils itself.]

If he has no illusions about the nature of the life to which
he is exposing himself, neither has he any about the nature of
his success, or the reasons for it. The last pages, indeed, are
a triumphant account of the final transformation of the country bumpkin into a gentleman. He has changed his appearance
as well as his name. He wears a silk doublet, a hat with a noble
silver brim and his hair comes down to his waist.

He goes on with even greater enthusiasm:

> Just imagine what has happened to a young rustic like me who
> in a mere two days has become the husband of a rich girl and the
> lover of two women of high social standing . . . the title of 'mon-
> sieur' with which I honoured myself, I who was known as 'Jacob'
> ten days or so ago, the amorous provocations of those two ladies,
> and above all the charming though impure heart that Mme de
> Ferval had used to seduce me . . .[1]

---

[1] In spite of the use of the words 'lover' and 'seduce' in this passage, it
should be understood that there is never an actual act of adultery in the
novel as we have it.

The greatest moment of all occurs at the very end of the novel, as we have it. Jacob saves the life of a man who is being attacked or, as we should say today, 'mugged' in the street by vandals—saves him with the sword that his wife has bought him as still another status symbol. The person whose life he saves turns out to be an aristocrat, who invites Jacob to go with him to a performance of Racine's *Mithridate* at the Comédie Française:

> Until then I had been more or less in possession of myself, had not entirely lost sight of myself; but this was stronger than I and the proposal to be taken grandly to the Comédie Française turned my head completely; I felt stunned by a great wave of joy, glory, fortune, worldliness . . .

Although *Le Paysan parvenu* like *La Vie de Marianne* remains unfinished, this is something like an apotheosis. Except for the job, which is bound to turn up, Jacob has well and truly reached his goal, which is far from being the case with Marianne. We know that there was to have been a sixth part, that the wife was to die very soon—presumably for the same reason that old men who marry very young girls often die in a couple of years—and that at the time of writing his 'memoirs', Jacob was an elderly man living in retirement in the country a long way from any relations. This leaves us with the impression that we have not missed very much, that there might have been only one more part describing the death of the wife and that for the rest of his life, whatever his sexual propensities, the protagonist enjoyed a successful career without the sort of excitement which got him into middle-class society.

There have been unfavourable criticisms of *Le Paysan parvenu*. Only one invites comment here. Many years ago, André Le Breton, who was something of a prude, complained that already in *La Vie de Marianne* 'one felt that the atmosphere was no longer healthy' and that 'in spite of our fondness for Marivaux we can hardly resign ourselves to seeing in *Le Paysan parvenu* what he himself put into it'.[1] He meant that the work

---

[1] *Le Roman au dix-huitième siècle*, 1898, p. 81.

was a 'sex novel'. He was right, but in the wrong way. It cannot be too strongly emphasised that there is absolutely nothing indecent or improper in *La Paysan parvenu,* that its great originality lies in the remarkable penetration with which the novelist analyses certain kinds of religious behaviour and the relations between religiosity and sexuality, which are both something which is still with us and likely to remain with us.

CRÉBILLON *FILS*

I. THE MAN AND THE WRITER

Crébillon est moins un romancier libertin qu'on romancier qui peint les libertins.[1]—HENRI COULET

'AT BOTTOM he is only an entertainer', Emile Henriot said of Crébillon *fils,* who finds himself in the same boat as Choderlos de Laclos, or what Henriot called novelists whose works belong to 'the second shelf', meaning that in his opinion they are both second-raters.[2] It is not exactly a bright judgement. Crébillon may not be a novelist of the same order as Laclos, who stands out as the author of one of the two greatest French novels of the eighteenth century, but it is hopelessly misguided to dismiss him as a minor performer. We shall see that though unfinished, *Les Egarements du coeur et de l'esprit* is a great novel whose author has been given far less credit than he deserves or, as Stendhal put it, whose novels are 'too neglected'. There can be no doubt that his supposed obscenity has been used to obscure his literary genius. He has suffered to an even greater extent than Laclos at the hands of the puritans. They branded him as an obscene writer whose name is still associated almost exclusively with *Le Sopha,* which is certainly not of the same order as *Les Egarements du coeur et de l'esprit* or anything like it.

Claude-Prosper Jolyot de Crébillon was born in Paris on February 14, 1707, a fortnight after his parents' marriage, and was baptised the following day at the church of Saint-Etienne du Mont. 'It was hoped', observed one writer, 'that the promptness with which the christening was accomplished would help to compensate for the delay of the wedding ceremony'.[3] His mother died when he was four years old and he was brought up by his father. Crébillon *père* was the author of a number of

1 Crébillon is less a licentious novelist than a novelist who gives a picture of libertines.
2 *Les Livres du second rayon,* 1948, p. 184.
3 J. G. Palache: *Four Novelists of the Old Régime,* 1926, p. 21.

73

turgid tragedies in verse which demonstrate the decadence of French classical drama, and was described unkindly by Boileau as a 'drunken Racine'. It did not prevent him from being elected to the French Academy or receiving better treatment than his more gifted son.

The father was also a decidedly eccentric character with a passion for pets. He used to wander around Paris picking up not women, but stray cats and dogs. It is said that at one time his grubby, ill-smelling house provided a home for twenty-two dogs, ten cats and several ravens.

The son's trouble as a writer began with the publication of *L'Ecumoire,* his second full-length novel, in 1734. It is an amusing and mildly licentious work, but on this occasion the cause of the trouble does not appear to have been licentiousness. In spite of the oriental setting and the description of it as an 'histoire japonaise', the author was suspected of using it as a disguised attack on a number of prominent personalities, who included the Duchesse du Maine, Cardinal de Rohan, Cardinal Dubois, and on the papal Bull Unigenitus. Crébillon was imprisoned for a few days and obtained his release through the intervention of the dowager Duchesse de Conti, who maintained that the supposed portrait of her daughter was not sufficiently lifelike to be recognisable.

There was more trouble with *Le Sopha,* which Crébillon discreetly called a 'conte moral'. In 1742, two years after its appearance, he was exiled from Paris on account of its alleged immorality and his omission to obtain a license to publish. The sentence was reduced, but he did not return to Paris until 1747.

In spite of his preoccupation in the novels with seduction, Crébillon himself seems to have behaved a good deal better than his characters and is not credited with many liaisons. Soon after leaving the Collège de Louis-le-Grand, where he was educated, he became engaged to an actress named Mlle La Gaussin. When, however, he produced the marriage licence, she told him that she had found a rich 'lover' whom she preferred to a poor 'husband'. His only liaison of any duration was with Mme de Murgy, whom he used as his model for Mme de Lursay in *Les Egarements du coeur et de l'esprit.* Then, in 1744, he met

Henrietta Maria Stafford, the daughter of an English peer who had been a chamberlain to King James II. She read *Le Sopha*, fell in love with the author and crossed the Channel in order to offer herself to him. He seems to have followed the example of his own parents. She was his mistress for four years before they were married on April 23, 1748. A child was born two years before they were married and died two years after it. Its death was followed a few months later by that of the mother. Little is known of the marriage, which is thought to have been a happy one in spite of the wife's lack of beauty. A contemporary described her as a 'person with a squint and shockingly ugly', but added that she was a 'thoroughly good creature, very gentle, very polite, and not lacking in good sense'.[1]

In 1749, only two years after his return from exile, Crébillon applied, somewhat surprisingly, to the chief of police for the post of censor, which had been held by his father. The application was ignored. In 1755, however, he was brought to the notice of Mme de Pompadour. Although she had disapproved of *Le Sopha,* she had him appointed royal censor for *belles lettres.* When Crébillon *père* died in 1762, she transferred the father's two-thousand-franc pension to the son. In 1774 he did even better. He became the police as well as the royal censor, which gave him still another pension. From all accounts he managed both censorships sensibly and well, except for minor trouble when one of the artists restored a couplet that he had banned in a play. His last novel was published in 1771. He died on April 12, 1777, at the age of seventy, at a time when he is said to have been poor and forgotten, and was buried 'without cere-mony' in the cemetery of Saint-Germain-l'Auxerrois.

During his lifetime opinion in France was divided about the literary merits of his work. Among the progressives, Vol-taire applauded him and d'Alembert commented shrewdly on the value of his work as social criticism. The Abbé Prévost re-viewed some of the novels unfavourably in *Pour et contre* at the time of publication. Marivaux caricatured him though not unkindly in *Le Paysan parvenu.* Diderot hit rather harder in

---

[1] Quoted, E. Henriot, *Op. cit.,* pp. 182–83.

Les Bijoux indiscrets, but the bitterest attack of all came, very inappropriately, from the Marquis de Sade, who described him as 'le scélérat des scélérats'.

His marriage to his English admirer is not without interest. English readers in general showed him more indulgence than his compatriots. He was admired by Horace Walpole, Laurence Sterne and Thomas Gray. Although he was later to lose his enthusiasm, Horace Walpole speaks, in a letter to Horace Mann in 1752, of 'my passion for the writings of the younger Crébillon'.[1] In another letter he said: 'We have at last got Crébillon's *Sopha*: Lord Chesterfield received three hundred of them and gave them to be sold at White's. It is admirable'.[2] In spite of her relations with Voltaire, that was far from the view of Mme du Deffand. 'You made me reread Crébillon's novels', she said in a letter to Walpole. '...there is nothing more disgusting, more obscure, more given to preciosity and more obscene'.[3]

This kind of unfavourable reaction was not confined to the eighteenth century. French authors of literary manuals adopted the same prim attitude towards him that they once did towards Laclos, but instead of abandoning it, as they eventually did with Laclos, it has continued down to our own time. His father is given a few lines; the son either goes unmentioned or is dismissed in a disparaging footnote. The procedure is not confined to the authors of school manuals. He even goes unmentioned in Paul Guth's highly entertaining history of French literature, which was certainly not written exclusively for schoolchildren. The result is that, at the present time, his novels are not popular or widely read by the general reader and with one or two exceptions are not readily available in French or English.

This does not mean that the position is without hope. Although there has been nothing in the nature of a genuine recovery, in the past few years there has been a change for the better among several of the more perceptive critics in France and the United States. In the admirable introduction to his edition of *Les Egarements du coeur et de l'esprit,* which was published in 1961, Etiemble describes it roundly as a 'master-

---

[1] *The Letters of Horace Walpole,* III, p. 105.　　[2] *Ibid.,* p. 178.
[3] *Lettres de la Marquise du Deffand,* I, p. 384.

piece' that he would never dream of relegating to 'the second shelf'. He also demonstrates very effectively that Crébillon is in no sense a pornographic writer. The novels, to be sure, are dominated by sexual relations, but with the exception of *L'Ecumoire* he was careful to avoid scabrous physical details and there is really nothing in them which could be called erotic.

It must always be remembered that Crébillon belonged to an extremely licentious society. It seems probable that without realising it, contemporaries like Mme de Pompadour and Mme du Deffand disapproved because they felt rightly that his work was a very damaging exposure of the society in which they lived and that it gave a bad impression of the French in general, who for a long time were regarded abroad as a people of loose morals. There are also grounds for thinking that the persistence of this unfavourable attitude is due to the ignorance of the authors of literary manuals, who have either read none of the novels, or none except *Le Sopha*, and have simply taken earlier criticism for granted.

II. THE NOVELIST

1 The Setting

ALTHOUGH Crébillon gave several of his novels a foreign setting, partly in order to avoid the difficulties which arose over *L'Ecumoire* and partly because oriental settings were fashionable at the time, his world is much narrower than Marivaux's. He confines himself almost exclusively to a single class, so much so that we do not even come face to face with the servants who surround the characters as we do repeatedly in Marivaux.[1] Whatever the setting or the disguise used, his real world is Parisian aristocratic society at the time of the Regency. It is desirable to take a general look at it before discussing his principal novel in detail.

During the last years of Louis XIV's reign the court became grimly puritanical, largely owing to the influence of his morganatic spouse. The Regency produced a prompt and vigorous reaction, or at least in that section of aristocratic society to which Crébillon devoted his work. Restrictions went by the board. Society was no longer governed by any genuine moral principles. Adultery ceased to be regarded as discreditable because society had abandoned its belief in the sanctity of marriage. Sexual promiscuity became its chief pastime in much the same way as sport in our own day.

Crébillon deals with a period in which there happened to be no European war. The aristocracy, who at the best of times were made up of the idle rich, found themselves without any serious occupation or any profitable way of filling in their time. They therefore devoted it to what I have called their 'sport'. Since there were no jobs for them as soldiers, the men concentrated on the civilian equivalent: the conquest of women. Although they continued to use traditional terminology, to speak of the 'victory' of men and the 'defeat' of women, it

[1] *Les Heureux orphelins* is an exception because the first part is an adaption of Mrs. Hayward's *The Fortunate Foundlings* and the second part also takes place in England.

78

was simply part of the game. Women were more than ready to co-operate with men in a game which provided both parties with plenty of fun. Some women gave in on the spot or practically threw themselves at men. The more sensible of them, however, felt that it was desirable to make a show of resistance, that every liaison should be marked by what one of Crébillon's characters calls the 'gradations', meaning the stages leading to imaginary defeat. Women who gave in too easily or too soon spoilt the fun and were treated with contempt. If they put up a formal resistance they could claim that they had been carried away in spite of themselves, that they had been truly 'vanquished', which had the effect of removing what was supposed to be 'remorse' and dissipating the slight sense of guilt which still lingered on even in that amoral society.

There is one aspect of Regency society on which Crébillon places special emphasis. It is the absence of love or any truly deep feeling on the part of the supposed lovers. The male protagonist puts it genially. He says of two people in *La Nuit et le moment*:

> They are attracted by one another and take one another. What happens if they get bored with one another? They part with as little ceremony as they came together . . . Love [*amour*] has played no part in all that . . . We know that in these days taste [*goût*] is the only thing that exists; if people still talk of loving one another, it is far less because they believe that it is true than because it is a politer way of asking one another for the thing they both need.

The Comte de Versac describes the position much more cynically in *Les Egarements*:

> As for love, it no longer exists, and after all I am not sure that we need regret its loss all that much. A great passion is no doubt something eminently respectable, but where does it lead us except to boring one another for a very long time?

His definition of the relationship is still more cynical:

> A form of intimate relations [*commerce*] . . . a lively friendship which resembles love by its pleasures, without having its stupid delicacies.

'Amour', 'goût' and 'commerce' are key words in the Crébillon vocabulary. 'Amour' is no longer anything more than a euphemism; it has vanished and been replaced by 'goût', which stands for sexual attraction accompanied by friendly feeling and nothing more. Instead of a union between the parties, there is simply 'commerce', meaning a form of relations which only lasts until the parties become tired or 'bored' with one another and decide, if they are amiable, to part in a friendly way and start off again with another partner. What Crébillon's characters are advocating is the elimination of the most important element in human relations: affection or devotion. It is clearly a deliberate policy of *impoverishment*. I place special emphasis on the word because we shall see, when later we come to examine Versac's view of society in its entirety, that impoverishment is by no means confined to emotions or sexual relations.

'Like myself', says Versac, 'men only seek pleasure. Fix it forever on the same object and you find yourself fixed too'. It is a neat summing-up of the general attitude of eighteenth-century society in these matters. There are moments of unexpectedly violent attraction which may lead the young and inexperienced to mistake 'taste' for 'love'. There are even couples who imagine that they are in love and marry. Yet in a year or two the husband is off on the hunt again and the marriage becomes a mere formality. The wife either follows the husband's example or sets up as a 'virtuous' woman in spite of the fact that for the male members of this society 'virtue' is almost a dirty word. The truth is that whether married or single nearly everybody's aim is 'commerce', which is no more than a temporary connection among the promiscuous. Its length depends on its novelty, on good looks and dexterity in bed. Boredom sets in the moment that novelty has worn off and the couple simply decide to part and start off again with someone else.

I have stressed Crébillon's preoccupation with society during the Regency. It was a time when people revelled lightheartedly in sexual relations, but Versac's cynical comment on the disappearance of love and his own conduct hint already at a coming change. Instead of simply removing any positive or enduring feeling from human relations, it is replaced by a negative and destructive impulse, by sadism, which is something like a 'foul' in sport. The words 'victory' and 'defeat' no longer belong to the language of the Regency: they take on a fresh and sinister meaning. Men concentrate on the domination, the humiliation and, finally, on the destruction of women, who are no longer partners, but 'victims' in the literal sense. A prime example is Lord Chester in Crébillon's *Les Heureux orphelins,* but the climax is reached in the *Liaisons dangereuses* in 1782, where sadism is far from being confined to the male protagonist. It is a climax because twenty years earlier Rousseau had set out to rehabilitate 'amour-passion' in *La Nouvelle Héloïse* which more than any other eighteenth-century work of fiction looked forward to the future.

2 *Les Egarements du coeur et de l'esprit*

Les Egarements du coeur et de l'esprit is by far the most impressive of Crébillon's novels. He makes a very effective use of the techniques employed by Marivaux in *La Vie de Marianne* and *Le Paysan parvenu,* but his purpose is different. Marivaux's protagonists, as we have seen, are two young people who have to fight to win places for themselves in society. The shortcomings of society are only of interest in so far as they place unfair obstacles in the way of the young persons' goals or, to put it another way, in so far as they try to keep the individual out of society. Crébillon's title is an excellent indication of his theme. It is an account of the 'aberrations' of the 'heart' and 'mind' of a young man who is neither an orphan nor an abandoned child, but a rich young nobleman who is making his début in society, to which he is fully entitled:

> I made my entry into society [he says] at the age of seventeen with all the advantages that attract attention there. My father had left me a great name whose fame he himself had increased, and I expected that a considerable fortune would come to me from my mother.

It is clear from the start that there is no question of his having to win a position for himself and that the last thing that anybody will do is to try to keep him out. His only problem is to find the proper way of fitting himself into society and adapting himself to its behaviour.

This provides the novelist with the opportunity of introducing his readers to a world which is even newer to them than it is to Meilcour.[1] He has no illusions about it. He uses his protagonist as the instrument for the exposure of a corrupt society. It is the psychological insight with which he describes its impact on the newcomer which makes the work such an effective piece of criticism—criticism which turns out to be not merely social and psychological, but moral.

In spite of his noble birth Meilcour, whose actual rank and christian names are never disclosed, is a remarkably naïve and inexperienced young man who has little idea of the way in which he should conduct himself in this new and confusing world:

> L'idée du plaisir fut, à mon entrée dans le monde, la seule qui m'occupa. La paix qui régnait alors me laissait dans un loisir dangereux. Le peu d'occupation que se font communément les gens de mon rang et de mon âge, le faux air, la liberté, l'exemple, tout m'entraînait vers les plaisirs: j'avais des passions impétueuses, ou, pour parler plus juste, j'avais l'imagination ardente, et facile à se laisser frapper.

> [When I made my entry into the world, the idea of pleasure was the only one that occupied me. The peace which reigned at that time left me in a state of dangerous leisure. The small amount of work that people of my rank and age generally undertake for themselves, the false air, freedom, example—everything led me in the direction of pleasure: I had impetuous passions or, to speak more accurately, I had an ardent imagination which easily allowed itself to be impressed.]

It is a highly perceptive account of the perplexity that a young man feels on his entry into society without a guide. It is also a good illustration of the elegance, lucidity and precision of Crébillon's prose. Meilcour is completely without the know-how which is one of the most striking characteristics of Marivaux's protagonists, who know exactly what they want. The first sentence tells us significantly that Meilcour is filled with

---

[1] I have shown that a similar method was used by Zola in *Germinal*, where the introduction of an outsider enables the novelist to examine the mining world in detail for the benefit of his readers (*The Art of French Fiction*, p. 166.)

desire for an undefined 'pleasure'. The second is a statement of
the concrete reasons for the situation in which he finds himself
and hints at the dangers that they cause. The third sentence
enlarges on the first two with a concise list of the factors at
work: 'peu d'occupation', 'rang', 'faux air', 'liberté', and
'exemple'—all drawing him in the direction of 'plaisirs'. The
close is particularly important. He possesses powerful impulses
described as 'passions impétueuses' and 'imagination ardente';
they are 'facile[s] à se laisser frapper', but there is still no def-
inite or reputable goal.

Next, the bewilderment which heightens the boredom:

> Au milieu du tumulte et de l'éclat qui m'environnaient sans
> cesse, je sentis que tout manquait â mon coeur: je désirais une
> félicité dont je n'avais pas une idée bien distincte; je fus quelque
> temps sans comprendre la sorte de volupté qui m'était nécessaire.
> Je voulais m'étourdir en vain sur l'ennui intérieur dont je me
> sentais accablé; le commerce des femmes pouvait seul le dissiper.

> [In the midst of the bustle and glitter which surrounded me
> unceasingly, I felt that my heart lacked everything: I had an urge
> for a form of happiness of which I had no very clear idea; for
> some time I was unable to understand the sort of pleasure that
> was necessary for me. I tried in vain to escape from an inner bore-
> dom which was overwhelming: relations with women was the only
> thing which could dissipate it.]

He feels dazed by the 'bustle' and 'glitter' of social life, but
instead of acting as a positive stimulant they simply bring
home to him his lack of communication with the new world,
his failure to fit in and the absence of any sense of direction. He
feels almost a prisoner, driven into himself, where he finds
nothing but emptiness, which emerges in the words 'm'environ-
naient sans cesse', 'tout manquait à mon coeur', 'l'ennui in-
térieur'. He is looking 'in vain' for a way out of the dilemma,
as we see again from the expressions he uses: 'une félicité dont
je n'avais pas une idée bien distincte' and 'sans comprendre la
sorte de volupté qui m'était nécessaire', while 'accablé' looks
back to 'tumulte' and 'éclat', re-emphasising their crushing
effect. The most pregnant observation is naturally the reference
to 'pleasure' ('volupté' as distinct from 'plaisir' in the earlier

passage) and 'le commerce des femmes'—a term to which I
drew attention when discussing society in general—as the only
means of rectifying the situation. It shows that society has
already begun to do its work and what will happen as soon
as any attractive woman shows an interest in him.

We can see now that the title of the novel is an accurate
description of what will continue to be Meilcour's dilemma.
He is potentially an intelligent person, but already in the third
paragraph of the work we are told that a 'rare thing' has happened to him; for no understandable reason his parents have
only provided him with a 'modest education'. It was clearly
responsible for his immaturity at the time of his entry into society and for the fact that he has no idea at all of what he
should undertake to make a name for himself, as well as enter-
ing into smart society. The result of his immaturity is that the
problems presented to him by society lead to the conflict between 'heart' and 'mind', with the 'mind' being constantly
overcome by the 'heart', which leads to the feeling, or rather
the illusion, that only 'relations with women' would enable
him to overcome his trouble and achieve something.

Meilcour has already seen and been excited by a number of
attractive-looking women, but was too timid to make an approach to any of them:

> My embarrassment had lasted for six months and would pro-
> bably have gone on much longer if one of the ladies, who had
> made the greatest impression on me, had not had the goodness to
> take charge of my education.

'Education' is a vital word. What we are about to see is that
society will impose its own particular form of education, which
will be successful precisely because of the 'modest' or, more accurately, the inadequate education provided by the parents.
The novel's main theme is in fact a young man's sexual education, which becomes the main condition of his entry into society. Inexperienced young men who made their first appearance
in this amoral society were regarded as something like social
neophytes. There was general agreement about one of the supposedly best ways of handling them. They underwent instruc-

tion at the hands of amiable, attractive and experienced wi-
dows who taught them the doctrines and practices of society.
Their instruction was completed by what might be called the
rite of initiation: sexual intercourse with the instructress. I
have used the word 'rite' because the practice which established
a young man as a full member of a free-thinking society was
like a caricature of religious instruction, with the lady replacing the priest who gives instruction for 'conversion' and then
performs the ceremony.

Mme de Lursay is the amiable, attractive and experienced
forty-year-old widow who becomes Meilcour's instructress. She
is a friend of his mother's, which has brought them together.
For two months they have met nearly every day and have had
pleasant but entirely innocent conversations. She is aware of
their secret inclination for one another and decides that the
time has come for action on her part.

Although she feels something like genuine affection for
Meilcour and intends to give herself to him, she is absolutely
determined to make proper use of conventional resistance or
the 'gradations'. The primary cause of their difficulties is the
correctness of her tactics and the clumsy reactions, or the
'égarements', of the neophyte. She is an instructress with a
difficult pupil and is obliged to use the authority which belongs to age. He appears to be mistaken in thinking that her
tactics are the result of her own uncertainty about herself, but
perfectly correct in describing them as a 'continual mixture of
severity and tenderness'.

The novel, as it comes down to us, consists of three parts
published in two instalments in 1736 and 1738. We know
from the author's preface that there were to have been several
additional parts and that they would have told the full story of
Meilcour's career from his entry into society to the time when,
after being 'led on by people interested in corrupting his heart
and mind...he has come back to himself and owes all his
virtues to an estimable woman'. We have never been told by
Crébillon, any more than by Marivaux, why his novel remains
unfinished. The loss is a matter for regret, but artistically it is
no more serious than it is for *Le Paysan parvenu*. The account
of Meilcour's relations with Mme de Lursay is as complete as
that of Jacob's with Mlle Habert, and in spite of the different

endings they provide each of the novels with its central theme.

Whatever the losses, Crébillon's novel is admirably constructed. The three parts are closely linked and there is not a single superfluous or unnecessary scene. It is built round Meilcour's meetings, or perhaps we should call them encounters, with Mme de Lursay and three other characters. It is a sign of the novel's economy and conciseness that though there has been a delay of two months before action starts, 'instruction' will be completed in ten meetings of varying lengths in something less than a fortnight.

An important aspect of the novel's structure is its circular movement. The protagonists go over the same ground again and again in varying moods, which has the effect of linking not only the different parts of the novel, but the different scenes. Mme de Lursay's alternation between 'severity' and 'tenderness' is matched by Meilcour's between meekness and moments of youthful hostility, expressed by words that he prudently keeps to himself: 'hatred', 'detest', 'aversion' and 'contempt'. The result is a succession of misunderstandings, tiffs and vacillations which reveal brilliantly the impact of society on Meilcour's personality, the trouble it causes and, most important of all, the changes that it produces.

The meetings with the three other characters, who belong to the same social circle and either join or are drawn into the inner circle, lead to a considerable increase in the couple's problems and the strain on the instructress. They are Meilcour's meetings with an extremely attractive girl of his own age; with the ogling Mme de Senanges, an unattractive middle-aged widow who does her best to 'get' him, and with Versac.

Although Mme de Senanges is a nuisance, the main complication, and one of the principal causes of *égarement,* is naturally Meilcour's attraction for the young girl. The situation is aggravated by Versac's virulent campaign against Mme de Lursay. He does plenty of damage in the first two parts. In the third he tries, in the course of a long conversation with Meilcour, to replace Mme de Lursay as his instructor and to persuade him to complete his initiation with Mme de Senanges.

We must anticipate a little by observing that the meetings with three different women reveal three different atttitudes to women in general. The young girl stands for love and purity; Mme de Lursay for 'taste' and an element of affection which is not love in any true sense; Mme de Senanges for 'taste' in its crudest sense and nothing more. The three different attitudes are a sign of the breadth of Crébillon's survey and the penetration that he reveals.

Mme de Lursay begins her instruction by adopting what sounds like a motherly attitude. She offers to act as Meilcour's guide and to give him impartial advice about any woman who attracts him. The inexperienced youth promptly blurts out the attraction that he feels for her. She immediately starts to play the game of artificial resistance. 'You are young', she tells him. 'There are many women for whom this would be an additional attraction.' She pretends that it does not apply to her. Even if she shared his affection, there would be the strongest reasons for not giving in. Either he would not love her enough or would love her too much. In either case the result would be disastrous for her and would bring about her downfall, owing to the follies, infidelities or indiscretions of youth. It is an argument to which she will return repeatedly and Meilcour's vacillations will demonstrate the rightness of her view. She concludes with these words:

> 'Therefore, Meilcour, what I advise you to do is not to think about me any more. I have a painful feeling that you are going to hate me, but I flatter myself that it will not be for long and that one day you will be grateful to me for my frankness. Don't you want to remain my friend?' she added, holding out her hand to me.

'She was convinced', he remarks, 'that in order to get me and even to keep me, it was essential to hide her love for me as long as possible'. The meetings which follow illustrate her tactics: hints that she loves him and suggestions that anything of the sort is out of the question; rebuffs followed by tender looks; affectionate talks brought to an abrupt end.

The first hint of love comes at the second meeting:

> 'Yes', she went on, giving me the tenderest look in the world, 'yes, Meilcour, you are right to complain: I do not treat you well; but ought you to be displeased by a little show of pride? Don't you

see how much it costs me? Ah! if only I believed it, how happy I
should be to tell you that I love you!'

In spite of all this pretty obvious hint he goes home feeling,
rather absurdly, that she 'hates' him. He is so upset that next
day he returns to her house immediately after dinner in the
hope of seeing her. He finds that she is out. He is bitterly disappointed. He goes off to the opera alone in a very bad mood,
catches sight of the unknown girl in the next box and falls for
her:

> Je ne sais quel mouvement singulier et subit m'agita à cette vue:
> frappé de tant de beautés, je demeurai comme anéanti. Ma sur-
> prise allait jusqu'au transport. Je sentis dans mon coeur un dé-
> sordre qui se répandit sur tous mes sens.

> [I do not know what strange and sudden movement agitated me
> at this sight: struck by so many elements of beauty, I remained
> dumbfounded. My astonishment was reaching the state of rapture.
> In my heart I felt a disorder which affected all my senses.]

It is a brilliantly pungent description of the young man's reaction, and a new example of *égarement*. The reflexions that he
makes shortly afterwards are even more revealing:

> Encore attaché à [Madame de Lursay] par le désir, tout rempli
> que j'étais d'une nouvelle passion, ou, pour mieux dire, amoureux
> pour la première fois, le peu d'espoir de réussir auprès de mon
> inconnue m'empêchait de songer à perdre totalement Madame de
> Lursay. Je cherchais en moi-même comment je pourrais acquérir
> l'une, et me conserver l'autre.

> [Still attached to Madame de Lursay by desire, filled as I was
> with a new passion or, more accurately, in love for the first time,
> the little hope that I had of succeeding with the unknown girl put
> a stop to the idea of giving up Madame de Lursay completely. I
> tried to think of a way of acquiring the one and keeping the other.]

It is a concise and penetrating account of what one feels
inclined to call a multiple conflict, which will dominate his
outlook for the rest of the novel or, as we shall see, beyond it.
It is a conflict between the innocent young man that he still is

and the member of a dissolute society that he is in the process of becoming; between deep and genuine feeling for the stranger and his decidedly mixed feelings for Mme de Lursay; finally, a conflict between two basically irreconcilable worlds which he will try in vain to reconcile, with the 'inconnue' and Mme de Lursay as their representatives—well brought out by the antithesis in the last sentence of 'acquérir' and 'conserver'.

He spends the next three days trying, unsuccessfully, to trace the 'inconnue' and does not go near Mme de Lursay. When he does, he gets it in the neck:

'For several days your behaviour to me has hardly been proper. In order to find you innocent, I had to look for offences on my part. I found none'.

Her words are a reversal of what she said at the second meeting, when she excused herself for not 'treating him well'. She goes on to address him as though he is a hardhearted seducer:

'You imagine that burning with impatience to be vanquished, I was only waiting for your declaration in order to make mine. Why do you flatter yourself that you could bring off such an easy victory? . . . But you don't love me; you have never loved me . . . I see through you at last. You hardly dare to look me in the face. Ah! Meilcour, is that the way one attacks a heart? Is that the way to make oneself loved?'

A few moments later there is a sudden change:

'You love me very much then', she replied, 'and you are burning to hear that your love is returned? I can only repeat what I have already said. My heart is still untroubled and I am afraid of seeing its peace disturbed. Still . . . No, I have nothing more to say to you: I forbid you to guess how I feel'.

As she finished speaking, Madame de Lursay left me. In doing so, she gave me the tenderest of looks.

The three passages are an excellent example of her method, with its sudden changes from 'severity' to 'tenderness'. The reasons are obvious. 'Severity' is necessary for instruction, but the move to 'tenderness' at the end of a talk is intended to pre-

vent him from forming a wrong impression of her real attitude
and from breaking with her. In this she is right. The danger,
as we are about to see, is not without substance. We should also
observe that paradoxically 'severity' tends to betray a nervous
woman's 'tenderness' and that, without really believing it, she
is perfectly correct in saying that he does not love her and has
never loved her in the true sense, as we know from his reaction
to the 'inconnue'.

At the end of the first part of the novel, Versac calls on Mme
de Meilcour and her son. He delivers a vicious attack on Mme
de Lursay's past, which makes her sound like the worst kind of
'pushover' even by eighteenth-century standards. When he has
gone, Mme de Meilcour, who is a symbol of true virtue, tells
her son that it is a lot of nonsense. This helps to keep Mme
de Lursay in the right perspective for the reader. The impetu-
ous youth, however, swallows the whole of the Versac story
and decides to make a name for himself by a sensational break
with Mme de Lursay.

'I left home', he tells us, 'determined not to spare Madame de
Lursay anything of the contempt that in my opinion she deserved ... I was convinced that I could only revenge myself
properly by creating one of those public scenes which destroy
a woman's reputation for ever'.

It is clearly a very unsuitable scheme for an inexperienced
young man. Although he knows perfectly well that his own
feeling for her is 'goût' and not 'amour' and that her feeling for
him is almost certainly superior to his for her, he is preparing
to break with her because of the allegation that in the past
she has indulged in the same feeling for other men that he now
indulges in for her. In spite, however, of the fact that he feels
'extremely moved by the beauty of a plan which would punish
a hypocrite and enable me to make a brilliant début in society', he begins almost at once to have doubts about his ability
to bring it off. He thinks that instead he had better pay her out
first by seducing her then by being unfaithful to her. He speaks
as a memoir writer when he goes on to observe that 'this vil-
lainous plan appeared the most agreeable and the most re-
liable'.

When he arrives at Mme de Lursay's, he finds that Versac

has preceded him and is busy making things unpleasant for her in spite of his own disreputable practices. As soon as Versac leaves and Meilcour finds himself alone with Mme de Lursay, he becomes the groveller. The inner picture is rather different:

> I had the feeling that my contempt for her had redoubled. But we were alone. She was beautiful and I knew that she was a woman of feeling. She did not inspire me with passion or respect; I was no longer afraid of her, but only desired her all the more . . . Never had she shown her tenderness for me more clearly; never had my response to it been worse.

It is an important passage in view of what is to come. It shows that however hostile his feelings towards her may appear to be, they do nothing to curb the violence of the physical attraction minus love that he feels for her, or rather that they tend to increase it. The last sentence is a sign that in spite of Versac and of his own private fulminations, there is still something of the decent young man in him who feels guilty about his ungracious attitude towards Mme de Lursay.

Mme de Lursay displays her usual skill in smoothing things over. She has just convinced her pupil of the necessity of 'gradations' when a lacquey announces the arrival of Mme and Mlle de Théville, and Meilcour suddenly finds himself being introduced to his 'inconnue'. She is Hortense de Théville, daughter of a former friend of his mother's. This brings us to something like a riddle. A day or two before the introduction, when Meilcour was wandering alone in the Tuileries, he had overheard a conversation between Hortense and the lady in charge of her in which she admitted that she felt a strong attraction for an unnamed man. Meilcour realised that she might be referring to him, as she had seen him at the opera without knowing who he was any more than he knew who she was. He remains convinced, however, that she must be in love with the Marquis de Germeuil, who visited her in the box at the opera and appears to be a frequent companion. Although Meilcour meets her several times after the introduction, her reception usually appears decidedly cool and he never discovers what her feelings are for him or, indeed, whether she has any feelings for him at all.

He manages to keep his attraction for Hortense a complete secret from Mme du Lursay by discreetly encouraging her jealousy over his supposed attraction to the odious Mme de Senanges, but at the beginning of the third part he makes what may well have been a major blunder. He is sulking and refuses a particularly gracious invitation from Mme de Lursay to spend two days in the country with a party that she has organised. He discovers too late that Hortense was one the party. It seems possible that her apparent coolness may have been caused by the fulsomeness with which on occasion he treated Mme de Senanges in her presence. It follows that if he had accepted the invitation, he might have been able to dispose of the misunderstanding and that if he was the unnamed person for whom she professed an attraction, he might have won her for good.

It is while the party is away in the country that Versac unexpectedly calls on Meilcour and sees him alone.

Versac's long conversation with Meilcour in the third part of the novel performs two functions. It stands out as the most sustained and damaging exposure of Regency society in the entire work. It is also, as I have already suggested, a second or rival form of instruction for the protagonist, in spite of the fact that they have to break off before Versac can deal in detail with what he regards as men's proper attitude to women.

Mme de Lursay's instruction might be described as a kind of personal and private conversion in order to make Meilcour her lover. Versac is attempting to do something very different and much more harmful. He is trying to turn Meilcour into a disciple, a person who like himself will seduce innumerable women instead of having a prolonged affair or being 'fixed' with any of them, which is an additional reason for his siding with Mme de Senanges against Mme de Lursay. When he makes his first appearance in the novel, Meilcour describes him in these terms:

> Worshipped by all the women whom he continually deceived and tore to pieces, vain, imperious, scatter-brained, the most daring coxcomb that one had ever seen and all the dearer, perhaps, in their eyes on account of these same failings, however much to their disadvantage they happened to be.

It is an honest, impartial and, one assumes, a final judgement on the part of the 'memoir writer' on achieving complete maturity. Yet Meilcour makes no attempt to conceal the fact that, as a young man, he felt a great admiration for Versac. There is, however, an element of ambivalence in his attitude. After describing his first appearance, Meilcour goes on to tell us that he himself has since 'followed very advantageously in Versac's footsteps'. But in the third part he remarks that he was beginning a conversation with him 'which had too much influence on the actions of my life'. These comments are clearly linked to a remark that he made earlier about Mme de Senanges, 'to whom, as will appear later, I had the misfortune to owe my *education*' (italics mine). The most important words are 'as will appear later'. It seems clear that Versac and Mme de Senanges are the people described in the novelist's preface as being 'interested in corrupting Meilcour's heart and mind'—a point to which we shall return.

Although it is a free-thinking society, we can hardly avoid the impression, at an early stage in the conversation, that Versac is something like the devil's advocate:

> It is an error to think that in the world of fashion one can preserve the moral innocence that is common to people when they make their entry, that one can remain always virtuous and natural without risking one's reputation and one's fortune. The heart and mind are forced to spoil themselves; everything is a matter of fashion and affectation; talents are purely arbitrary; one can only succeed by continually disfiguring oneself. These are the principles of which you must never lose sight; but it is not sufficient to know them in order to be a success; you must make yourself ridiculous. You must study with care the tone of the world in which our rank has placed us; the absurdities which best suit our condition; those, in short, which are approved, and the study of them demands more shrewdness and attention than one can imagine.

The opening sentence is not a mere generalisation: it is a dogmatic statement which is apparent from the use, in an inverted sense, of the word 'error'. It is also decidedly startling. Versac is telling Meilcour that it is an 'error' not only to preserve traditional moral virtues, but also the human qualities

which normally belong to sensible and intelligent people and
which are dismissed as 'arbitrary'. (This is what I had in mind
when I spoke earlier of Versac's policy of 'improvement'.) The
only way to achieve success in this world is to make oneself
'ridiculous', but ridiculous, as we shall see, in a special manner.
In the last two sentences Versac clearly assumes the role of instructor and uses the instructor's language, with 'you must'
occuring three times.

He tries to impress his pupil by describing his own experience:

> I was born a very different person from what I now appear to
> be, so that it was not without extreme pain that I succeeded in
> spoiling my mind. I blushed sometimes over my impertinence: I
> only spoke ill with timidity. I was truly conceited but without
> grace, without brilliance like many others, and was still far from
> the superiority of the kind that I have since acquired.
>
> It is no doubt easy to be conceited because anyone who is afraid
> of doing so needs to keep a continual watch on himself, and yet
> there is nobody who does not have his own particular form of
> conceit; but it is not so easy to acquire the sort that I needed. Be-
> cause it has no model, this bold and unusual form of conceit is the
> only kind that is worthy as serving as one.

The second of these three pronouncements by Versac is particularly important. It shows that the 'égarements du coeur et
de l'esprit' are not confined to Meilcour. Versac decided to in-
tegrate himself into contemporary society. It was in no valid
sense a positive action. He found that he was born 'a very different person from what I now appear to be' and 'that it was not
without extreme pain that I succeeded in spoiling my mind'.
That is precisely what he is trying to persuade Meilcour to do.

There are several other words which stand out in the three
passages. 'Spoil' and 'disfigure' mean something much more
painful and more humiliating than lightheartedly disregarding
moral precepts and indulging in womanising. The neophyte is
expected to degrade himself by what amounts to ruining his
natural talents, or rather his mental talents and his genuine
emotional attraction for the right kind of woman. 'Ridiculous'
and 'absurdities', which are elevated into standards of behaviour, are a sign that social life has degenerated into an unpleasant kind of farce. The great success is the man who makes him-

self into a sort of buffoon by inventing a new form of 'conceit'. It sounds like a comedian doing a fresh turn and reminds us of Versac's own performance at parties in the first part of the novel. It does not, however, prevent Versac from taking the view that the painful factors are confined to the period of self-education, or boasting about what he calls 'the superiority that . . . I have since acquired' for his fatuous performances.

What emerges from all this is that instruction means not the cultivation of one's inborn talents, but their degradation or even removal. It is a frightening lesson for a young man, but there is even more to come. Not surprisingly society turns out to be depressingly low-brow. Nothing makes a worse impression in a man than a show of intelligence, which is compared damningly to 'virtue' in women:

> While nothing is more ignoble in a woman than to be virtuous, nothing is more indecent in a man of good form than to be regarded as learned.

The ban on learning leads to another misuse of the mind. 'The only thing which occupies the mind of society at present', says Versac, is 'scandalmongering'. The true test of what passes for 'good form' is peoples' 'manner of talking scandal'. 'Good form' is an expression which is constantly on Versac's lips. It is the standard that he uses for all his judgements of society and it re-appears in what might be called a summing-up:

> . . . it is better to subscribe to the errors of one's century, or at least to conform to them, than to display virtues which would appear strange or would not be in keeping with good form.

I have spoken of the way in which Versac's picture reduces social life to an unpleasant kind of farce, but it is clear from the start and from the tone in which he speaks that he is absolutely serious and means every word he says. What it all adds up to is corruption. He is teaching a form of nihilism. Traditional values are dismissed as 'errors', but instead of replacing them by anything which can be described as positive, the alternative is no more than to subscribe to the 'errors of one's century'. What appeals to him, what he hopes will appeal to his pupil, is

society's frivolity, its flightiness, its fickleness, its shallowness
and its spitefulness. Virtue and intelligence are replaced by
reckless and unfeeling seductions, prompt abandonments and
'scandalmongering'. For the values of this society are so wrong
that to show virtue or intelligence brings you into conflict with
spurious 'good form' and turns you into an outsider. The only
cure, the only way to succeed, in finding one's way into society,
which is Meilcour's aim, is to behave like a half-wit, which in
this half-witted society will pass for brilliance.

What it all adds up to is that though Versac tries to represent
himself as a decidedly original contributor to the formation of
a new society, his pronouncements have exactly the opposite
result. They turn out to be an absolutely damaging criticism of
contemporary life, which is exactly the reverse of his intention.

The ending is the most impressive part of this highly impressive novel. Meilcour's inner conflict is analysed with great brilliance and no attempt is made to suggest that it has been re-
solved.

The party has returned from the country. Meilcour hurries
to Mme de Lursay's house. His purpose is twofold: he hopes to
meet Hortense and is determined once again, or so he believes,
to break off relations with his instructress. If this had happened,
it would have meant the rejection of an amoral in favour of a
moral life. There are plenty of guests, but no sign of Hortense.
Mme de Lursay's reception is cool. He naturally begins to wilt.
For a moment he thinks that he will abandon his plan for a
break. Then he changes his mind and decides to stay behind
and have it out with her.

On a previous occasion, at Mme de Lursay's suggestion, he
had stayed behind secretly when the other guests had left to be
alone with her and only his own misunderstanding had prevented a premature completion of the 'rite'. This time both the
beginning and the ending are different. He makes a totally unexpected reappearance when everybody else has gone.

He feels that his return is not exactly welcome, is terrified
and begins to wish that he had avoided 'shutting himself in'
with Mme de Lursay. Her handling of the situation is masterly.
She is very much the instructress. She solemnly makes the pupil
feel that his behaviour has not been too good. She defends her

resistance on moral grounds, which is a pretence, and on account of her doubts about the young man's reliability, which is just. She speaks with her usual candour. She makes no attempt to conceal the fact that she has had liaisons in the past, as Versac had suggested. If Meilcour had asked her, she would have told him. 'My one great regret', she says, 'is that my heart is not as new as yours and that I cannot offer you the first fruits'. This leads to a repetition of the proposal made at the first session that they should just be 'friends'. There is the customary move from 'severity' to 'tenderness' with plenty of 'tender looks' and for the first time even a few tears.

We know that Meilcour has long been aware that, whatever his mood, nothing can curb the violent physical attraction that he feels for her. This time it becomes positively overwhelming or, as I feel tempted to say, almost hypnotic. We know, too, that in a literal sense he has always been something of a groveller. Once again the man who was determined to break with her is at her feet. He looks up and is dazzled by her beauty. She looks down at him. There is 'such love in her eyes' that he is bowled over, seized by 'an indescribable agitation' and for a moment is unable to speak or even to listen to what she is saying.

A few moments later, the instructress completes her work:

> Ses regards, ses soupirs, son silence, tout m'apprit, quoique un peu tard, à quel point j'étais aimé. J'étais trop jeune pour ne pas croire aimer moi-même. L'ouvrage de mes sens me parut celui de mon coeur. Je m'abandonnai à toute l'ivresse de ce dangereux moment, et je me rendis enfin aussi coupable que je pouvais l'être.

> [Her looks, her sighs, her silence all showed me, though a little late in the day, the extent to which I was loved. I was too young not to think that I was in love myself. The workings of my senses appeared to be the workings of my heart. I abandoned myself completely to the intoxication of this dangerous moment and ended by making myself as guilty as I could be.]

Crébillon's insight is evident in the references to the way in which Meilcour mistakes the 'workings' of his 'senses' for those of his 'heart'. The excitement creates the illusion that he is really in love with his instructress. What must be emphasised is that it is precisely this illusion and the 'intoxication' which

produced it that conceal the real problem temporarily without
leading to anything like a final solution:

> Je paraissais transporté, et peut-être je n'aimais pas. Etait-elle
> forcée de convenir que l'aimais, elle n'en était pas plus tranquille.

> [I seemed to be carried away, and perhaps I did not love. If she
> was forced to admit that I did love her, it did not make her any
> calmer.]

It is a sign of Meilcour's integrity that he makes no attempt
to excuse himself:

> Je l'avouerai: mon crime me plut, et mon illusion fut longue,
> soit que le maléfice de mon âge l'entretînt, ou que Madame de
> Lursay seule le prolongeait. Loin de m'occuper de mon infidélité,
> je ne songeais qu'à jouir de ma victoire.

> [I will admit it: my crime pleased me and my illusion was a long
> one, either because the wickedness of my age preserved it or be-
> cause Madame de Lursay alone prolonged it. Far from thinking
> about my unfaithfulness, I only thought about enjoying my vic-
> tory.]

The words 'coupable', used earlier, and 'crime' both have a
double meaning. They stand for the feeling of moral guilt produced by the fall and for the conviction that he has been 'unfaithful' to Hortense.

The passages invite three other observations. The feeling of
moral guilt shows that though the 'rite' has taken place, 'conversion' is by no means complete. The link with the world into
which Meilcour was born remains. It is provided, as I suggested
earlier, by the person of Hortense, who has become its representative—a slightly remote representative—for him.

The theme of 'amour' and 'goût' is not of course the exclusive preserve of Regency society; it is a perennial element in
human nature. In the past few years it has been brilliantly
portrayed by Eric Rohmer in a famous series of films which he
calls 'contes moraux'. Although he uses the same label as Crébillon used for Le Sopha, the process is reversed. In the films
'amour' triumphs over 'goût' without a fall by the male pro-

tagonists. Jean-Louis's chaste night in the same room as Maud in *Ma Nuit chez Maud* is very different from Meilcour's night with Mme de Lursay in spite of the fact that Maud like Haydée in *La Collectionneuse* and Chloé in *L'amour l'après-midi* has a good deal in common with Mme de Lursay. Jean-Louis's later night in a room with Françoise is as chaste as his night with Maud. The same cannot be said of Françoise's nights with Maud's husband, for whom she fell before meeting Jean-Louis and whom she abandoned on religious grounds at the right moment for her future, which was a happy marriage with Jean-Louis.

Lastly, the chaste manner in which Crébillon describes Meilcour's fall is in itself an answer to those critics who have branded his novels as obscene.

It is something like a pause in the 'rite' which brings Meilcour back to the question of his relations with Hortense:

> Quelque enchanté que je fusse, mes yeux s'ouvrirent enfin . . . Hortense, cette Hortense que j'adorais, quoique je l'eusse si parfaitement oubliée, revint régner sur mon coeur. La vivacité des sentiments que je retrouvais pour elle me rendait encore moins convenable ce qui s'était passé. N'est-ce pas dans la seule espérance de la voir, que je suis venu chez Madame de Lursay, me disais-je? Et pendant leur absence, n'est-ce pas elle seule que j'ai regrettée? Par quel enchantement me trouvais-je engagé avec une femme qu'aujourd'hui même je déteste?

> [However enchanted I was, my eyes opened at last . . . Hortense, the Hortense whom I worshipped in spite of the fact that I had forgotten her completely, returned to reign over my heart. The strength of my feeling for her made what had gone on seem even less proper. Was it not simply in the hope of meeting her that I came to Madame de Lursay's, I said to myself? And while they were all away, was she not the only person whom I missed? By what kind of enchantment did I find myself tied to a woman whom even today I detested?]

'Enchanté' and 'enchantement' are really the equivalent of 'hypnotic'. The verb 'détester' is particularly significant in the present context. Even when allowance is made for Meilcour's

excitability, it brings out the gulf between 'amour' and 'goût'.
You may 'detest' or think that you detest a woman, but neither
hostility, moral scruples nor pride will protect you against the
irresistible physical attraction. In spite of the mark of interroga-
tion, the word 'enchantement' shows that its hynotic quality is
unlikely to spoil the fun entirely.

When the memoir-writer looks back on the incident, he suggests that there might have been a different view from the one
that he took:

> What I believe today is that if I had had more experience,
> Madame de Lursay would simply have brought me down more
> quickly. For what we call good breeding makes us more clear-
> sighted because it has done more to corrupt us.
>
> It would therefore have made me feel more strongly how dis-
> graceful it is to be faithful. I should not in truth have been seized
> by feeling; it would have appeared ridiculous with Madame de
> Lursay and, in order to conquer me, it would have been necessary
> for her to have been as contemptible as she had avoided appearing
> to me to be. Far from the memory of Hortense being banished for
> a moment from my mind, I should have enjoyed thinking about
> her. In the midst of the excitement into which Madame de Lursay
> would have plunged me, I should have lamented the custom which
> does not allow us to resist a woman whom we please; I should
> have preserved my heart from the disorder of my senses and, by
> means of these delicate distinctions which might be described as
> the quietism of love, I should have abandoned myself to all the
> charm of the occasion without running the risk of being unfaithful.

In this passage 'experience' is equated with 'corrupt'. Meilcour is telling us that if he had had more experience, he would
have behaved in the way recommended by Versac, whose influence is evident in the reference to the 'disgrace' of being
faithful. He would have been careful to avoid any personal
feeling for Mme de Lursay, which was the cause of the conflict
and the feeling that he was guilty of infidelity towards Hortense. This brings us to an important divergence. Unlike Versac, Meilcour believes in 'love'. Instead of advocating his policy
of 'impoverishment', the complete substitution of 'goût' for
'amour' by the removal of affection, he is arguing that they are
separate and that you can indulge in both of them with differ-

ent persons without there being any question at all of unfaithfulness to the beloved.[1]

The word 'corrupt' is of particular importance. It looks back to Meilcour's use of 'guilty' and 'crime'. It also reminds us of the statement that the conversation with Versac 'has had too much influence on the actions of my life'. The inference is that if the remaining parts of the unfinished novel had been written, they would have described a rakish period of relations with Mme de Senanges and her like before Meilcour was reformed by an 'estimable woman'. It also leads to the further inference that the final parts of the novel were never written because they would have been much less interesting than the subtle analysis of the performance of Meilcour as a neophyte.

Whatever the correct interpretation, the declaration only serves in retrospect to emphasise the pain of the immediate situation. Meilcour tries to persuade himself that his conduct is innocent so far as Hortense is concerned because she does not love him and because he himself has promised her nothing and cannot believe that he will ever owe her the same gratitude that he owes Mme de Lursay. It does not help:

> I convinced my mind easily enough that the reasoning was right, but I could not deceive my heart in the same way. Overwhelmed by its secret reproaches and unable to suppress them, I tried to distract myself, to drown the importunate memory which occupied me in spite of myself, by plunging into a new surge of intoxication. My efforts were in vain and every moment made me more guilty without feeling the least calmer.

The last words of the novel demonstrate forcibly that in spite of all his guilty feelings, the neophyte has been well and truly defeated:

> Several hours had passed and the day was beginning to dawn, but I was still far from being at one with myself. Thanks to the proprieties, which Madame de Lursay always observed very strictly, she eventually sent me away. I left her promising, in spite of my remorse, that I would see her early the next day, very determined, what is more, to keep my promise.

[1] It recalls Jacob's view when he was on the verge of adultery with a *fausse dévote* two days after his marriage.

We have seen that Mme de Lursay and Versac became rival instructors. Although we remain convinced that in virtually every respect she is a better person than the count, there is one important fact to which we cannot close our eyes. In spite of the fact that Versac tries to replace Mme de Lursay as Meilcour's instructor and in spite of the genuineness of her feelings for the neophyte, ironically they both try in their different ways to lead Meilcour in the same direction, to set him up in the same world and to make him submit to 'rites' which are *morally* identical. The irony is underlined by the fact that if, as I have already suggested, Meilcour had accepted Mme de Lursay's invitation to go to the country with her party, or even if Hortense had turned up at Mme de Lursay's house on the party's return from the country, he would have won over Hortense, abandoned Mme de Lursay, avoided the moral fall and undergone a different form of initiation: union with the beloved by marriage in church.

It is apparent from all that has been said that Crébillon's admirable achievement needs to be summed up by a number of observations. Etiemble, as we have seen, is perfectly correct in saying that the novelist is not a pornographic writer, but we must go on to observe that though he provides a highly penetrating study of the peculiarities of high society in the eighteenth century, he does so without adopting a formal moral attitude. There is no comedy in his outstanding novel as there is in *L'Ecumoire* and *Le Sopha*. He adopts a completely impersonal attitude without any praise or condemnation of the different attitudes, and it is precisely the fact that criticism of society does not depend on personal views that makes it much more effective and damaging.

Versac argues that 'amour' should be dropped and replaced by 'goût', but though there is no admission that there is anything immoral about it, he has to admit that the process of adapting himself to the practices of society led to 'extreme pain' and to 'spoiling my intelligence'. It appears that with other people there is an attempt to avoid these troubles by combining 'amour' and 'goût'. 'Amour' may lead to a happy marriage, but does not necessarily exclude 'goût' which is treated as a form of 'sport'. Meilcour, as we have seen, tries it on, but has to admit that 'I should have lamented the custom which does

not allow us to resist a woman whom we please'. It is precisely
the conflict provoked by his 'fall' with Mme de Lursay which
suggests that at bottom he is superior in virtually every way to
Versac and that in spite of the loose period to follow, he would
have ended as an impressive member of society making a happy
and virtuous marriage with Hortense if Crébillon had only
been able to make himself conclude his unfinished novel.

3 *Other Works*

I have dwelt on the superiority of *Les Egarements du coeur et
de l'esprit* and have only room to glance briefly at Crébillon's
other works of fiction.

L'Ecumoire is an amusing piece of entertainment: partly a
religious-political allegory, but mainly a fairy story for adults
in which the fortunes of the protagonists depend on the outcome of a clash between good and bad fairies. The setting is the
imaginary oriental kingdom of Chécian. Crébillon's irreverence
is apparent from the fact that the country's god is a monkey
and that the characters use the word 'Singe' instead of 'Dieu'.
The patriarch is believed to stand for the Pope, the high priest
for the French Cardinals de Rohan and Dubois, and the absurd
skimming ladle—the 'écumoire' of the title—for the Bull Unigenitus.

Tanzaï, the king's son and heir, is warned by a good fairy
that he must not marry until he is twenty-one. He finds that he
cannot wait. There is a competition in the oriental manner
with an assembly of princesses from other realms. He chooses
the beautiful Néadarné. He is told that before the wedding
ceremony he must insert the huge skimming ladle, presented by
a good fairy, into the mouth of a revolting old woman, who is
one of the bad fairies, and the high priest. The high priest refuses; the prince proceeds with the wedding. The trouble begins when he enters the nuptial couch. He finds that he is im-
potent. Not in the sense of a Stendhalian 'fiasco': his sexual
organs have vanished and the skimming ladle is clamped to his
body in their place.

An oracle sends him to a magic forest. The skimming ladle is
detached. It is only the first part of the cure. He must go on to
another place, where he is to have sexual intercourse with a

person who turns out to be the revolting bad fairy into whose mouth the skimming ladle was forced before the wedding. He is made to work hard—thirteen goes with the horrible Concombre—but his virility is restored. He returns to Chécian and pretends to his wife that it was only an unpleasant dream. The trouble is by no means over. The second time that he enters the nuptial couch, he finds that a similar misfortune has overtaken his wife. 'La porte des plaisirs est murée', is the way in which he explains it to his father!

The oracle tells them that Néadarné must visit a male fairy named Jonquille in his island and allow him to do as he pleases with her. Néadarné displays all the scruples and resistance of the virtuous woman. In the end she gives in. Jonquille is a highly attractive male fairy and she has to admit to herself that the cure was not altogether unenjoyable. She returns to the husband and pretends like him that it was all a dream. In order to complete the deception another good fairy, whose lover Néadarné rescued when she escaped from Jonquille's island. gives her a formula which will restore her virginity. She creates a minor obstacle by reciting it too frequently, but finally everything comes right and the story has a happy ending based on unavoidable mutual deception. It is not difficult to see how it fits in with Crébillon's general picture of Regency society. One is tempted to remark, indeed, that genuine 'amour' is restored by compulsory 'goûts' for husband and wife!

Crébillon wrote three epistolary novels. I have already shown that *Lettres de la Marquise de M * * * au Comte de R * * ** , his first full length novel, is one of the outstanding epistolary novels of the century. *Les Lettres de la Duchesse de * * * au Duc de * * ** is much less successful, but the two novels form a pair. We know that the Marquise was a naturally virtuous woman who was brought down by a count who turns out to be a heartless libertine. The Duchesse is also a virtuous woman who not only preserves her virtue, but in spite of her attachment to him when she becomes a widow she refuses to have anything more to do with the Duc (who is a widower) because she has discovered that when trying to conquer her he was having affairs with other women. The third epistolary novel is the *Lettres athéniennes,* published in 1771. It is the only one of the three with more than a single correspondent, but though it

has greater variety than the other two, it is basically uninteresting: a vast correspondence about the flightiness of Hercules.

I have already suggested that *Le Sopha* has had too much
attention.What puts the reader off is the absurdity of the work's
conception: a young Brahmin is turned, as a punishment, into
a spirit who is forced to live in the bodies of sofas. He is free
to change sofas as often as he pleases, and we simply have a
series of seductions by different couples with the usual prolonged conversations. Some of them hold our attention, like the
fall of the ostensibly prudish couple, but it is too much of a
good thing and is made more tiresome by the foolish comments
of the sultan to whom the liberated Brahmin relates his tales.
Much the same is true of *Ah! quel conte!,* Crébillon's second
longest novel.

The first part of *Les Heureux orphelins,* as already observed,
is based on Elisa Haywood's *The Fortunate Foundlings.* This
explains what has been called the 'sanctimonious tone' of the
first part, but it enabled the novelist to bring out the contrast
between English and French society. Although the setting of
the second part is still England, it is almost a separate work in
the usual Crébillon style: the seduction of an English noble-
woman, whose offer of marriage is refused, by an Englishman
who has been brought up in France and, as I have already indicated, behaves like one of the most ruthless of seducers. The
link between the two parts is so flimsy that the whole work
reads like an unfinished novel in the Marivaux manner and the
'heureux' of the title is meaningless.

In *La Nuit et le moment* and *Le Hasard du coin du feu,* both
written about 1737, but not published until 1755 and 1763,
Crébillon displays his versatility by the rediscovery of another
form which was invented at the end of the fifteenth century by
Fernando de Rojas, author of the Spanish masterpiece, *La Celes-
tina,* and which was to be used again by Roger Martin du Gard
in *Jean Barois* in 1913. It is a novel in the form of a dialogue
or, as Crébillon calls the second of these works, a 'dialogue
moral'.

They are both works about susceptibility or, to use the familiar term, 'goût'. In *La Nuit et le moment,* which is the more
amusing of the two entertaining dialogues, a gentleman who is
staying as a guest at a lady's house appears unexpectedly in his

hostess's bedroom and begins the usual autobiographical discussion about his sexual adventures. It grows cold; the servant
is sent away at the gentleman's request. He moves on to the bed.
Later on, he pulls off his dressing gown, shocks the lady by
showing that he has nothing on underneath and insists on getting into bed with her. The lady goes through a somewhat
abridged range of 'gradations' with switches from 'severity' to
'tenderness', but in the end the conversation about 'goût' is
translated into action. In the second dialogue it is the lady who
is the seducer or potential seducer. She finds herself at the 'fire-
side' alone with the marquise's lover, who arrives just as the
marquise has to leave in order to go and look after her mother,
who is unwell. The 'hasard' to which the duke succumbs is not
a performance, but an arrangement to take on Célie in due
course as his Number Two.

For some critics the dialogues are Crébillon's two best works.
Although they do not appear to me to be of the same order as
Les Egarements, they are undoubtedly two of the most attractive
of his works and deserve to be much better known than they
are. In fact, one would like to see *Le Hasard du coin du feu*
translated for the first time into English and published in the
same volume as a fresh translation of *La Nuit et le moment.*

ROUSSEAU

JULIE OU LA NOUVELLE HÉLOÏSE

1

'LETTERS OF two lovers living in a small town at the foot of the Alps'. Rousseau's description of his theme appears at the beginning of each of the novel's six parts. It is a useful guide to an understanding of its nature and scope. It is a highly original love story which was different from all the other eighteenth-century novels and was to have a great influence on Rousseau's successors. Etienne Gilson has put it well:

'Rousseauism is a profound revolution of the classic conception of man which French society of the eighteenth and seventeenth centuries had inherited from scholasticism, that is to say, from Aristotle and Plato'.

He goes on:

'Rousseauism is the resignation of reason . . . the whole of psychology must be reconstructed on a completely new basis where sensibility will play the directing role that in earlier times was entrusted to reason'.[1]

We shall find that there is a succession of conflicts and contrasts which will continue throughout the novel and contribute largely to its unity: moral and social conflicts provoked by love; contrasts between Clarens, the 'small town at the foot of the Alps', and the great city of Paris, and between Julie d'Etange's father and her husband.

What needs to be said is that La Nouvelle Héloïse, published in 1761, is the first great Romantic novel. Although Rousseau's psychological insight is admirable, we can see that from Gilson's point of view the many conflicts and contrasts will be provoked not by 'reason', but by 'sensibility'. It is brought out by the fact that the conflicts and contrasts have virtually nothing in common with the youthful 'égarements' of Crébillon fils's Meilcour.

Rousseau's scope is much wider than that of his predecessors. The small town is not without its shortcomings, but when the

[1] Les Idées et les lettres, 1932, pp. 277–78.

young lovers are forced to separate and Saint-Preux accompanies Lord Bomston to Paris, Rousseau will use him to bring out the differences between the moral qualities of the two settings. He will also use him to underline his personal enthusiasm for Italian and his profound dislike for French music. What is more we shall find that in the last three parts of the novel he works on the contrast between the two settings with the idea of creating a utopia—a tiny community whose behaviour is intended as a model for the rest of the world and is clearly a reflection of his own sensibility. Finally, it must be emphasised that the novel is impregnated with Rousseau's own profound and genuinely moral outlook—genuine in spite of the fact that his own life had not been exactly exemplary.

Although the novel divides into six parts, the most important division comes between the first three parts and the last three. We can anticipate by saying that the first three parts deal with what must be called the 'fall' of the lovers and its aftermath, and the last three with what might fairly be described as their 'redemption'. Rousseau's conception of 'redemption' was a personal one, but it underlines very effectively the novel's moral attitude.

We must look next at the characters. The structure has been compared in one important respect to French classical drama. Julie and Saint-Preux are the protagonists, but Julie's Cousin Claire and Saint-Preux's English friend, Lord Bomston, clearly resemble the confidants in seventeenth-century tragedy. Their social position naturally gives them greater weight and they play a major role in advising the protagonists, curbing the violence of their feelings and in the case of Lord Bomston preventing Saint-Preux from committing suicide. They naturally write a good many letters, particularly Claire. The remaining characters only write occasionally. This does not alter the fact that M. de Wolmar, the elderly nobleman whom Julie is compelled to marry against her will, also plays what might be called a vital role in the second half of the novel.

We must not be misled by what superficially appears to be the inconsistence and contradictions of the protagonists. They are one of the clearest indications of Rousseau's extreme penetration as a psychological novelist. We can see from the start that Julie is the dominant character whose name is used for both titles of the novel. *La Nouvelle Héloïse* might be regarded as the novel's alternative title, but it is the most popular one with nearly all commentators. The reason is sound. What Rousseau set out to do and did with supreme ability was to give what for him was a modern version of the medieval love affair of Héloïse and Abélard.[1] Julie is dominant not only on account of her remarkable complexity. Her view of life is highly moral; she becomes, significantly, in a highly personal manner, very religious, but remains in spite of herself highly sensual. Notwithstanding intense feelings of despair, she is a much stronger character—it is apparent in the violence of her language—than Saint-Preux. The difference is well brought out by the description of her—a description that she herself endorses—as a 'prêcheuse' and of him, slightly ironically, as a 'philosophe'. He holds sound moral views, is fond of theorising about everything in life, but in spite of his moral views there are moments when he becomes violently sensual. His main weakness is one that is not infrequently found in intellectuals: in spite of her strength of character, Julie gives in on purely emotional grounds to her father, which is the ruin of the love affair, but unlike Saint-Preux she never dreams of suicide.

There is a good deal of confusion in the novel over chronology and the ages of the protagonists. It is a fair inference that, at the start of the novel, Saint-Preux is twenty-one and Julie and her cousin eighteen. In spite of their youth the tutor and his pupil are decidedly sophisticated and unexpectedly well-informed for their age, which prompts Claire to say to Julie: 'It seems to me that for our age, we have done a lot of thinking'. They seize every opportunity of supporting the arguments and observations in their letters with quotations from Italian poets. The style in which they write is distinctly mature. That is not all. What is most surprising is the discovery that this couple, who have both been strictly brought up in a puritanical country like Protestant Switzerland, have not only included Plutarch's work on love in their studies, but that the tutor has admitted to his teenage pupil, at a very early stage and before there is any question of their love, that he indulges in solitary

---

[1] See *The Loves, Amours and Misfortunes of Abélard and Héloïse* (collection of their letters), 1947, and Régine Pernoud, *Héloïse et Abélard*, 1970.

vice. The result is that when they are obliged to part after their own fall, Julie urges him not to return to his vices!

It will be apparent from what I have said that the novel is not without a number of improbabilities. It should be emphasised, however, that they are minor and do not seriously detract from its merits or alter the fact that in spite of its enormous *longueurs* it is one of the greatest French novels of its century.

2

'Il faut vous fuir, mademoiselle, je le sais bien: j'aurais dû beaucoup moins attendre; ou plutôt il fallait ne vous voir jamais'.[1]

The first sentence of the first letter of this epistolary novel takes us straight into the drama. It reflects the tone of much of the novel and is the start of the series of highly complex conflicts which are at the heart of the work. The most important of them is the moral conflict which will continue until Julie's death in the last part. There is the fear that they will be carried away and succumb to temptation, which is what happens in the first of the six parts, and the fear that they may be guilty of adultery in the later parts, from which they were probably only saved by Julie's death. There is also the assumption, which turns out to be correct, that there will be insuperable obstacles in the way of marriage.

Saint-Preux's agitation is important for another reason. We saw, in discussing Crébillon *fils*, that in contemporary French society 'love' had been largely abolished and replaced by 'taste'. One of the most striking things about *La Nouvelle Héloïse* is that 'love' in its fullest and most genuine sense has been restored or, to put in a rather different way, the individual has been put together again. Whatever their shortcomings, Saint-Preux and Julie can fairly be described as *belles âmes*. They are in many ways an admirable couple who are perfectly suited to one another, as their 'confidants' are quick to see. Their love is deep and genuine in the sense that it is the restoration of the feeling lacking in Crébillion's section of society and, as we shall

[1] 'I must fly from you, Mademoiselle; I know perfectly well that I should have waited far less time; or rather it was necessary never to see you'.

see, in Saint-Preux's picture of Paris society. It is naturally accompanied by 'taste', but instead of meaning a superficial sexuality, in the present context 'taste' stands for a strong physical attraction, which is an essential factor in true love and, ironically, the source of tragedy in Rousseau's novel.

In this puritanical society physical attraction is, inevitably, associated with temptation. The love affair divides into six stages. There is an initial stage of agitation on both sides which is provoked by Saint-Preux's declaration; it is followed by the first 'lover's' kiss; the first and second 'falls'; the aftermath, which follows the separation; and, finally, Saint-Preux's return to the home of Julie, who has been married for some years to Wolmar.

We saw that in the novel's opening sentence Saint-Preux spoke of running away from Julie's home and giving up his post of tutor in order to avoid trouble, which of course he will eventually have to do. Julie is just as much in love with him as he is with her, but though she is badly shaken by his declaration she is even more upset by the suggested departure. This is the sense in which the first stage is dominated by agitation. The couple are determined to avoid temptation, to engage as far as possible—it naturally proves impossible—in a form of Platonic love. The nature of the conflict is reflected in the choice of vocabulary. There are five groups of interrelated words. Love is seen as a perpetual danger and is described as 'piège', 'poison', 'gouffre', 'précipice', 'abîme'. Words of moral praise alternate with words of moral condemnation: 'vertu', 'pureté', 'honnête', 'sacré', 'divin', 'saint', on the one hand; 'coupable', 'corrompt', 'criminel', on the other. They are matched by the alternation of words of devotion and recrimination. Saint-Preux uses some of the most moving expressions of devotion; Julie, a mixture of devotion and the fiercest recriminations: 'ma douce amie', 'fille incomparable', 'âme céleste' (Saint-Preux) : 'mon doux ami', 'aimable ami', 'vil séducteur', 'barbare', 'tyran' (Julie).

In his first letter Saint-Preux provides a brilliantly concise illustration of the way in which contradictory words are matched when he speaks of love as

La source du poison qui me nourrit et me tue.

[The source of poison that nourishes and kills me.]

'Poison' reappears in Julie's first full-length letter, but with a different emphasis:

> Dès le premier jour que j'eus le malheur de te voir, je sentis le poison qui corrompt mes sens et ma raison . . . de ce premier pas je me sens entraîner dans l'abîme.

> [The first day that I had the misfortune to see you, I felt the poison which corrupts my senses and my reason . . . from this first step I feel myself drifting into the abyss.]

For Julie there is no question of love 'nourishing' as well as 'killing'; it simply spells death and the 'abyss'.

In the letters that follow, we find Saint-Preux trying hard to eliminate the conception of love as a 'poison' and to reconcile it with 'virtue':

> . . . je vois avec transport combien, dans une âme honnête, les passions les plus vives gardent encore le saint caractère de la vertu! . . . s'il fallait choisir entre votre coeur et votre possession même . . . je ne balancerais pas un instant. Mais d'où viendrait cette amère alternative, et pour quoi rendre incompatible ce que la nature a voulu réunir?

> La sagesse a beau parler par votre bouche, la voix de la nature est la plus forte. Le moyen de lui résister quand elle s'accorde à la voix du coeur?

> [. . . I see with rapture how much in an honest heart the liveliest passions still retain the holy character of virtue!

> . . . if it was necessary to choose between your heart and your possession even . . . I should not balance for a second. But from where would come this bitter alternative, and why treat as incompatible what nature wishes to bring together?

> Wisdom speaks in vain through your mouth, nature's voice is the strongest. The means of resisting it when it is in agreement with the voice of the heart?]

We must remember that we are reading the letters of a young couple who are passionately in love. In spite of their maturity, we must not look for logical arguments; they simply rely on intuition for finding ways of reaching their real goal. It does not alter the excellence of the pattern. In the first of these three passages Saint-Preux sees love and virtue united in Julie. In the second, he places 'heart' above physical 'possession', but promptly suggests that 'what nature wished to bring together' should not be treated as 'alternatives' or 'incompatible'. The picture is completed in the third passage. 'Sagesse' is brushed aside. 'Nature', meaning physical possession, is not merely the 'voix...la plus forte'; 'elle s'accorde à la voix du coeur', and is therefore acceptable.

Julie, as we should expect from the passage about the first meeting, adopts what on the surface looks like a more rigidly moral attitude:

> J'entends: les plaisirs du vice et l'honneur de la vertu vous fer-aient un sort agréable. Est-ce là votre morale?

> [I understand: the pleasures of vice and the honour of virtue would provide you with an agreeable lot. Is that your moral?]

Far from wishing to unite the 'heart' and Saint-Preux's 'nature', she means to keep them apart:

> . . . deux mois d'expérience m'ont appris que mon coeur trop tendre a besoin d' amour, mais que mes sens n'ont aucun besoin d'amant.

> [. . . two months of experience have taught me that my heart, which is too tender, needs love, but that my senses have no need of a lover.]

She rubs it in with

> L'amour, cet amour fatal qui me perd te donne un nouveau prix: tu t'élèves quand je me me dégrade; ton âme semble avoir profité de tout l'avilissement de la mienne.

> [Love, this fatal love which brings me down, gives you a new prize: you rise while I degrade myself; your soul seems to have taken the benefit of the whole of the degradation of mine.]

In spite of this, they end by coming to a similar conclusion. Saint-Preux sums up his views by bringing together what he regards as virtue, emotion and physical love:

> . . . ce divin accord de la vertu, de l'amour et de la nature qui ne se trouve qu'en vous.

[. . . this divine harmony of virtue, love and nature is only found
in you.]

It is endorsed considerably later by Julie:

> Je ne sais si je m'abuse, mais il me semble que le véritable
> amour est le plus chaste de tous les liens. C'est lui, c'est son feu
> divin qui sait épurer nos penchants naturels, en les concentrant en
> un seul objet . . .

[I do not know whether I am abusing myself, but it seems that
true love is the most chaste of all relations. It is this, it is its divine
fire which knows the way to purify our natural leanings by con-
centrating them on a single object.]

The two pronouncements are clearly an expression of the
Romantic conception of love: the conviction that if two people
are genuinely in love, consummation even outside marriage is
no longer a sin. It is apparent in Saint-Preux's linking of 'vertu', 'amour' and 'nature'. Julie is even more explicit with her
statements that 'le véritable amour est le plus chaste de tous les
liens', that 'son feu divin . . . sait épurer nos penchants naturels'
by concentration on a single person or, as she puts it, 'un seul
objet'. It remains to add that the deliberate blending of what
are usually regarded as opposites is an excellent illustration of
Gilson's view that in Rousseau 'sensibility will play the directing role that in earlier times was entrusted to reason'.

Julie's pronouncement invites one other comment. Although,
as I have said, she usually adopts a more rigidly moral attitude
than Saint-Preux in her *language,* her attitude will be somewhat different when it comes to *action.* For not the least of the
novel's virtues are the surprises that it brings. Julie has remarked primly to Saint-Preux that she must warn him that
they cannot go into the 'bushes' together unless they are accompanied by her *'inséparable cousine'* (italics Rousseau's). Yet
when they arrive there we find that instead of an arrangement
for the preservation of virtue, it is Julie and Claire— the pretended victim and the supposed chaperone—who between them
have organized the first lovers' kiss. It is carefully planned.
Saint-Preux is made to kiss Claire first, no doubt as a form of
concealment. Julie's kiss is far more violent and the effect on

both of them is shattering. Julie faints. This is how Saint-Preux reacts:

> Mes sens sont altérés, toutes mes facultés son troublées par ce baiser mortel . . . C'est du poison que j'ai cueilli sur tes lèvres; il fermente, il embrasse mon sang. Il me tue, et ta pitié fait mourir.
>
> Une faveur? . . . c'est un tourment horrible . . . non, garde tes baisers, je ne les saurais supporter . . . ils sont trop acres, trop pénétrants; ils percent, ils brûlent jusqu'à molle . . . Un seul, un seul m'a jeté dans un égarement dont je ne puis plus revenir.

> [My senses have changed, all my faculties are troubled by this mortal kiss . . . It is poison that I have collected on your lips; it ferments, seizes my blood. It is killing me and your pity makes one die.
>
> A favour? . . . it is a horrible form of torture . . . no, keep your kisses, I would not know how to support them . . . they are too bitter, too penetrating; they pierce, they burn as far as the flesh . . . One only, one only has thrown me into a state of frenzy from which I can no longer escape.]

It is a remarkably impressive passage. It shows that the change from meditation on love to what can only be called mild action has completely reversed for the time being Saint-Preux's attitude. The violence of the change is evident in phrases like 'toutes mes facultés sont troublées par ce baiser mortel' and 'C'est du poison que j'ai cueilli sur tes lèvres'. The extent of the change caused by no more than a kiss is still another sign that reason has no power over sensibility.

It must be observed that Saint-Preux's last sentence is in its way the most important. It suggests that in view of the couple's feeling that marriage between them will be strongly opposed by Julie's father they have taken an irrevocable step downhill.

What must also be observed is that though in the past Julie adopted a strictly moral attitude and inflicted severe criticisms on Saint-Preux, it is she who has not only taken what will turn out to be the first real step downhill, but will be responsible for bringing about the moral 'falls'. In spite of this, Julie is aware for the moment of the danger and makes Saint-Preux leave the 'little town' for a few days. In spite of her past recriminations, she finds his absence so emotionally painful that she becomes ill and Claire has to recall him. Claire, who is trying to prevent Julie from going what she regards as 'too far', is herself obliged to go away for a short time just when Saint-Preux returns. This leads to the first real 'fall', which is first revealed in a letter from Julie to Claire. This time Julie realises, or rather admits, that she is not without blame:

> . . . he is not to blame: it is I alone who am; all my misfortunes are my own doing. I have no one to blame except myself.

She also realises that it is another step downhill from which there is no return:

> . . . it is in this way that a moment of frenzy has lost me forever. I have fallen into the abyss of ignominy from which a girl cannot return; and if I live, it is to be unhappy.

In her next letter to Saint-Preux, she refers to the 'fall' in these terms:

> . . . my regret is much less to have given up too much to love than to have taken away its greatest charm from it. This gentle enchantment of virtue has vanished from it like a dream: our fires have lost that divine ardour, which animated them by purifying them; we have hunted for pleasure, and happiness has run far away from us.

Julie's recriminations, particularly her unjust description of Saint-Preux in one of the earliest letters as a 'vil séducteur', leave us with the suspicion that she was trying, no doubt unconsciously, to impute to him her own sense of guilt. She makes something like amends by the completeness with which she places the blame on herself for the first 'fall' in her letter to Claire. In this passage from the letter to Saint-Preux she seems to begin by suggesting that she was responsible for anything that had gone wrong and then goes on to suggest mildly that it is a matter of joint responsibility. The use of the moral vocabulary—'virtue', 'divine ardour', 'purifying'—is an attempt to say that they concentrated so much on the physical side of love that the moral ethos, which they try somehow to preserve in spite of themselves, disappeared. What really inspired the pronouncement was the fact that, probably because Julie was

still a virgin, the first experience of physical love did not bring
them anything like the pleasure that they were expecting. The
issue is of special importance. In her letter to Claire, Julie was
trying to say that the moral 'fall' had cast her into an 'abyss'
from which on account of her sense of guilt there was no return. The truth is that the pleasure she got from it was so poor
that, in spite of her confession to Claire and her apparent feeling that she had sinned, she is determined to remedy her disappointment, which paves the way for the second 'fall' that will
be the result of her ingenious planning!

The first sign is the excited announcement, shortly afterwards, that Julie's parents are about to go away together for a
few days and that she will not be able to go with them, meaning
that the lovers will be left to themselves. She begins with some
words which are in strong contrast to the primness of other
letters:

> Kiss this letter, and jump for joy for the news that I am about
> to give you.

In the next letter there is a characteristically prim reference
to the departure:

> They left this morning, this tender father and this incomparable
> mother, in covering a beloved daughter, who does not deserve
> their goodness, with the tenderest of kisses.

She comes cleaner in the next sentence with an antithesis:

> . . . this ungrateful and unnatural heart sparkled with odious joy.

Then she turns on her lover:

> Ah! tyrant, you desire in vain to enslave completely this tender
> and too weak heart . . .

But she realizes that this is not a fair attitude:

> Forgive me, O my gentle friend! these involuntary movements . . .

We know that the parents' departure turned out to be a disappointment, that the lovers had no time to be alone because Saint-Preux had to go away himself to rescue the fiancé of Julie's servant from military service, and that when he returned he learnt that the parents', or rather the mother's absence, was to be cut short. This leads to what is perhaps the most startling incident in the entire novel. We suddenly find that in spite of all her moralising and her persistent feelings of guilt, Julie is absolutely determined not to be thwarted by the cutting short of the parents' absence:

> Far from rebutting my courage, so many obstacles have irritated it; I do not know what new force is animating me, but I feel a toughness inside me which I have never had before and, if you do not fear to share it, this evening can fulfill my promises, and pay once only the debts of love.

We see from this that the supposedly modest and virtuous Julie, whose only 'fall' was described by her as the result of 'un instant d'égarement', is deliberately taking the initiative and giving Saint-Preux an 'assignation' not in the 'châlet', as he suggested before learning of the mother's early return, but in her bedroom. The most striking thing about the passage is the language: the extreme vigour of the tone and the vocabulary with its revealing references to the 'obstacles' which have stood in the way of their making love and have 'irritated' her 'courage' and introduced a 'new force' and a 'toughness' which were previously unknown to her. What it all adds up to is that the lovers are perfectly suited to one another and that the 'obstacles'—Julie has already learnt that her father intends to marry her off to a friend—which will very unreasonably prevent them from marrying, are totally unjustified and are bound to exasperate them. At the same time, the toughness of the language once again demonstrates that in spite of the sense of guilt and the desire to be 'virtuous', Julie is an extremely sensual woman, which is underlined by the statement that the assignation in her bedroom means that they will 'pay *once only* the debts of love' (italics mine).

It is decidedly a risky affair, which emphasises Julie's sensuality. Saint-Preux has got himself into Julie's bedroom by passing through her mother's room when everybody is out of the way and having dinner. The main danger is that they may be caught in the act by the father, who is back. If this happens, he is expected to draw his sword in a rage and murder the pair of them. In the event everything goes well. Saint-Preux reaches the bedroom and somewhat comically rejoices in the discovery of pen, ink and paper so that he can write a letter to Julie while waiting for her to appear:

> . . . here I am in the sanctuary of all that my head admires . . . What happiness to have found ink and paper! I express what I feel in order to keep down excess. I give the change to my transports in writing.

The effect of love-making on them is very different this time:

> Oh! mourons, ma douce amie! la bien-aimée de mon coeur! Que faire désormais d'une jeunesse insipide dont nous avons épuisé toutes les délices? Explique-moi, si tu peux, ce que j'ai senti dans cette nuit inconcevable; donne-moi l'idée d'une vie ainsi passée, ou laisse-m'en quitter une qui n'a plus rien de ce que je viens d'éprouver avec toi.

> [Oh! let us die, my sweet friend! Let us die, the beloved of my heart! What are we to do in the future with an insipid youth of which we have exhausted all the joys? Explain to me, if you can, what I felt during this inconceivable night; give me the idea of a life spent in this way, or let me abandon one which no longer has anything of that which I have just experienced with you.]

We must go on to say that the lyrical tone has a special importance in the present context. Saint-Preux is no doubt speaking for both the lovers. We know that they have been strictly brought up, that their concern for morals is genuine and is based on religion, and that they are highly sensitive beings. It is well known, as I have said in discussing *Le Paysan parvenu*, that strong religious feeling is frequently accompanied by strong sexual feeling. It is suggested in this novel by the way in which Saint-Preux continually attempts not merely to defend love by the use of moral terminology, but to exalt it by the use of a religious-moral terminology: the already quoted '*divin* accord de la vertu, de l'amour et de la nature' and in other places the 'feu pur et *sacré*', 'douces *extases*' and 'ravissements *célestes*'. For our present purpose there are also two par-

ticularly revealing phrases: Saint-Preux's suggestion, before
learning of the early return of the parents, that they should
make a 'pilgrimage' to the *châlet* and his description of Julie's
bedroom as a 'sanctuary'. They mean something like a 'pilgrimage' to the temple or 'sanctuary' of Venus. They have both been
carried away by passionate sexual feeling. The result therefore
can only be described as an ecstasy—a commendable but
plainly a profane ecstasy of the kind experienced by people
with a strong religious as well as strong sexual feelings. It is
seen here, rightly, but not for the reasons that they imagine, as
a summit of their experience which can never be equalled
again and which will make the rest of their lives seem boring
and uninteresting. That is the significance of 'insipide' and
'épuisé'.

What emerges from this is that 'love' and 'taste' have been
brought together by compelling 'sensibility', which has also
removed the initial clashes between the pair.

3

This brings us to the second conflict. One of the characteristics
of French social life in the eighteenth century was its extreme
rigidity. It emerges in various ways in all the leading novelists
of the period. A recurrent theme is the parent, usually the
father, who is determined for social reasons to prevent sons and
daughters from marrying the person of their choice and forcing
them to marry an unsuitable partner of his own choosing. In
one of her earliest letters to Julie, Claire remarks of the father:

> The Baron d'Etange consents to give his daughter, his only
> child, to a little bourgeois who is without wealth!

It is a conventional reaction to the suggestion that Julie's
father might allow his daughter to marry Saint-Preux, or
rather Claire is jeering at the idea which never rouses any hope
on the part of either Julie or Saint-Preux. The baron is anything but an admirable figure and Claire will be the first to
tell us about his vices in a much later letter to Saint-Preux:

> Unfaithful and inconsistent for a long time, he squandered the
> fire of youth on a thousand creatures less worthy to please than his
> virtuous companion . . .

Although the father has been an out-and-out womaniser, it does nothing to diminish his outrageous snobbery or his puritanism when it is a matter of his daughter's morals, as we saw from the risk that the lovers ran by meeting in Julie's bedroom.

The real trouble begins when Lord Bomston, the sensible, intelligent and liberal English peer, tells the baron that his daughter and Saint-Preux are perfectly suited and should marry. It is the father's first knowledge of the lovers' attraction for one another. There is an explosion. It is followed by violent scenes in which he brutally beats his daughter. The beating leads to a miscarriage, which is kept secret and only conveyed to the reader first by a highly discreet reference in a letter from Julie to Claire and then by a more forthright statement to Saint-Preux at a much later stage. The father may feel ashamed of his treatment of his daughter, but never for a moment does he dream of abandoning his plan to marry her to M. de Wolmar, the Russian nobleman who is thirty years older than Julie and has been responsible at some time or other for saving her father's life.

Julie's devotion to her parents is very much a part of the contemporary social picture and is clearly the result of her puritanical upbringing. Her devotion to her mother is right. The mother who discovered her relations with Saint-Preux before they were ever brought to the father's knowledge by Lord Bomston, would like the couple to marry, but is far too timid to stand up to her ferocious and unfaithful husband. Julie nevertheless speaks of her 'tender' father, the pleasure that she will have in seeing again 'the best of fathers' on his return home and makes an odd declaration to Saint-Preux:

'O toi que j'aime le mieux au monde après les auteurs de mes jours'.

[Oh you whom I love most in the world after the authors of my days'.]

In the second section of the novel Lord Bomston comes forward with his suggestion of a runaway marriage and his very generous offer of an estate and an income if they take his advice, marry and emigrate to England. He gives a very acute and convincing reason why they should do so in the letter to Julie in which he makes his offer:

Love has worked itself too far into the substance of your soul for you ever to be able to drive it out; it intensifies and penetrates all stretches like a strong and corrosive water [*comme une eau forte et corrosive*]; you will never remove the deep impression without removing at the same time all the exquisite feelings that you have received from nature; and when there no longer remains any love in you, nothing estimable will remain in you.

The key phrase is 'comme une eau forte et corrosive'. The last word recalls the vocabulary of the lovers with words like 'abîme' and 'précipice' or, more obviously, 'poison' and 'corrompt'. Once it has taken root, true love is inescapable, but paradoxically its action is 'corrosive' unless it, or rather 'nature', which is its source, is fully satisfied by marriage. Once again, we must observe that his comments are an indication of what is to come.

Julie thanks him in the most generous terms, but turns the offer down, apparently and rather surprisingly on Claire's advice:

I should abandon pitilessly those by whom I breathe, those who preserve for me the life that they have given me and make it dear to me; a father who is almost sixty, a mother always languishing! I, their only child, should leave them without help in the solitude and boredom of old age, when it is time to return to them the tender cares that they have bestowed on me!

I have described the second conflict as social. It would be more accurate to call it social-and-moral in the sense that it is the result of the father's social snobbery and succeeds from his point of view on account of a strongly conventional moral streak which persists in Julie's make-up in spite of her passionate love and her toughness.

That it is conventional in the most literal sense is evident from the oscillations in her attitude to her father. The discovery that he is planning to marry her to Wolmar, as we have seen, almost certainly led to the decision to offer Saint-Preux the bedroom assignation. Before the marriage actually takes place, there is not merely an angry reference to 'obstacles', but a switch from 'tender' and 'best of fathers' to this:

Père barbare et dénaturé! . . . mon père m'a vendue! il fait de

sa fille une marchandise, une esclave! il s'acquitte à ma dépense!
il paye sa vie de la mienne.

[Barbarian and unnatural father! . . . my father has sold me! he
is treating his daughter as a piece of merchandise, a slave! he is
discharging his debt at my expense; he is paying for his life with
mine.]

When the marriage to Wolmar is imminent, she says in a
letter to Saint-Preux:

. . . un père esclave de sa parole et jaloux d'un vain titre dispose
de ma main qu'il a promise.

[. . . a father who is the slave of his word and jealous of a vain
title disposes of my hand, which he has promised.]

'Jaloux d'un vain titre' is the heart of the matter, but since
Julie fails to put up the resistance that it deserves it is left to
the unhappy Saint-Preux to pass judgement—on her:

Oui, c'est l'honnêteté de ton coeur qui nous perd; les sentiments
droits qui le remplissent en ont chassé le sagesse. Tu as voulu con-
cilier la tendresse filiale avec l'indomptable amour; en te livrant
à la fois à tous penchants, tu les confonds au lieu de les accorder,
et deviens coupable à force de vertu.

[Yes, it is the honesty of your heart which has defeated us; the
upright feelings which fill it have driven wisdom out of it. You
wished to conciliate filial tenderness with undefeatable love; in
delivering yourself at the same time to all your leanings, you con-
fuse them instead of making them agree, and become guilty as a
result of virtue.]

One should add that the passage is a particularly good
example of Rousseau's style. The case against Julie is stated
with remarkable lucidity and conciseness in a series of antitheses: 'l'honnêteté' and 'perd'; 'sentiments droits' and 'sagesse';
'tendresse filiale' and 'l'indomptable amour'; 'coupable à force
de vertu'. What Saint-Preux is perhaps too charitable to mention is that it was after all Julie who was the real 'seducer' and
got him into her bed and is now abandoning him out of respect for her supposed duty to her parent.

4

At the end of Part I, Claire very prudently arranges for Saint-Preux to leave in a hurry with Lord Bomston. The correspondence between the main parties goes on during the next two parts. It does a number of things. It enables Rousseau to use Saint-Preux to bring out what are for him the differences between the 'little town' and Paris, where he has gone with Lord Bromston. Saint-Preux and Julie engage in a profound discussion of their past, which once again is a mixture of devotion and recrimination, including Saint-Preux's judgement on Julie quoted above, while the 'confidants' work hard to control the lovers' despair.

Saint-Preux's letters about life in Paris, the excellence of Italian opera and his dislike of French music, err on the side of length—there are times when even Julie shows signs of boredom—but the contrast between Paris, or smart life, and Clarens are, as I have already suggested, particularly relevant to the plan of the novel and the way in which it will develop in the three final sections. In spite of their length, Saint-Preux's letters contain some very pertinent criticisms of Parisian society's morals and manners. Its members are decidedly hypocritical:

> Thus no one ever says what he thinks to other people, but what it suits him to make them think; and the apparent zeal for truth is never with them anything but hidden interest.

Again:

> . . . no man dares to be himself. *It is necessary to behave like others*—that is the first maxim of the wisdom of the country. *That is done, that is not done*: there's the supreme decision.

In this society, 'the whole of morality is a matter of pure verbiage'.

> Adultery does not cause any revolt: one does not find in it anything contrary to what is proper.

> Love itself, love has lost its rights and is not less unnatural than marriage.

He enlarges on society's attitude to love in a passage of particular interest:

> Even the words love and lover are banished from the descriptions of the intimate relations between members of the two sexes, and are relegated with the words *chain* and *flame* to novels which one no longer reads.

If his comments on society's hypocrisy recalls Versac's lecture to Meilcour in *Les Egarements du coeur et de l'esprit,* this observation is clearly an echo of the disappearance of love and brings out not merely one of the essential differences between Rousseau's novel and those of other eighteenth-century novelists, but the change that was beginning to take place among more reasonable people. It is emphasised by another pronouncement on the next page which draws a distinction between the ideal of the young lovers and the practice of high society:

> O Julie! such a woman who has not been afraid of soiling the marriage bed a hundred times would dare to accuse with unclean mouth our chaste love, and condemn this union of two sincere hearts which never knew such a thing as lack of faith.

In the letters that she herself wrote to Saint-Preux while he was in Paris, Julie was very much the 'prêcheuse', particularly when she learnt that at a party he had deliberately been made drunk and was seduced by one of the boldest women guests without his knowing what was happening to him. The most important of her letters, however, is the very long one near the end of section three in which she reviews the whole of their love affair. The description of her vigorous resistance to marriage with Wolmar illustrates conclusively what I have said about the reasons for giving in to her father:

> He saw that I had taken my line and that he would gain nothing from me by authority. For a second I believed myself delivered from his persecutions. But what became of me when I suddenly saw the severest of fathers at my feet, full of tenderness and bursting into tears? Without allowing me to rise, he clasped my knees and fixing his eyes dripping with tears on me, he said to me with a touching voice that I can still hear inside me: 'My daughter, respect the white hair of your unhappy father; do not make him

go down to the grave in grief like her who carried you in her womb; ah, do you wish to bring death to all your family?'

It is clear from this that Julie's decision was not the result of logic or morality in a strict sense, but of emotional feeling for her unworthy father in spite of his bad treatment of her when he first heard of her devotion to Saint-Preux.

The most significant part of the 'sermon' is the description of the wedding ceremony, which is also stylistically among the most impressive passages in the whole novel:

> Dans l'instant même où j'étais prête à jurer à un autre une éternelle fidélité, mon coeur vous jurait un amour éternel, et je fus menée au temple comme une victime impure qui souille le sacrifice où l'on va l'immoler . . .

> Qui me permet enfin d'aspirer encore au titre d'honnête femme, et me rend le courage d'en être digne? Je le vois, je le sens, la main secourable qui m'a conduite à travers les ténèbres et celle qui lève à mes yeux le voile de l'erreur, et me rend à moi malgré moi-même . . . L'auteur de toute vérité n'a point souffert que je sortisse de sa présence, coupable d'un vil parjure: et, prévenant mon crime par mes remords, il m'a montré l'abîme où j'allais me précipiter.

> [At the very moment when I was ready to give a pledge of eternal fidelity to another, my heart swore eternal love to you, and I was escorted to the temple like an impure victim who soils the sacrifice to which she is about to be surrendered . . .

> Who allows me at this last stage to go on aspiring to the title of honest woman, and gives me the courage to be worthy of it? I see it, I feel it, the helping hand which has led me through the darkness and which lifts from my eyes the veil of error and restores me to myself in spite of myself . . . The author of all truth has not allowed me to leave his presence, guilty of vile perjury: and in preventing my crime by my remorse, he has shown me the abyss into which I was going to fling myself.]

This was the scene that I had in mind when I spoke of the element of profane 'ecstacy' that Saint-Preux revealed in the letter immediately after the second 'fall'. I am not suggesting that the experience is mystical in the sense of direct revelation.

What I am suggesting is that in an accepted sense it is a spiritual ecstacy. What we are in fact witnessing is a psychological conversion inspired by Julie's genuinely religious feelings, which will have become much deeper by the time we reach the second half of the novel. It is brilliantly expressed by the contrast between the woman, who is still deeply in love with Saint-Preux, being led 'like an impure victim who soils the sacrifice to which she is about to be surrendered' in the temple where she is about to swear the oath of eternal fidelity. There is a sudden psychological change in the image of the divine, but invisible hand uncovering the 'wrong' and restoring her to her virtuous self. What is true is that there is a genuine determination to be faithful, as she will be in practice (in spite, as we shall see much later, of a narrow escape), to the man whom she is being forced to marry. She is therefore convinced, and in a sense she is right, that she had undergone a moral change, that in giving way to her father she has, so to speak, done penance for what she now regards as the sins of her two 'falls' with Saint-Preux.

That is not all. One of the most important images in the novel is the 'veil'. In all the preceding letters it is a word which stands for the physical darkness that hides the sight of the lover on his way to his mistress's bedroom or for something like a psychological barrier which hides the lovers' moral troubles and moral dangers from them. Julie uses the word a good deal more frequently than anybody else. When she is arranging the assignation, she says:

> Enfin la nuit de cette saison est déjà obscure à la même heure; son *voile* peut dérober aisément dans la rue les passants aux spectateurs, et tu sais parfaitement les êtres de la maison.

> [Finally, the night at this season is already dark at the same time; its *veil* can easily hide the passers-by in the street from spectators, and you know the people of the house perfectly.]

It is she, too, who is most concerned with the moral troubles:

> . . . tu sens bien qu'il n'y a que le délire de la passion qui puisse me *voiler* l'horreur de ma situation présente.

> [. . . you are fully aware that there is only the delirium of pas-

sion which could *veil* from me the horror of my present position.]

Again:

> Le coeur ne suit pas les sens, il les guide; il couvre leurs égare-
> ments d'un *voile* délicieux.

> [The heart does not follow the senses, it guides them; it covers
> their bewilderment with a delicious *veil*.]

On another occasion Saint-Preux uses the image in the same
sense:

> J'avais dompté les fougueuses saillies d'une imagination témé-
> raire; j'avais couvert mes regards d'un *voile* et mis une entrave à
> mon coeur; mes désirs n'osaient plus échapper qu'à demi.

> [I had tamed the fierce bursts of a rash imagination; I had
> covered my looks with a *veil* and put a shackle on my heart; my
> desires no longer dared to escape except by half.]

In the present letter there are two contrasted uses of the
image. The first of them precedes the account of the marriage
ceremony:

> Mon bon ami, laissons retomber ce *voile*: avons-nous besoin de
> voir the précipice affreux qu'il nous cache pour éviter d'en ap-
> procher?

> [My good friend, let this *veil* fall again: have we any need to
> see the frightful precipices that it hides in order to prevent an
> approach?]

We can see at once that the appearance of the image in the
description of the wedding ceremony is not merely a contrast
with the previous use, but points to something like a reversal
of the process. The 'veil' is no longer an instrument which is
introduced to protect the lovers from being seen or from seeing
their own failings. The invisible hand lifts the 'veil' for a moment to show Julie the dangers from which she has been saved
by divine intervention, or so she believes. The fact that it contradicts the earlier use in the same letter emphasises the conversion and looks forward to what is to come.

5

Although Julie's farewell letter at the end of the third part, in which she announces that as a result of 'inflexible duty' the lovers will never see or have any communication with one another again, is a prelude to a long and complete silence between them, the sequel is very different from what she expected. When Saint-Preux returns to Switzerland after nearly four years' service in the British navy, which he owed to Lord Bomston and which took him all round the world, he promptly receives an invitation from Wolmar to visit Clarens.

There is no immediate reference in the fourth part to 'veils', but we can see at once that metaphorically the 'veil' has been lifted and that Saint-Preux finds himself in a new world. It would be going too far to describe it as an earthly paradise, but it is evident that, as I have already suggested, Clarens has been transformed into something like a miniature utopia. Saint-Preux describes it in great detail in several letters to Lord Bomston of inordinate length. He places the emphasis, significantly, on the setting and the mood of the inhabitants. The natural setting is beautiful and matches their way of life. It is a feudal world which is run with extreme benevolence. The servants and other workers are treated generously, partly from charitable feelings and partly to keep the community intact by preventing them from seeking their fortunes in other places. If servants or workers fail in their duties and are dismissed by Wolmar, they have a right of appeal to Julie, who on occasion reverses her husband's decision. The owners are well off, but they are not grasping money-makers. Food is partly the product of their own farm and partly the product of exchanges of their own goods for those of other landowners. Saint-Preux sums up briefly in these terms:

> . . . a simple, well-arranged house where order, peace and innocence reign . . . Everywhere the useful has been substituted for the agreeable, and the agreeable has almost always been the winner.

Finally:

> What has struck me first in this house and most strongly is to find ease, freedom, gaiety, in the midst of order and exactness.

The nine substantives, 'order', 'peace', 'innocence', 'useful', 'agreeable', 'ease', 'freedom', 'gaiety' and 'exactness' do, indeed, suggest something like a perfect world which possesses all the virtues and none of the vices attributed to polite society in Saint-Preux's letters about Paris, which means a strong contrast between two worlds deliberately undertaken by Rousseau. Julie appears to be a changed woman. She is an exemplary wife and mother who is truly devoted to husband and children. She actually describes her husband, in a letter to Claire, as 'the man of the world who is the dearest to me'. Claire herself compares Julie for the second time to Héloïse:

> Cousin, you were a lover like Héloïse, now you are devout like her. God grant that this will have more success.

It is true that Julie has become genuinely and overtly devout. She is distressed by the unbelief of her husband, who will not be converted until after her death.[1] It does not alter the fact that he is in many ways the outstanding character whom we meet for the first time in the second half of the novel. His wisdom, kindness, generosity and gentleness, his tolerant and liberal outlook turn him into something like a benevolent monarch in this tiny world, while Julie's father (who makes his peace with Saint-Preux) is reduced to an amiable and harmless nonentity, bringing out the contrast mentioned earlier. We can see that the metaphorical 'lifting of the veil' had in fact revealed everything. It was not until she had been married for several years that Julie was able to make up her mind to confess to her husband that she had been Saint-Preux's mistress. She did not know until she made her own confession that her father had discovered the secret and informed his friend before the marriage actually took place. Wolmar's reaction is typical of the man. He commends his wife for her confession, but his knowledge of the liaison has done nothing to make him feel hostile towards her lover. Without any arrogance or boasting,

[1] There will be another reference to him near the end of the novel when she exonerates his unbelief by declaring that 'God himself has *veiled* his face'—a contrast with the 'unveiling' of her own at the marriage. She adds, significantly, that 'at the price of her blood' she would like him converted. This is what happens, but being dead she will not 'see' the converted husband.

he quietly makes up his mind to have a good look at Saint-Preux in order to be sure that there is no danger in allowing him to spend time with Julie.

Wolmar is a man of considerable insight, confirming the view already expressed that there is something of the novelist in Saint-Preux, Julie and Wolmar. His insight prompts Julie to say of him that he possesses 'some supernatural gift which enables him to read down to the bottom of peoples' hearts'. He is soon satisfied about Saint-Preux, but decides to consult the wise Claire. His views strike us as a remarkable paradox:

> If I tell you that my two young people are more amorous than ever, it is doubtless nothing marvellous to say to you. If I assured you on the contrary that they are completely cured, you know what reason and virtue can do; it is not that either is their greatest miracle. But these two conflicting views are true at the same time; that they burn more ardently than ever for one another, and that there reigns between them an honest attachment; that they are still lovers and not more than friends; it is, I suspect, what you will have found more difficulty in understanding, and yet it is nevertheless the exact truth.

He completes his picture by another passage devoted particularly to Saint-Preux:

> It is not Julie de Wolmar with whom he is in love; it is Julie d'Etange . . . The wife of another is not his mistress; the mother of two children is not his former pupil. It is true that she must resemble her and that she often reminds him of the memory of it. He loves her in time past: that is the real solution of the enigma. Take away his memory, and there would no longer be any love.

It is an intriguing piece of psychological analysis. Wolmar sees that Héloïse and Abélard are as much in love as ever, but he is convinced—this is important in view of what is to come—that they are 'completely cured' in the sense that they do not love one another in the same way, or rather that it is not the two present personalities who are in love, which means that for Wolmar love will eventually vanish and be replaced by a different feeling. He is satisfied that there is no danger of adultery or of his marriage being damaged in any way. He therefore decides that instead of keeping the lovers apart, which would be a provocation and might undo the good work, they must spend the rest of their lives together under his benign rule and that the best way of doing it is for Saint-Preux, whose career began as Julie's tutor, to become the tutor of the children of Julie and himself.

It appears to be a sensible plan based on the virtue of the couple and therefore deserves to succeed. There are, however, other passages which deserve a careful look. The statement that Saint-Preux is in love not with Julie de Wolmar, but with Julie d'Etange is an echo of a declaration that Julie herself made in an earlier letter to Claire:

> . . . I love him as tenderly as ever without loving him in the same manner.

It means two things: that she is subscribing to Wolmar's view of the change, which he believes has taken place in their personalities, and that she believes that physical attraction has gone, which will turn out to be an illusion.

In his own letter to Claire, Wolmar makes a statement about Julie which has far greater implications than he realises or could be expected to realise:

> When I say them, it is above all the young man that I mean; for one can only speak of your woman friend by conjecture; a *veil* of wisdom and honesty makes so many folds round her heart that it is no longer possible for the human eye to penetrate, or even for her own eye.

Wolmar's moral estimate of the couple is sound in its way; they are determined to behave in exemplary fashion, but no one in this world, not even the perceptive Wolmar, can forecast with absolute certainty what will happen to a pair of once passionate lovers in a moment of *égarement*. In order to put his views to the test, or rather to confirm them, he does two things. He takes the couple to the *bosquet* where, as he knows, the first lovers' kiss took place. Next, he finds an excuse for going away, leaving them to themselves, recalling the parents' departure in the first part and their drawing blank for more creditable reasons. The visit to the *bosquet* shakes them both badly. When they are on their own, a moment of violent attraction points to a return to the previous couple, consisting of Héloïse and Abélard or Julie d'Etange and Saint-Preux, who were supposed to have been transformed, with the result that they only just manage to escape the most serious 'fall' of all.

This enables us to understand the situation in the last phases of the novel. We have seen that Wolmar's analysis suggested that each of the lovers contained, as it were, two personalities: the youthful and the mature personalities. He recognised that the youthful pair still loved one another, but was convinced that they were in the process of being replaced by mature personalities. The mistake, as we have seen from the narrow escape from a 'fall' during Wolmar's absence, lay in believing that youthful personalities would be prevented by mature personalities from being themselves again. It is revealed in what must be called the conflict between Julie's real and her supposed feelings. When she says that she loves Saint-Preux 'as tenderly as ever, but not in the same manner' she is trying to convince herself that the passionate love of their youth has been transformed into something like an *amitié amoureuse*. Wolmar's observation about the impossibility of anybody, including Julie herself, seeing into the depths of her heart explains the nature of the illusion. It is in fact a Freudian situation. Julie's 'sagesse' and 'honnêteté' act, significantly, as a 'veil' which conceals her real feelings, meaning her unconscious feelings, from herself and are purely the result of her determination to behave properly and to avoid temptation.

The effect on both lovers is extremely painful. Although Julie describes her husband as 'the man of the world who is the dearest to me', living together with Saint-Preux and being sexually separated from him can only make a sensual woman, who was forced to marry a man for whom she felt no sexual attraction and who was much older than she, decidedly unhappy, and the unhappiness is almost certainly increased by an uneasiness which is really an unconscious feeling of guilt. In the last letter that Saint-Preux receives from her before her death, she says:

> I will admit to you straightforwardly that the last six months that we have spent together have been the sweetest of my life.

Then, a few pages later, she contradicts herself and comes close to the truth:

> Everywhere I see only subjects of satisfaction, and I am not satisfied; a secret languish infiltrates itself into the depth of my heart. I feel that it is empty and swollen . . . My friend, I am too happy; happiness bores me.

In what has become a growing sense of desperation, she decides to defend herself by trying to persuade Claire, now a widow, and Saint-Preux to marry. She emphasises the danger of the situation in which they are living by suggesting to Saint-Preux that unless he marries Claire there might be a series of 'falls' with other women, particularly those belonging to the more modest classes, such as servants.

Inevitably, for their own reasons and in spite of their great affection for one another, both Saint-Preux and Claire refuse the suggested marriage.

We cannot say with any certainty whether Wolmar's plan would have succeeded in the end. It seems, however, that even if it had, it would hardly have brought happiness to the couple, that at best it could only have succeeded in the negative sense of avoiding adultery and the disruption of the marriage, but that the youthful personalities would have remained unchanged at least until old age, that they would have been the real personalities with maturity as no more than a 'veil'.

The dénouement is of course Julie's unexpected death, supposed to be the result of pleurisy caused by jumping into a lake to save one of her sons from drowning. It is a strange episode. Although she is dying, Julie displays plenty of energy. She gathers the family together for meals in her bedroom, tidies it up herself and has a long and somewhat controversial discussion about religion with a clergyman who comes to visit her on her deathbed, from which it emerges that like the novelist himself she is what is known as a 'Christian deist' rather than an orthodox Christian. One cannot avoid saying that such a bunch of activities, physical and verbal, would have been impossible for a woman who was known to be within a day or two of incurable death.

We must take a final look at the important image of the

'veil'. Saint-Preux has left Clarens on a journey to Rome with Lord Bomston, his rather unusual 'confidant' whom he will save, somewhat oddly, from an unfortunate marriage with either of his two Roman women friends. Although he does not know it, he has seen Julie for the last time. One night he has a terrifying nightmare, which he describes in a letter to Claire and which will turn out to be a premonition of what is to come. He dreams that he is looking at Julie's mother (who died in the first half of the novel) on her deathbed. He suddenly finds that instead of the mother it is the daughter:

> Je voulus lever les yeux sur elle, je ne la vis plus. Je vis Julie à sa place; je la vis, je la reconnus, quoique son visage fût couvert d'un *voile*. Je fais un cri, je m'élance pour écarter le voile, je ne pus l'atteindre; j'étendais les bras, je me tourmentais et ne touchais rien.

> [I wanted to raise my eyes to her, I no longer saw her. I saw Julie in her place; I recognised her though her face was covered by a *veil*. I gave a cry, I rushed forward to tear off the *veil;* I couldn't reach it; I stretched out my arms, worried myself and didn't touch anything.]

He is in such a state that Lord Bomston takes him back to Clarens so that he can satisfy himself that nothing has happened to Julie:

> Allez, visionnaire . . . hâtez-vous; je vous attends; mais surtout no revenez qu'après avoir déchiré ce fatal *voile* tissu dans votre cerveau.

> [Go, visionary . . . hurry up; I am waiting for you; but above all, don't come back until you have torn away this fatal *veil* of tissue in your mind.]

Saint-Preux does not actually see Julie, but hears her talking to Claire in the garden:

> De peur de lui laissir une défiance, je lui ai caché que je ne vous avais point vues. Quand il me demanda si le *voile* était levé, je l'affirmai sans balancer, et nous n'en avons plus parlé. Oui, cousine, il est levé pour jamais, ce *voile* dont ma raison fut longtemps offusqué.

[For fear of defying him, I concealed from him the fact that I hadn't seen you. When he asked me if the *veil* was lifted, I confirmed it without hesitation, and we said no more about it. Yes, cousin, it is lifted for ever, this *veil* by which for a long time my reason was obscured.]

The last sentence appears to be a suggestion on Saint-Preux's part that mature life has been a *veil* hiding to some extent the youthful personalities. What we are about to see is that all his statements made above look forward in an extremely striking way to what is to come.

In his long letter to Saint-Preux in which he gives a detailed account of Julie's death, Wolmar explains that the body was beginning to decay and that he asked Claire to cover the face. She leaves the bedroom:

Je la vis rentrer un moment après, tenant un *voile* d'or brodé de perles que vous lui avez porté des Indes. Puis, s'approchant du lit, elle baissa le *voile,* en couvrit en pleurant la face de son amie, et s'écria d'une voix éclatante: 'Maudit soit l'indigne main qui jamais lèvra ce *voile!* maudit soit l'oeil qui verra ce visage défiguré!'

[I saw her re-enter a moment later, holding a golden *veil* decorated with pearls that you brought her from the Indies. Then, moving towards the bed, she lowered the *veil,* covered her friend's face with it in tears and cried in a shrill voice: 'Cursed be the unworthy hand which ever lifts the *veil!* Cursed be the impious eye which will see the disfigured face'.]

Her words are repeated a 'thousand times' by the people of the household.

It is a remarkable piece of irony. The nightmare is not merely prophetic; Saint-Preux's statement that the '*veil* which had long obscured his mind had been lifted for ever' is followed by the spectacle of Claire 'lowering the *veil*' over the face of the dead Julie. Her call for a curse on anyone who 'lifts' it even looks back to Bomston's phrase telling Saint-Preux not to come back until he has 'torn away the fatal *veil*'.

Although the word is not used, there is something like a posthumous lifting of the 'veil' in Julie's last letter to Saint-Preux, which does not reach him until she is dead:

I dare to honour myself with the past; but who would have replied to me about the future? One day more perhaps, and I was guilty! What did this amount to in relation to the whole of life spent with you? What dangers I risked without knowing it! To what greater dangers I was going to be exposed! No doubt I felt for myself the fears that I was feeling for you.

I have called the second half of the novel the period of 're-demption'. The lovers have fought nobly against temptation and have suffered greatly. The 'veil' first used as a form of con-cealment was lifted to reveal what appeared to be a new and happy world, but turned out to be decidedly painful. A dream disclosed something like 'redemption' by death. We should ob-serve, too, that until Julie's death every use of the image of the 'veil' is abstract and metaphorical. The covering of the dead Julie with a *real* 'veil', which was significantly a present from Saint-Preux, is something like the lowering of the curtain at the end of a tragedy. The posthumous lifting of the metaphor-ical 'veil' shows Julie as she really was and had come to see her-self, which confirms the impression that death was a 'redemp-tion' in the sense that it saved her from what would have been a real sin. It remains to add that this final letter displays the error of Wolmar's analysis of the couple and that it was only death which prevented the youthful personalities from becom-ing the dominant pair again and removing the false 'veil' of the mature personalities.

What emerges from all this is that the 'veil' is the most im-portant image in the novel and reflects perfectly the relations between the protagonists and between the protagonists and their world. It naturally confirms what I said about 'montage' in relation to Rousseau in the opening chapter of the book (p. 24).

6

We know that one of the most striking features of *Les Liaisons dangereuses* is the variety of tone of the different correspon-dents. It is so marked that, as I said earlier, we have the impres-sion that we can almost hear the tone of their voices, in par-ticular the contrast between the voices of the immature young persons and the cynical balanced tone of Valmont or Mme de Merteuil. This is something that is not to be found in *La Nou-*

velle Héloïse. There are, as we have seen, plenty of changes of
mood, with the protagonists rapidly moving from one extreme
to another, but basically the style of all of them is the same. It
is the same in order to enable the novelist to achieve his aim.
That aim is the profound analysis of the feelings of the lovers
and the reactions of Claire, Lord Bomston and Wolmar. It is,
indeed, the maturity of style which brings out the contrast between the youth of the lovers in the early stages of their love
and their sophistication.

It does not detract in any way from Rousseau's achievement.
He is generally recognised as a master of French prose. A casual
glance at two statements by Saint-Preux is sufficient to show
that his prose is essentially musical and that the perpetual conflicts do nothing to reduce the effect of the music:

> Je suis à la fois soumis et téméraire, impétueux et retenu; je ne
> saurais lever les yeux sur vous sans éprouver des combats en moi-
> même. Vos regards, votre voix, portent au coeur, avec l'amour,
> l'attrait touchant de l'innocence; c'est un charme qu'on aurait
> regret d'effacer.

> [I am at the same time submissive and reckless, impetuous and
> cautious; I should not know how to raise my eyes to you without
> running into conflicts within myself. Your looks, your voice, go to
> the heart with love, the touching attraction of innocence; it is a
> divine charm that one would regret to lose.]

Again:

> Mais cette carrière de douleurs est couverte des ténèbres de l'av-
> enir: le terme qui doit la borner se dérobe à mes faibles yeux . . .
> le soleil se lève, et ne me rend plus l'espoir de te voir; il se couche,
> et je ne t'ai point vue; mes jours, vides de plaisir, s'écoulent dans
> une longue nuit. J'ai beau vouloir ranimer en moi l'espérance
> éteinte, elle ne m'offre qu'une ressource incertaine et des consola-
> tions suspectes.

> [But this career of sufferings is covered with the darkness of the
> future: the end which must restrict it conceals itself from my weak
> eyes . . . the sun rises and does not increase my hope of seeing you;
> it goes down, and I haven't seen you, my days, empty of pleasure,
> elapse during a long night. It is in vain that I try to revive in me
> the lost hope, it only offers me an uncertain resource and doubtful
> consolations.]

Rousseau's musical prose comes as something of a relief after the decidedly dry prose that we find in some of the most distinguished of eighteenth-century writers. One of its merits is that it is never loosely lyrical in the manner of his successors. We can see from the opening sentence of the first of the two passages that there is no relaxation of the care with which Rousseau chooses his vocabulary. The antithesises between 'soumis' and 'téméraire', 'impétueux' and 'retenu' are characteristic of the lovers and in this case lead to a striking rhythmical eulogy of Julie in the second sentence of the first of the two passages. Another passage from a letter of Julie's becomes something like an explanation:

> Privée de toi, je reste sans ressource, sans appui, sans espoir; le passé m'avilit, le présent m'afflige, l'avenir m'épouvante. J'ai cru tout faire pour notre bonheur, je n'ai fait que nous rendre méprisables en nous préparant une séparation plus cruelle. Les vains plaisirs ne sont plus, les remords demeurent; et la honte qui m'humilie est sans dédommagement.

> [Separated from you, I remain without resource, without help, without hope; the past degrades me, the present pains me, the future terrifies me. I believed that I had done everything for our happiness, I have done nothing but make us contemptible in preparing for us a still more cruel separation. The vain pleasures no longer exist, the remorse remains; and the shame which humiliates me is without compensation.]

It is at once apparent that this is an example of traditional style or what, technically, could be described as traditional 'rhetoric'. First there are the ternary phrases, 'sans ressource, sans appui, sans espoir'. They are strengthened by the next ternary phrase with its past, present and future. What we also observe is the perfection of the choice of vocabulary. The ternary phrases are not mere repetitions used by way of emphasis; they are visible distinctions between 'ressource', 'appui' and 'espoir' which reveal the full nature of the sense of despair. The same is true of the next phrase, where each word is a perfect rendering of Julie's reactions to three separate phases of life. The passage goes on to antitheses: the attempt to win happiness is defeated and leads to 'méprisables', and 'une séparation plus cruelle'. It is completed by the final sentence with 'les vains plaisirs ne sont plus, les remords demeurent' and 'la honte qui m'humilie', which carry the analysis of her state of mind to its end, while 'sans dédommagement' places the seal on the ultimate defeat. Finally, we should notice the extreme concision with which Julie sums up in three short sentences all the main feelings that she has experienced.

The only other aspect of Rousseau's style on which I wish to comment is his use of nature. We all know that his descriptions of nature look forward to the Romantics. What deserves stressing is that his descriptions of nature are organic in the sense that they reflect the actual mood of the speaker and are not simply picturesque. When Julie sends Saint-Preux to Vervai in order to avoid the difficulties, as she mistakenly hopes, caused by the first 'kiss of love' he spends his time tramping round the countryside and draws on the sight of it to express his sadness caused by the temporary separation:

> On n'aperçoit plus de verdure, l'herbe est jaune et flétrie, les arbres sont dépouillés, le séchard et la froide bise entassent la neige et les glaces; et toute la nature est morte à mes yeux, comme l'espérance au fond de mon coeur.

> [One no longer sees greenery; the grass is yellow and withered, the trees stripped, the dryness and the north wind heap up snow and ice; and in my eyes the whole of nature is dead like the hope at the bottom of my heart.]

It is no doubt a matter of pure chance that the temporary banishment took place during a wintery season, but what Saint-Preux sees clearly corresponds to his profound depression. There is nothing slapdash about the description; it is extremely logical. The general statement about the absence of 'verdure' is followed by the details which reflect his mood perfectly: 'l'herbe jaune et flértrie', 'arbres . . . dépouillés', the cold north wind which piles up snow and ice leading to the final summing up, which has the effect of binding man and nature: 'toute la nature est morte à mes yeux, comme l'espérance au fond de mon coeur'.

It is matched by the highly cheerful description of nature when he returns under the impression that the absence of Julie's parents will leave them to themselves:

Je trouve la campagne plus riante, la verdure plus fraîche et plus vive, l'air plus pur, le ciel plus serein; le chant des oiseaux semble avoir plus de tendresse et de volupté ... on dirait que la terre se pare pour former à ton heureux amant un lit nuptial digne de la beauté qu'il adore et de feu qui le consume.

[I find the countryside more smiling, the greenness fresher and more living, the air purer, the sky more peaceful; the singing of the birds seems to have more tenderness and delight ... one might say that the earth is offering itself in order to provide your happy lover with a nuptial bed worthy of the beauty that he adores and the fire which consumes him.]

The procedure is identical with that of the previous passage, but this time is used to express a mood which is exactly the opposite. The general description of the countryside as 'plus riante'—the comparison is clearly important and will be repeated—is followed by adjectives which are the opposite of those used in the other passage with their emphasis on life: 'plus fraîche', 'plus vive', 'plus serein'. The sound of the wind is replaced by the sound of birds singing, which is used to link nature with human feeling in the transit to 'plus de tendresse et de volupté', which is a clear reflection of the pleasure that in spite of Julie's feelings he experienced at the first 'fall'. Instead of 'hope being dead in the depths of his heart', he is full of energy and hopefully asking for more. The 'lit nuptial' of course looks forward to the second 'fall', which both of them were to enjoy enormously.

Great writers, as we know, always divide the critics at one stage or another in their careers. *La Nouvelle Héloïse* was an extremely popular novel at the time of its publication and although Rousseau had become a highly controversial figure in political and intellectual circles, it did not prevent large numbers of general readers assembling in order to welcome him publicly when they knew that he was passing through their town. His reputation seems to have declined in the latter part of the nineteenth century. André Le Breton explains in his study of the eighteenth-century novel that Rousseau owed his great popularity to the fact that the novel 'a jailli du plus profond de son être' and goes on to observe that it 'no longer has practically any readers' because 'it is full of dissertations or sermons in the form of letters of twenty-five to thirty pages long'.[1] Although Rousseau's novel appears to be less popular with English readers than the *Confessions,* it has come back into its own in France. For Jean-Louis Lecercle 'many of its pages are out of date today', but it is 'certainly the greatest novel of the century and one of our masterworks'.[2] Henri Coulet describes it as 'le plus beau roman français du XVIIIe siècle' and refuses to admit that there is anything superfluous in it. 'The Rousseauist vision of life', he declares, 'would be incomplete in *La Nouvelle Héloïse* without the letter about Opera, the letter on Elysée, the letter on domestic economy at Clarens, and the letter on education of children and so on'.[3] I myself subscribe to the view of René Pomeau, which is similar to that of M. Lecercle: 'Great novel for which it is necessary to have the courage to overcome the *longueurs*'.[4] The *longueurs* could well have been avoided without the omission of far-reaching criticisms of high society in Paris, which M. Coulet rightly regards as an essential part of the work. The *longueurs* are obviously a defect partly because they certainly try the reader's 'courage' and his patience, but still more seriously because they tend to obscure the novel's technical accomplishment—the way in which the different episodes look back or forward to one another and the very effective use of recurrent words and images, as well as the way in which length and repetition on occasion detract from the force of a particular incident or pronouncement.

Yet the novel deserves all the praise that it has received. Its scope is much wider than that of even the most distinguished of Rousseau's contemporaries; it gives a deeper and richer view of human nature than we find in the social novels in which the characters are largely confined to *salons;* its style and technical accomplishment were to have a great influence on later novelists and, finally, as I observed at the beginning of this study, the novelist somehow gives the impression of bringing the whole of life into his work instead of simply telling what on every account is a highly remarkable love story treated in an extremely original manner.

1 *Le Roman du dix-huitième siècle,* 1898, p. 239.

2 *Rousseau et l'art du roman,* 1969, p. 308.

3 *Le Roman jusqu'à la Révolution,* Tome I, 1967, pp. 401, 406.

4 Antoine Adam, Georges Lerminter, Édouard Morot-Sir (Editors): *Littérature française,* Tome I, 1967, p. 370.

STENDHAL'S LAST NOVEL

LAMIEL

1

'CES AVENTURES sont peu édifiantes et cette nouvelle est un mauvais livre'.[1] Stendhal must have smiled grimly to himself as he scrawled these words on the manuscript of his last novel. *Lamiel* is certainly not an edifying story, and there have been sharp differences of opinion about its value. It is difficult to believe that even if Stendhal had managed to finish it, it would have been a work of the same calibre as his three principal novels; but if it is an absurd exaggeration to claim that 'he wrote nothing more significant', it is also an exaggeration to dismiss it as 'boring'.[2] It remains a fragment, but a fragment which contains some of the best and some of the worst of Stendhal. This gives it its peculiar interest. For like all unfinished or minor works of a great writer it tells us a good deal about his method, as well as about his strength and weakness.

We know comparatively little about its genesis. Henri Martineau thought that the idea might have come to Stendhal in April 1838 when he was collecting material for his *Voyage dans le midi de la France*. According to a remark in that work, he spent three days at Toulouse, where a mission was in progress, in order to document for himself a projected history of his own time. The mission of Toulouse may have suggested the mission and the 'miracle' of the fireworks in the opening chapter of *Lamiel,* when twenty crackers went off behind the altar while a priest was preaching and were greeted by his words: 'L'enfer, mes frères!'

Early in 1839 when he was drawing up a list of 'works in preparation' for inclusion in *La Chartreuse de Parme*, Stendhal mentioned a novel called *Amiel* which was described as *sous presse,* though he had not in fact begun to write it. He

---

[1] 'These adventures are hardly edifying and this novellette is a bad book'.
[2] André Gide in his introduction to *Lamiel* (Les Classiques du XIXe siècle), Paris, 1947, p. 32: Armand Caraccio in *Stendhal l'homme et l'oeuvre* (Connaissance des Lettres), Paris, 1951, p. 188.

returned to Civita-Vecchia on August 10 of the same year, and on October 1 he started work on the novel. A note on a copy of *Mémoires d'un touriste* shows that in the early part of January 1840 over three hundred pages of the manuscript had been dictated. Work went on until May, but it seems to have been largely the work of revision and the story did not go any further than the point reached at the end of 1839. Stendhal had evidently hoped that he would be able to write it with the same ease and rapidity as *La Chartreuse de Parme*, but the great élan which had produced that masterpiece seems to have faltered and died. The book was laid aside, taken up again in 1841 and 1842, but he could make no real progress. On March 9, 1842, less than a fortnight before his death, he wrote some further notes which show that he was still undecided about certain fundamental points, and was actually toying with the idea of making Dr. Sansfin the principal character of the book instead of Lamiel.

When we turn to the book it becomes easier to understand his hesitations and his indecision. We know that Stendhal is always concerned with the fate of the 'outsider' in a corrupt society. In *Armance* the protagonist is denied a full life as a result of impotence, which today is regarded with few exceptions as a psychological malady, but in the three great novels he is a metaphysical rather than a social outcast.[1] We know, too, that in those books Stendhal examined the social-political scene from three different angles by making each of the three principal characters a member of a different social class, and had also dealt with what he regarded as the three most important 'moments' in recent political history. He had therefore completed his survey and wanted to do something different. This produces a change in the well-defined pattern of the novels. He makes his principal character a woman in the belief that this will produce a fresh approach to experience; but the political situation is studied obliquely through provincial society instead of the centre.

The provincial setting is of particular importance in *Lamiel* and the importance is by no means purely political. Sansfin, the

---

[1] One of the principal exceptions is impotence caused by congenital syphilis.

local doctor, is clearly a product of the Enlightenment and something like a *philosophe* who is in conflict, morally and socially, with the people of traditional views who surround him. There is a sense in which Lamiel herself is also a child of the Enlightenment and her trick with her confessor when she is trying to satisfy her curiosity about love is evidently a borrowing from the *Liaisons dangereuses*.[1] What is more important, however, is that we have the impression, in spite of Sansfin's name, that the period is somehow an aftermath in which all the previously dominant ideas appear to be crumbling. It is precisely this that provides Lamiel with a stimulant which produces a change of life for her.

One of the most curious things about the novel is the beginning. The first two chapters are related in the first person, who is unnamed, but appears to be the novelist imitating the autobiographical novelist on a tiny scale. It is curiously effective. It provides an introduction to provincial life at Carville, which is the most important of the novel's settings. At the end of the second chapter we are told that the anonymous narrator had inherited a fortune from an uncle living in America. After five years spent at a provincial town called La Havane, he suddenly feels that he wants to live as a rich man in Paris and also to learn what is happening to Carville. 'All these adventures', he says, 'for there have been adventures, are related to the little Lamiel, who was the adopted child of the Hautemares, and I took upon myself the fantasy of describing them in order to become an *homme de lettres*'. He closes with a highly amusing remark:

'Therefore, O benevolent reader, I say good-bye to you. You will not hear any more talk about me'.

It is entirely correct. The novel becomes the work of an omniscient narrator.

It is a good introduction. *Lamiel* is the story of a foundling who is brought up by the village beadle and his wife and who turns into an adventuress. She comes under the influence of the sceptical doctor who offers the only possible escape from the

[1] *Les Liaisons dangereuses*, (Pléiade), Letter LXXXI, p. 201.

boredom of Carville. She seduces the son of the local *châtelain*, the young Duc de Miossens, and runs away to Paris where she has other affairs; but they all leave her cold.

She does not fall in love, does not even grasp the meaning of the word until she is nearly murdered by a robber who has broken into her room. Stendhal draws on the personality and career of a notorious criminal named Lacenaire for his portrait of Valbayre as he had drawn on the Berthet affair in *Le Rouge et le noir*. Lacenaire was precisely the sort of person to kindle Stendhal's imagination. He was a bandit, an enemy of society, but he was also a man of culture who shared Stendhal's enthusiasm for the theatre and admired his favourite authors. Valbayre, who reminds us of Ferrante Palla in the *Chartreuse de Parme*, declares proudly that he reads Corneille and Molière —significantly Stendhal's personal taste, which omitted Racine —that he has too much education to do manual work, and he drives Lamiel into a frenzy of delight by taking her to the theatre when the police are at his heels. The chapters describing Lamiel's adventures as a member of Valbayre's gang were never written, but Stendhal's notes show that the novel was to have ended by Lamiel's setting fire to the prison in an attempt to rescue her lover and perishing in the flames.

Lamiel is the only novel, but not the only work, in which Stendhal's protagonist is a woman. He had tried something of the sort in an early story called 'Vanina Vanini' in the *Chroniques italiennes*, in *Mina de Vanghel* written shortly after *Le Rouge et le noir*, and again in *Le Rose et le vert* which was written in 1837. In a valuable essay Jean Prévost has discussed Lamiel's resemblance to the heroines of these stories and to Mathilde de la Mole. They are all examples of what he calls 'l'Amazone stendhalienne'. 'She is', he said, 'the woman whose head is roused rather than her heart and who becomes the *ennemie aimée* rather than the true lover'.[1] 'She is a woman who is completely feminine by her beauty and her grace, and completely masculine by her intelligence and her energy'.[2] When he describes Lamiel as a 'feminine incarnation of Julien Sorel', he also stresses her resemblance to the male protagonists of the

[1] *Essai sur les sources de Lamiel: les Amazones de Stendhal: le Procès de Lacenaire*, Lyon, 1942, p. 9.
[2] *La Création chez Stendhal*, New edition, Paris, 1951, p. 378.

novels.[1] She, too, is an 'outsider' at odds with society, and in spite of her charm she possesses the same ruthlessness. We know that though Stendhal put a great deal of himself into his heroes, he never put the whole of himself into any one character.[2] There is not only something of him in both Fabrice and Mosca, but also in Lucien and M. Leuwen, Lamiel and Dr. Sansfin. This means that in general he identified himself simultaneously with youth and its illusions and with the disillusioned middle age. *Lamiel* is to some extent an exception. There is a good deal of Stendhal in his heroine, but she has fewer illusions than Fabrice or Lucien in *La Chartreuse de parme* or *Lucien Leuwen* and the novelist's connection with Sansfin is far closer than his connection with Mosca or M. Leuwen in the same two novels. Sansfin like Stendhal has been brought up on the 'ideologists'. Jean Prévost was surely right in thinking that his hump was a sardonic reference to Stendhal's own ugliness, and the education of Lamiel a memory of Stendhal's endeavour to instil the principles of 'ideology' into his sister Pauline.

I think that we can begin to see what Stendhal was trying to do and why he failed to do it. The figure of the 'Amazon' had an immense fascination for him, but it had its sources in the complications of his personal life. It was the fascination of the timid bungling seducer who was always hoping that a strong woman would seduce him as Mathilde seduced Julien. *Lamiel* was a determined attempt to make the Amazon the central character of the novel, and the similarity between Lamiel's disguise and Mina de Vanghel's shows that the earlier story was very much in his mind. It seems possible that the personal element accounts both for the comparative failure of the early stories and for the last minute hesitations between Lamiel and Dr. Sansfin. There is, however, another explanation of Stendhal's failure to finish the novel and of the unsatisfactoriness of the later chapters. We know from the other novels and from the *nouvelles* that he had an immense admiration for the heroic figures of the middle ages and the Renaissance, but there was no place for them in the nineteenth century. The hero therefore undergoes a transformation. He is either replaced by the uninspiring figure of the honest merchant in Balzac's *César*

---

[1] *Ibid.*, pp. 375–76.　　[2] *The Novel in France*, p. 161.

Birotteau, or he turns into a bandit. Mathilde de la Mole and
the Duchesse Sanseverina are heroines who were born out of
due time, but when he came to the reign of Louis-Philippe,
Stendhal found that he could not repeat the success.[1] It is
already apparent that Lucien Leuwen dreaming nostalgically
of the Age of Louis XV is a man of a different stamp from
Julien or Fabrice. There was only one opening for Lamiel, and
she took it. She became a gangster's 'moll'.

2

Stendhal thought at one time of calling his novel *Un Village
normand,* and the opening paragraph explains why:

> Je trouve que nous sommes injustes envers les paysages de cette
> belle Normandie où chacun de nous peut aller coucher ce soir. On
> vante la Suisse; mais il faut acheter ses montagnes par trois jours
> d'ennui, les vexations des douanes, et les passeports chargés de
> visas. Tandis qu'à peine en Normandie le regard, fatigué des symé-
> tries de Paris et de ses murs blancs, est accueilli par un océan de
> verdure.

> [I think that we are unfair to the countryside of our lovely Nor-
> mandy where each of us could go and spend the night. People
> speak highly of Switzerland; but its mountains have to purchased
> at the price of three days of boredom, the annoyances of the cus-
> toms and passports covered with visas. Whereas we are scarcely in
> Normandy before our eyes, wearied by the symmetry of Paris and
> its white walls, are greeted by an ocean of verdure.]

It seems strange that a critic who has examined Stendhal's
workmanship as carefully as Jean Prévost should be able to say
that the opening of *Lamiel* is 'purely picturesque, more mo-
tionless than the description of Verrières at the beginning of
Le Rouge et le noir'.[2] Stendhal's openings not only state some of
the essential themes of the novels; the ending is already implied
in them. The calm of Verrières and the disturbances that follow lead logically to the macabre execution of Julien; the great

1 We remember the ironic description of Mathilde as 'ce personnage . . .
imaginé bien en dehors des habitudes sociales qui parmi les siècles assure-
ront un rang si distingué à la civilisation du XIX° siècle'.
2 *Essai sur les sources de Lamiel,* p. 25.

élan with which the *Chartreuse de Parme* opens to the muted
note on which it closes; the placidity of Carville in this book
to the discovery of Lamiel's bones among the ashes of the
prison. The passage seems to have been tossed off with Stendhal's
usual casualness and facility, but when we look into it we per-
ceive its artistry. The first sentence describes the ease and comfort with which the weary Parisian can reach Normandy. Then,
like a shot from a film, the Swiss mountains pass across the
screen, but we also see the long tiring journey with carriages
toiling up steep roads, the troublesome customs' officials, the
stamping of passports. The third sentence stresses the sharp
contrast between the annoying formalities, the monotony of
urban life and the irregular beauties of the countryside. The
effect depends on the opposition of 'fatigué' and 'accueilli',
'symétrie... de ses murs blancs' and 'océan de verdure'. The
last phrase in particular, with its image of wide, lush, undulat-
ing plains coming immediately after the image of the dry dusty
city, produces a strong sense of release.

In the second paragraph we read:

> Les tristes plaines grises restent du côté de Paris, la route pén-
> ètre dans une suite de belles vallées et de hautes collines, leurs
> sommets chargés d'arbres se dessinent sur le ciel non sans quelque
> hardiesse et bornent l'horizon de façon à donner quelque pâture
> à l'imagination, plaisir bien nouveau pour l'habitant de Paris.

> [The sad grey plains remain in the direction of Paris, the road
> runs through a succession of lovely valleys and high hills, their
> tops covered with trees are etched, not without a certain boldness,
> against the sky and block the horizon in such a way as to provide
> food for the imagination—a pleasure that is quite new for the
> inhabitant of Paris.]

It is a striking example of the classic artist at work. There is
none of the detail, the careful building up of atmosphere that
we find in Rousseau and in the novelists who followed Stendhal. He uses simple colourless words and still contrives to produce his effect with a few brief strokes where another writer—
Fromentin is a good illustration—would have needed pages
of description. The 'sad grey plains' are behind us, but the release produced by 'océan de verdure' in the first paragraph

begins to fade. We feel that we are 'penetrating' into a sanctuary. The 'bornent' reinforces the word 'pénètre' because it suggests that we are going somewhere where, in spite of the 'pâture à l'imagination', we shall be shut in. This impression is developed in the fourth paragraph:

> Si l'oeil, qu'éveille aux beautés des paysages le charme des lointains, cherche les détails, il voit que chaque champ forme comme un enclos entouré de murs de terre, ces digues établies régulièrement sur le bord de tous les champs sont couronnés d'une foule de jaunes ormeaux.

> [If the eye, which the charm of distance awakens to the beauties of the countryside, looks for details, it sees that each field forms as it were an enclosure surrounded by earthen walls, the dykes built in regular fashion along the edges of all the fields are crowned by a mass of young elms.]

The Swiss mountains are far behind us. The long shot of the 'charme des lointains' changes to a close-up of 'les détails'. The key words are 'un enclos entouré de murs de terre' and 'ces digues établies régulièrement'. For in spite of the opulence of the surrounding country, we are already conscious of something faintly oppressive in the atmosphere. We are in a village 'lost in the midst of apple trees, [which] lies at the bottom of the valley', shut in by 'walls' and 'enclosures', cut off from the great world. We shall find that as the novel unfolds, this atmosphere of isolation and suffocation becomes more and more pronounced, is in fact one of the principal themes.

'Carville', writes the novelist, 'is a place which will not be found on the map and of which I ask for permission to describe the horrors, that is to say, part of the truth'. I have already suggested that in this novel the political comment is indirect. Stendhal proceeds to give a picture of a Norman village which under the Restoration has relapsed into a sort of feudalism and is dominated, symbolically, by the Château of the Duchesse de Miossens. The visitor who had left urban life in search of peace will find little among the Norman country folk:

> The shrewdness, the sordid calculations of these Normans provided me with scarcely any relief from the complicated life in Paris.

There are decent people everywhere, even in Normandy where, to tell the truth, they are much rarer than in other places.

He fills in the moral picture of the individual members of the community with the same rapid mischievous strokes. This is the Duchess:

The Revolution of 1798 and Voltaire were not something which was odious to her; they were something that had not happened.

We catch a glimpse of the doctor at the bedside of a handsome young man who has been struck down by apoplexy:

The doctor spent the night at his bedside, and, although he applied the appropriate treatment, he had the pleasure of seeing the handsome being die towards daybreak.

'There's a fine body vacant', he said to himself; 'why can't my soul enter it?'

It is a personal touch in which Stendhal reminds us of his own ugliness.

The beadle is 'le meilleur et le plus parfaitement dévot des hommes'; his wife 'était encore, s'il se peut, plus petitement dévote'.[1] They decide to adopt a child, but their motives are by no means wholly charitable:

'I should do well to adopt a little girl, a tiny little girl. We'll bring her up in the fear of God: we shall really *give her a soul,* and when we're old she'll look after us'.

They intend to 'form' the child according to their own ideas, but the book is a conflict between the individualistic 'outsider', who has a 'soul' of her own, and the 'horrors' of provincial society. The pair depart for the *Enfants Trouvés* at Rouen where, observes Stendhal ironically, they chose a little girl of four, duly vaccinated and already the sweetest little thing'.[2]

[1] 'The best and most meticulously devout of men; [his wife] was even more feebly devout, if that is possible'.

[2] In Stendhal the 'outsider' first becomes aware of his difference in the home. Lamiel and Fabrice are illegitimate; Octave and Lucien are only children who do not quite 'hit it off' with their fathers. Julien is neither an only child nor illegitimate, but he hates his father and his brothers.

We know that Stendhal's novels are built up round certain key words on which he sets his personal stamp, giving them a special resonance which echoes all through the book. The 'singulier-singularité' of *Armance* and *Le Rouge et le noir,* the 'médiocre-médiocrité' of *Lucien Leuwen* are matched in *Lamiel* by the words 'âme' and 'ennui':

> Les esprits sont précoces en Normandie; quoique à peine âgée de douze ans [Lamiel] était déjà susceptible d'ennui, et l'ennui, à cet âge, quand il ne tient pas à la souffrance physique, annonce la présence de l'âme.

> [Minds are precocious in Normandy; although barely twelve years old, Lamiel was already susceptible to boredom, and boredom at that age, when it was not the result of physical suffering, reveals the presence of a soul.]

In Stendhal 'âme' is the principle of vitality, 'ennui' the sense of frustration caused by the pressure of a 'mediocre' environment which threatens to stifle it. All the principal characters in *Lamiel* are afflicted by it. The Duchess is bored; Sansfin is bored; Lamiel falls ill from boredom.

> 'Voici un cas bien rare en Normandie, se dit-il [Sansfin]. C'est *l'ennui,* et l'ennui malgré le commerce de la duchesse, l'excellent cuisinier, les primeurs, les beaux meubles du château . . .'

> [Here's a case that's very uncommon in Normandy, he said to himself. It's *boredom,* and boredom in spite of the company of the Duchess, the excellent cook, the early vegetables, the splendid furniture of the château . . .]

It is 'ennui' that causes the revolt of Sansfin and Lamiel. For in this book, as surely as in the *Liaisons dangereuses,* the characters divide into two parties—'le parti prêtre' on one side, the rebels and enemies of convention on the other. Sansfin sets to work to cure Lamiel of her 'ennui', and in the process he manages to dissipate the duchess's 'ennui' as well as his own.[1] This provides Stendhal with his opportunity. He was at pains to ex-

---

[1] Sansfin's comment on Lamiel, who has gone to live at the château as an antidote to the duchess's 'ennui'.

plain that he was essentially an 'improviser'; he was not concerned with the orderly unfolding of feelings. 'The page I am
writing, he said, 'gives me the idea of the next'. He was interested in feelings in action. His aim was to seize a feeling
the moment that it came into being, to show impulses pulling
simultaneously in different directions, the conflicting potentialities of a situation. Sansfin is determined to assert himself,
to achieve a position in society in spite of his deformity. He
thinks of marrying the duchess, then decides against it:

> 'Grand Dieu, combien je me trompais en me donnant une nou-
> velle imposture à soutenir! Je serais bien plus heureux en dé-
> veloppant mes qualités naturelles. Si la nature m'a donné une
> triste envelope, je sais manier la parole et me rendre maître de
> l'opinion des sots, et même,' ajouta-t-il, avec un sourire de satis-
> faction, 'de l'opinion des gens d'esprit . . .'

> ['Good heavens, what a mistake I was making in assuming
> another spurious role! I should be much better occupied in de-
> veloping my natural qualities. If nature has given me a poor ap-
> pearance, I know how to turn a phrase and mould the opinion of
> fools and even', he added with a smile of satisfaction, 'the opinion
> of clever people . . .']

All Stendhal's characters, as we know, are engaged like the
novelist himself in an effort to penetrate beneath the conventions and false personalities—the 'impostures' which society
tends to impose on them and to discover the real being underneath. This is the source of the rebellious attitudes of all his
protagonists. There is therefore a contrast between 'imposture'
and 'qualités naturelles'. For underlying Stendhal's work is a
belief in the genius of the individual, the innate qualities
which promise success whatever the society in which he is living. The doctor decides that while working out his plan to win
a great position, he must amuse himself:

> 'Pendant que je vais suivre ce grand dessein, il faut me donner
> les prémices du coeur de cette jeune fille'.—Pour parvenir à toutes
> ces belles choses, Sansfin fit durer pendant plusiers mois la pré-
> tendue maladie de Lamiel; comme l'origine du peu de réel qu'il
> y avait dans cette indisposition fort simple était l'ennui, Sansfin

sacrifia toute chose au désir d'amuser la maladie; mais il fut étonné
de la clarté et de la vigueur de cet esprit si jeune: la tromper
était fort difficile. Bientôt Lamiel fut convaincue que ce pauvre
médecin d'une figure aussi burlesque était le seul ami qu'elle eût
au monde. En peu de temps, par des plaisanteries bien calculées,
Sansfin réussit à détruire toute l'affection que le bon coeur de
Lamiel avait pour sa tante et pour son oncle Hautemare.

['While I'm carrying out the grand design, I must have the first
fruits of the heart of this girl'.—In order to accomplish all these
fine things, Sansfin managed to spin out Lamiel's supposed illness
for several months; as boredom was the origin of what little was
genuine in her very simple indisposition, Sansfin sacrificed everything to his desire to entertain the patient; but he was amazed at
the clarity and vigour of her young mind: it was extremely difficult to deceive her. Lamiel was soon convinced that the poor doctor, who had such a funny face, was her only friend in the world.
In a short time, by means of carefully calculated jokes, Sansfin
succeeded in destroying all the affection that Lamiel's kindly heart
had for her aunt and uncle Hautemare.]

Stendhal is concerned here not merely with the differences
between 'real' and 'counterfeit' feelings, but with the degrees
of reality of the different feelings and qualities. The 'peu de
réel qu'il y avait dans cette indisposition' is a key to the interpretation of the passage. It moves smoothly along to the words
'amuser la malade'; then there is a pause. We literally feel the
impact of 'la clarté et . . . la vigueur de cet esprit si jeune', as
though the doctor had struck a physical obstacle. The impact is
intensified by 'la tromper était fort difficile'. There is another
alteration which is reflected this time in the changed disposition
of Lamiel, and the attention shifts from what is happening in
the doctor's mind to what is happening in hers. The last sentence
but one abruptly announces that he has got past her defences
and convinced her that he is really her only friend. He pushes
home his advantage and 'destroys' her affection for her devout
foster parents. 'Détruire' is a characteristically Stendhalian
use of a transitive verb to record the destruction of one set of
feelings or one mood which is replaced by another. The effect,
as usual, is achieved by the skilful balancing of words against
each other. We must glance back at the earlier passage. Compared with 'imposture', the 'qualités naturelles' stand for some-

thing real; but when we go on to compare them with 'la clarté et . . . la vigueur de cet esprit si jeune', we realise that the final advantage lies entirely with Lamiel. The doctor is naturally more experienced and more mature—he is master of 'plaisanteries bien calculées'—but there is nothing 'calculated' about her 'clarté' and 'vigueur'. Potentially, she is vastly superior to him. It is not difficult to see why. In spite of the tragedies of Julien and Fabrice and the apparent success of Mosca, the youthful heroes and heroines are the idealised beings that Stendhal would like to have been; the middle-aged cynics are ironical portraits of the man he was.

3

'The central problem', writes an American critic of the Stendhalian heroes, 'is always the same: the education of youth for life; the formation of his mind and the character under the blows of experience; his début in society'.[1] His words are equally true of Stendhal's heroine in this book. In speaking of Stendhal the term 'education' must be understood in the humane sense of developing the innate qualities of character. Lamiel's education is much more sympathetic than that of the characters in the other novels. She is placed in the hands of two men of opposing views, but though they both try to 'instruct' her, they are unable to impose their views or 'form' her, as Valmont and Mme de Merteuil 'form' Cécile in the *Liaisons dangereuses*. She is much too independent and her own qualities are developed by the friction of her mind on theirs, by playing off one against the other.

It might be supposed that the competition between Sansfin and the gentle Abbé Clément would be hopelessly unequal, and that the influence of the crafty doctor would predominate; but this is to underrate the subtlety of Stendhal's method.

> Ce jeune prêtre, fort pâle, fort pieux, fort instruit . . . avait un cruel défaut pour son état . . . il avait beaucoup d'esprit . . .

> [The young priest, very pale, very pious, very learned . . . had a fault which was very unfortunate for his state . . . he was highly intelligent . . .]

[1] Matthew Josephson, *Stendhal or the Pursuit of Happiness*, 1946, pp. 391–92.

It enables him to appreciate the potentialities of his charge:

> Il fut frappé de la grâce qu'il y avait dans la réunion d' un es-
> prit vif, audacieux et de la plus grande portée, avec une ignorance
> à peu près complète de toutes les choses de la vie, et une âme par-
> faitement naïve.

> [He was struck by the grace that he found in the combination of
> a mind which was lively, bold and of the greatest range, with an
> almost total ignorance of everything in life, and a soul which was
> completely naïve.]

Stendhal's principal characters exist at two different levels,
and possess qualities which seem at first to be contradictory.
They possess the admirable qualities signified by words like
'clarté', 'vigueur', 'audacieux' and 'vif'; theirs are minds which
are potentially 'de la plus grande portée'; they are driven on by
an insatiable curiosity about themselves and other people. But
these qualities go together with an extraordinary lack of experience, a naïveté which makes them so engaging. Now the
positive qualities contribute to their poise and resilience, and
the process of education is in fact the development and application of these qualities to the conquest of naïveté and inexperience. For underlying their inexperience is a very healthy scep-
ticism and a decidedly critical outlook:

> Lamiel's first reaction at the sight of a virtuous person was to
> take him for a hypocrite.

The great aim of Stendhal's heroes and heroines is to become
integrated beings. This can only be achieved by taking what
each of the different educators has to give, and because they are
fundamentally superior to the individuals who surround them
their gifts cannot be developed by any one educator. Lamiel's
education is therefore a process of sifting and testing what
Sansfin and the Abbé Clément offer. At every moment we find
her instinctively comparing their teaching:

> His teaching [we are told of the abbé] was very different from
> that given by Dr. Sansfin. It was not hard, cutting, going back to
> the principles of things like Sansfin's; it was gentle, insinuating,

full of grace, there was always a little maxim preceded by a pretty little story of which it appeared to be the consequence, and the young teacher took good care to let the young pupil deduce this consequence for herself. She often fell into a profound reverie which the abbé could not explain. It happened when something taught by the abbé seemed to be in contradiction with one of the doctor's terrible maxims.

The abbé's 'pretty little storie(s)' alternate in her mind with the 'terrible maxims' of the doctor:

> For example, according to the latter, the world was only a bad play, performed without grace, by rogues without grace, infamous liars...
> 'How many girls die before they are twenty-three', he used to say to Lamiel, 'and then what's the good of all the restraint they've imposed on themselves and since they were fifteen, all the fun they missed in order to gain the good opinion of eight or ten old women...'
> We have fun, which is the sole object for which the human race has been placed on earth...'

She responds readily to the gentleness and grace of the abbé's teaching:

> 'There's a grace that the doctor has never known. What a difference between his gaiety and the Abbé Clément's! The Sansfin's only really gay when he sees some misfortune overtake his neighbour; the good abbé, on the contrary, is filled with goodwill for all men.'

Yet at bottom she finds the abbé's teaching unsatisfying. The 'maxims' and the 'anecdotes' come pat, but it is all a little too neat. It does not go to the roots—'to the principles of things'— like Sansfin's:

> Instead of thinking of the poverty of his arguments compared to the unbreakable, granite-like reasoning of Dr. Sansfin, she saw him as young, full of naïveté and forced by his poverty to repeat ridiculous arguments in which perhaps he did not believe.

Sansfin's arguments represent the less brilliant side of the

Enlightenment, and we shall see that the stress laid on them accounts for some at least of the weaknesses of the novel. To Lamiel, however, his reasoning seems 'the unbreakable, granite-like reasoning' compared with the 'ridiculous arguments' of the abbé. She has no illusions about the doctor, but her objections are not intellectual. The combined effect of the teaching of the two men on her is summed up in an interesting passage:

> La méchanceté trop découverte du docteur heurtait un peu cette âme encore si jeune, et elle voulait la force incisive des idées du docteur, revêtue de la grâce parfaite que l'abbé savait donner à tout ce qu'il disait.

> [Dr. Sansfin's malice, which was too evident, jarred a little on a mind which was still very young, and she would have liked the incisive power of the doctor's ideas clothed in the perfect grace which the abbé was able to give to everything he said.]

What needs to be stressed is that Lamiel's education is an organic process. She is exposed to two conflicting systems, but we are not simply *told* the views of her teachers; they are *enacted* through the language used, and we feel their direct impact on her mind and even more on her sensibility. 'Dur' and 'tranchant' are balanced against 'doux', 'insinuant', 'rempli de grâce'; 'remontant aux principes des choses', 'raisonnement inébranlable comme le granit' and 'force incisive des idées' against 'jolie petite anecdote', 'idées si douces' and 'grâce parfaite'. They are not absorbed uncritically, they are carefully scrutinised; some are accepted, others rejected. In this way we see a mind developing and a personality emerging which are distinct from those of her teachers. She has taken what they had to give. The doctor is her *intellectual* mentor; but the abbé, who appeals strongly to something in her own make-up, educates her *sensibility*. He contributes at least as much as the doctor to turning her into the true Stendhalian heroine:

> Elle voyait tout en beau dans la vie, tout à coup ses rêves de plaisir recevaient le démenti le plus cruel. Son coeur n'était point tendre, mais son esprit était distingué.
> A vrai dire, elle n'avait point eu le temps d'acquérir de l'expérience; c'était un coeur et un esprit romanesques qui se figuraient

les chances de bonheur qu'elle allait trouver dans la vie; c'était là les revers de la médaille.

[Everything in life seemed wonderful to her, then very suddenly her dreams of pleasure were cruelly disappointed. Her heart was not tender, but her mind was distinguished.

To tell the truth, she had not had time to acquire any experience; her heart and mind were romantic and imagined the chances of happiness that she would find in life; it was the other side of the medal.]

'C'était là le revers de la médaille'. There are two sides to the picture. On the surface gentleness, kindness, grace, naïveté: underneath a ruthless pursuit of happiness, a refusal to be taken in, to accept anything at its face value until it has been thoroughly tried and tested.

The Stendhalian heroes have one thing in common. They are intensely preoccupied not merely with love, but with their own capacity for love. They are immensely susceptible, but they are haunted by the fear that there is something lacking in their make-up which prevents them from being able to love. At other moments they turn on love as being something too soft, as something unworthy of their fundamental superiority and congratulate themselves, in a way which is reminiscent of Laclos' characters, on their imperviousness to such a weakness. Lucien, we are told, in *Lucien Leuwen*, 'had never thought of love except as a dangerous and contemptible precipice into which he was certain not to fall'. 'My heart', he says in another place, 'is not made for love'. This attitude, as I have already suggested, is the reflection of something personal in the novelist. Now Stendhal was fond of projecting himself into his characters in different situations to see what it felt like. It is not surprising that in *Lamiel* he varies the formula. Lamiel shares the curiosity of the other characters, but appears to be without their susceptibility. We are told:

At that time Lamiel's one passion was curiosity.

It recalls Laclos' account of Mme de Merteuil's girlhood:

'My head alone was seething with excitement; I had no desire for pleasure, I wanted to know . . .'

The novelist's other pronouncements on his heroine are not less interesting:

> She had no disposition for love; what she enjoyed above everything else was an interesting conversation. A story of war in which the heroes braved great dangers and accomplished difficult things set her dreaming for three days on end, while she showed no more than a passing interest in a love story.

When she meets the Abbé Clément again during her escapades in Paris and is scolded by him, this is her reply:

> I didn't think that there was anything wrong in giving myself to young men for whom I felt no attraction. I want to know whether love is possible for me.

These passages deserve attention because they have a bearing on what I shall have to say later. In the unfavourable comparison between 'love' and 'adventure' Lamiel appears to be echoing Lucien Leuwen, but there is a difference. Lucien is susceptible and though he does at times feel doubts about his capacity to love, he also tries to convince himself that he prefers many exercises and adventures. Lamiel, on the other hand, appears to be frigid. This impression is confirmed by the second passage. She has by this time had several affairs, but she is still genuinely trying to find out whether 'love is possible' for her. Her defence is even more interesting. There is nothing wrong in what she has done, she thinks, because she did not feel any 'attraction' for the young men. In other words, she did not experience any 'pleasure'. From this we can turn to the famous incident earlier in the book where she tips a peasant to instruct her:

> The following day she met Jean in the wood; he was wearing his Sunday clothes.
> 'Kiss me', she said to him.
> He kissed her. Lamiel noticed that in accordance with her orders, he was freshly shaved; she told him so.

'Oh don't mention it', he said brightly. 'Mademoiselle is the mistress; she pays well and she's so pretty!'

'Certainly, it's your mistress I want to be'.

'Ah! that's different', said Jean in a businesslike way; and then without raptures, without love, the young Norman made Lamiel his mistress.

'There's nothing else?' said Lamiel.

'No', replied Jean.

'Have you already had lots of mistresses?'

'I've had three'.

'And there's nothing else?'

'Not that I know of. Will Mademoiselle want to see me again?'.

'I'll let you know in a month's time. But no gossiping. Don't talk about me to anyone'.

'Oh! I shouldn't be such a fool', said Jean Berville. His eye shone for the first time.

'What! Love's nothing but that?' Lamiel said to herself in astonishment. 'It's hardly worth forbidding it so strongly. But I'm deceiving this poor Jean: in order to see me again, he may turn down a good job'. She called him back and gave him another five francs. He was overcome with gratitude.

Lamiel sat down and watched him go away (she wiped away the blood and scarcely thought about the pain).

Then she burst out laughing, and kept on saying to herself over and over again:

'So that's all it is, this famous love!'

I have suggested that Lamiel suffers from frigidity. There are obvious similarities between frigidity in women and impotence in men. Frigidity like impotence, as I have already said, is a psychological condition. It may be partial or complete. There are women who are frigid with some men and not with others. It may be due to a variety of causes: to misplaced *pudeur* or an inadequate sexual education, to a fixation on the father, to the fact that the woman is in love with someone else, to latent homosexuality or—this is of particular importance in the present instance—to that primitive antagonism between the sexes known as 'the sex war'. We cannot say with certainty what happens to Lamiel in the incident with the peasant, but it is obvious that there is no orgasm on her side. The fiasco may be the result of the peasant's brutality or incompetence or of Lamiel's personal peculiarities. The last alternative appears by far the most likely, and is supported by Lamiel's experiences with the young men in Paris, which got her into trouble with the Abbé Clément. We remember that Lamiel is a woman 'whose head is roused rather than her heart', that she prefers 'adventure' to 'love', that she is given to celebration—'curiosity was her one passion'—and we also remember that she was not 'attracted' by the young men with whom she experimented. It must also be remembered that the 'outsider' is by definition a 'superior' individual. The innate superiority of the outsider brings into play the sex war—the desire of the male to dominate and the refusal of the female to submit to someone whom she feels to be inferior to herself. The meeting between Valbayre and Lamiel seems to be conclusive. For Valbayre is recognised instinctively as another 'outsider'. She submits to him because he possesses the mental and, what I should like to call in the wide French sense, the 'moral' qualities which appeal to her imagination and which in her case are an essential condition of love.

'Comment, ce fameux amour, ce n'est que ça!' The spectacle of the bleeding Lamiel laughing over her encounter in the wood strikes another characteristic note. Nearly all Stendhal's heroes begin their careers with a *déception* of this kind. Stendhal himself was passionately anxious to see Italy, Fabrice to fight at Waterloo, but when the great moment comes it is a disappointment. 'So that's all it is', says Stendhal when he looks down from the mountains on Italy, and Fabrice can scarcely believe that he has really been present at a battle at all. The clash between dream and reality was a favourite theme of the Romantics; but though the *données* are the same, Stendhal's reactions are the reverse of the Romantics'. The Romantics, dismayed by the shock, fell into a state of melancholy resignation. With Stendhal the initial disappointment provokes his immense power of attack. He goes forward through his heroes in the determination to make the dream come true. So it is with Lamiel. Her disappointment is repeated over and over again, but her 'natural qualities' prevent her from becoming, as many women do in similar circumstances, a psychopathic case. She 'bursts out laughing', shrugs her shoulders and tries again. And, in the end, she meets Valbayre.

This is the crux of the matter. We have seen that education in the fullest sense is a matter of prime importance for Stendhal's heroes. We have also seen that Lamiel's education was undertaken by two people of conflicting views and that she adopted a decidedly critical attitude towards both of them. The important decision was not only that neither satisfied her, but that though she absorbed something from both, a compromise between the two would not have provided her with the sort of life that she wanted. That was the point at which the 'outsider' emerged. She rejected the traditional religious attitude of the priest and the tough attitude of the *philosophe,* broke with both of them, abandoned the provinces and made her way to Paris, where she met Valbayre, who seemed to be able to provide her with the sort of life—the life of 'adventure'—that she wanted. I have already commented on the resemblances between Valbayre and Ferrante Palla in *La Chartreuse de Parme.* They are both bandits. The important thing is that, in spite of the fact that he had a concern for the poor which is lacking in Valbayre, Ferrante Palla is no more than a minor character whom the Duchess of Sanseverini uses to destroy the ruler who has become her principal enemy. Valbayre is a major character whose goal is purely negative: the destruction of the society in which he lives, which if achieved would simply have produced chaos and helped nobody. It is precisely the inadequacy of the goal compared with that of other Stendhalian heroes which accounts for the wrongness of Lamiel's choice and the peculiar deficiencies of the novel.

4

There is at present a tendency among some of Stendhal's admirers to work up an esoteric cult for the master's lesser works, to argue not merely that they are unique of their kind and deserve to be more widely read, which is true, but that they are in some respects superior to the great masterpieces. Gide's predilection for *Armance* is one example: Comrade Aragon's tendentious eulogy of *Lamiel* is another. Stendhal's peculiar spell does not often fail. 'A magnificent fragment' is a fair description of *Lamiel,* provided that it is confined to the first part of the novel, but once Lamiel leaves Carville, Stendhal does not know what to do with her and the interest of the book evaporates. He does not know what to do with her because, as I have

already said, there was no place for her in the France of Louis-
Phillippe. For we may suspect that he felt obscurely that Lamiel's adventures with Valbayre would have produced an entertaining *nouvelle,* but not a novel of the calibre of the three
masterpieces.

In spite of his assertion that Stendhal 'wrote nothing more
significant', a more serious criticism comes from André Gide.
'There are certain strata of the soul', he said, 'into which Stendhal did not seek to penetrate because he was unaware of them;
the profound regions where we find religious feelings that he
treated so lightly . . . the raptures and exaltations'. Those mysterious regions, he went on, may only exist in our imagination,
but without them the human being is impoverished. 'Now in
this book Stendhal suddenly and unwittingly makes us understand and feel the frightful void caused by their absence'.[1]
Terms like 'profound', 'mysterious regions', 'raptures', 'exaltations' and 'frightful void' must be used with circumspection.
It is not by any means certain that the *Chartreuse de Parme*
would have been improved by an infusion of pious sentiments,
and it is not a novel that anyone except perhaps Claudel would
accuse of lack of 'depth'. It is a story of tragic individuals in a
comic setting. The tragic note comes largely from the desperation with which they cling to personal relationships, and their
sense of the void beneath. 'My philosophy', we remember Stendhal saying, 'belongs to the day on which I happen to be writing'. When he sat down to write a novel, he soon forgot Cabanis
and Tracy, and followed the promptings of his sensibility. In
the *Chartreuse de Parme* the 'philosophy' belongs to the comic
setting and serves to heighten the tragic note. It is far otherwise in *Lamiel.* The 'philosophy' is at the centre of the book
and because it was a poor thing it becomes, artistically, an irre-
parable weakness.

[1] *Op. cit.,* p. 35.

FLAUBERT

I. THE NOVEL, THE SYMPHONY
AND THE CINEMA

IN A letter to Louise Colet on September 7, 1853, Flaubert said that he was working on the Comices Agricoles, which was to become one of the most admired scenes in the whole of *Madame Bovary*. He was finding it a very exacting task:

> I have included *all* my characters moving about and talking, mixing with one another. and above them a great stretch of country which envelopes them. But if I succeed, it will be quite symphonic.

'Symphonic' is clearly a keyword. Flaubert enlarged on the theme in another letter to Louise Colet on October 12:

> If ever the effects of a symphony have been brought into a book, it will be there. It is necessary that the thing should bawl together, that we should hear at the same time the bellowing of the bulls, the sighs of love, and the words of administrators. The sun is shining over all that, and gusts of wind are making large bonnets flap.[1]

Some forty years later Zola made a similar comparison. He did not confine himself to a single scene, but applied it to his novels as a whole as described in a letter to a certain M. Bonnet:

> What you describe as repetitions are to be found in all my books. It is in fact a literary device which I used sparingly to begin with and later was perhaps inclined to overdo. In my opinion it gives a work more body, a closer unity. It resembles in a way the leitmotifs in Wagner, and if you happen to know a musician who can explain their use to you, it will give you a good idea of my particular literary device.[2]

[1] *Correspondance:* Troisième Série (1852–1854), Louis Conard, 1927, pp. 335, 365.
[2] *Correspondance 1872–1902*, in *Oeuvres complètes*, Vol. 49, Bernouard, 1929, p. 765.

The discovery by two novelists of a connection between their own art and music is matched by a similar discovery by one of the greatest living film directors. In the introduction to a volume of his scenarios, Ingmar Bergman writes:

> Now we come to essentials, by which I mean montage, rhythm and the relationship of one picture to another—the vital third dimension without which the film is merely a dead product from the factory.

He goes on:

> Music works in the same fashion. I would say that no art has so much in common with film as music. Both affect our emotions indirectly, not via the intellect. And film is mainly rhythm; it is inhalation and exhalation in continuous sequence.[1]

We can see that in addition to commenting on the relations between their own art and music, all three writers place a special emphasis on the importance of the relations between images which are responsible for giving a work 'body', 'unity' and 'rhythm', which is already a suggestion that all the arts have a good deal in common.

Bergman's reference to the relations between film and music is of particular interest. The introduction of music in the days of silent film was one of the first important developments which was to bring film closer to other arts. Music, as Ernest Lindgren reminds us, began because of the need of viewers of the silent film to hear music. This meant that it began as a distraction for simple viewers by a musician playing a piano or something of the sort as a mere accompaniment of the film, but when Edmund Meisel's original scores for *Battleship Potemkin* were introduced they had such an effect in the film that in some European countries the film itself was passed for exhibition, but the music banned, presumably because it was so effective that it would encourage violence in the countries where it was shown. Ernest Lindgren goes on to observe 'that it is not the intrinsic quality of the music in a film which is so important as its dramatic appropriateness and a proper synchronization between its

1 *Four Screen Plays of Ingmar Bergman,* Eng. tr., 1960, pp. xvi, xvii.

rhythm and the visual rhythm of the film. Music which is so good that it calls attention to itself at the expense of the film is out of place; hence the common observation that the best film music is that which is not heard', meaning music which becomes an integral part of the film, but does not interfere with the integrity of the film's experience.[1]

The introduction of music in film was naturally followed in due course by the introduction of dialogue and colour, which produced some perceptive comments from Eisenstein: 'Sound sprang from the inner urge present in the silent film to go beyond the limits of plastic expressiveness alone . . . As the silent film cried out for sound, so does the sound film cry out for colour . . . We regard colour as an element of the film's dramaturgy'.[2] This confirms the view that the introduction of sound and colour was not only an extension of the development of film, but showed clearly that it was introducing elements which would bring it still closer to the other arts.

The view that both the novel and film resemble music naturally suggests that there must be some marked resemblances between the novel and film. Although Bergman declares categorically that 'film has nothing to do with literature', other directors have taken a very different view.[3] Pudovkin and Eisenstein insist that 'montage' means not only the relations between images in film, but between words in writing. Commenting on a scene in Maupassant's *Bel-Ami* in which Georges Duroy is waiting to meet Suzanne at midnight, Eisenstein says that its effectiveness is achieved 'entirely through montage'.[4] What is much more interesting for our present purposes is his view of the Comices Agricoles. He explains that the theatre, particularly musical comedy, was of special value in teaching him the importance of sharp changes. 'Strangely enough', he says, 'it was Flaubert who gave us one of the finest examples of cross-montage dialogues used with the same intention of expressive sharpening of idea'.[5] He does not confine himself to prose fiction. Pudovkin's *Eugene Onegin* 'is a model of expressiveness, achieved by a purely montage method and with purely montage

1 *The Art of Film,* fourth impression 1970, p. 139.
2 *Notes of a Film Director,* 1959, pp. 114, 116, 123.
3 *Op. cit.,* p. xvii.   4 *The Film Sense,* Eng. tr., 1943, p. 27
5 *Film Form,* Eng. tr., 1951, p. 12.

means', while *Paradise Lost* itself is a 'first-rate school in which to study montage and audio-visual relationships'.[1]

What emerges from all this is that in Eisenstein's opinion montage was not the invention of film directors, but their application in the right way to their own art of a form used in other arts.

Pudovkin and Eisenstein used to argue vigorously about one aspect of montage. Pudovkin insisted that it was the 'link' between images; Eisenstein that it was their 'collision'.[2] Jean Cocteau took something like the middle way. 'The cinematograph', he said, 'requires a syntax. This syntax is obtained through the connection and clash between images'.[3]

Eisenstein's films, particularly *Strike,* are outstanding examples of 'collision' between images. Federico Fellini's *La Dolce Vita* is a good example of what Cocteau calls 'connection and clash'. The film begins with a helicopter flying in the direction of Rome. A huge statue of Christ the Worker is suspended from it and sways to and fro as the helicopter seems to change height, to be seen from different angles and to receive different reactions, none of them serious and some of them flippant, from the people below. It is an ironic sequence. The film is the story of life in the Holy City: a succession of orgies, love affairs, prostitution, an apparently reasonable and civilised man who murders his two children and then commits suicide. The image of Christ the Worker looks forward to a series of other images. An immense crowd is assembled outside Rome, where the Madonna is supposed to have appeared to two children; the gathering ends with a huge fire followed by a violent rain storm and the death of the person who had come hoping for a miraculous cure, which makes this part of the film look like a sceptical attitude toward appearances of the Madonna at Lourdes and at other places. We see the protagonist listening to the future murderer of his children playing Bach on an organ in church. An all-night orgy by youthful visitors in a palace near Rome is followed by long-distance shots of the chaplain on his way to say Mass in the palace chapel early in the morning: he pauses for a moment to look at the youths emerging from the palace

---

[1] *The Film Sense*, pp. 49, 52.   [2] *Film Form*, pp. 37–38.
[3] *Cocteau on the Film*, Eng. tr., 1954, p. 15

after their orgy. Finally, another orgy at the seaside is followed
by the spectacle of a monstrous fish lying dead on the beach,
which seems to look back to the statue of Christ the Worker. It
is underlined by the hero's failure to link up with a simple
country girl who attracts him. 'She smiles and beckons him',
writes John Russell Taylor; 'he shakes his head and is drawn
away, back into whatever further hell may be in store for him.
The film closes on her, looking after him—the lost innocence
and freshness of childhood to which, even if he wanted to, he
could never return'.[1] There is a 'collision' or 'clash' between
secular and religious images: the growth of the 'permissive
society' in and around the Holy City and the failure of religion
to curb it. For Fellini, Christ is detached from the world and
has no influence on it. The childrens' vision is a false one and
merely adds to the general confusion. The priest does not even
try to do anything with the revellers and is followed into the
chapel by a solitary woman church-goer. The monstrous fish
seems to stand for the ugliness of the world and its death.

In spite of the achievements of film directors and their illuminating pronouncements, the view still persists in some quarters—mainly among aestheticians—that film is simply a mech-
anical invention and has nothing to do with art.[2] This is the
reverse of the truth. 'Montage', as Cocteau says, 'is style. A
director who doesn't edit his own film allows himself to be
translated into a foreign tongue'.[3] 'Two film pieces of any kind,
placed together', says Eisenstein, 'inevitably combine into a new
concept, a new quality; arising out of juxtaposition', which
turns 'juxtaposition' into 'creation'.[4] His claim to have discovered montage in four different writers is amplified, or perhaps we should say clarified, by R.J. Sherrington. In discussing
Flaubert's limitations as a playright, he remarks: 'What Flaubert needed, of course, was the cinema, not the theatre'.[5] It suggests that in spite of the great impression that his art made on
Eisenstein, the novelist's experience had reached the point when
a different medium was necessary to provide the perfect means

---

1 *Cinema Eye, Cinema Ear*, 1964, p. 42.
2 See Peter Wollen, *Signs and Meaning in the Cinema*, 3rd ed., 1972, p. 8.
3 *Cocteau on the Film*, p. 104.   4 *The Film Sense*, p. 16.
5 *Three Novels by Flaubert*, 1970, p. 338.

of communicating it and that unlike Robbe-Grillet in our own time Flaubert's only alternative was the theatre, which in his case proved a failure, as it did later with Henry James. It follows that the invention and development of the cinema were due to the fact that it fulfilled an existing human need: it offered the most effective way of communicating certain aspects of the artist's experience. Put in another way, it was a form of vision, which is native to man, that created the camera and not the camera that created the vision. We know that Flaubert's influence on the novel has been immense, but in spite of Eisenstein's eulogy, it is unlikely that he has seriously influenced directors. What can be said, what we shall find when we come to examine *Madame Bovary,* is that to a much greater extent than the other three writers named by Eisenstein he *anticipated* the methods of the film director and spoke more truly than he knew when he described the drafts of *Madame Bovary* as 'scenarios'.

The views of the novelists and the film directors are an indication that there are not simply resemblances between the methods used in literature, music and film, but that montage is *generic* and probably applies in different degrees to virtually all the arts. The crux of the matter is that art of its nature is vision, experience, pattern. The expression 'technical devices' can be misleading and needs to be used with circumspection. It is necessary for a proper understanding of an artist's or a writer's work to isolate certain aspects of his style, but it must be remembered that 'style' itself is a method of apprehending experience and that in any successful work what we loosely describe as 'technical devices' are an integral part of the artist's style and therefore of his vision.

It is time to take a closer look at the sort of experience that we expect from film.

'A film', said Cocteau, 'whatever it might be, is always its director's portrait'.[1] It reminds us of Flaubert's 'Madame Bovary, c'est moi', and the strong personal or even autobiographical element which is known to exist in most of Fellini's films.

There are in fact two kinds of director. There is the director

---

[1] *Cocteau on the Film,* p. 77.

who makes popular commercial films. He is a mere technician who uses all the main film methods, but has no personal experience to communicate. The second kind of director is essentially an artist and is sometimes described as *auteur*. The films of the first kind of director are roughly the equivalent of detective stories; those of the *auteur* correspond to the work of the serious novelist.

Fellini is clearly speaking of himself as *auteur* when he says:

> We have to get away from the slavery of the five senses, the alleged naturalism of the camera. It is completely phoney, anyway; no camera and no tape recorder are 'true to life', thank God. In fact, our apparatus is much less objective than the human eye.[1]

Fellini's 'alleged naturalism of the camera' and his statement that 'our apparatus is much less objective than the human eye' clearly point to the personal experience that the director is determined to communicate to the audience as surely as a serious novelist does to his readers. It also recalls what I said earlier about 'realism' and the distinction between verisimilitude and the artist's insight into his characters' deeper feelings. In every work of art there must clearly be a link with the world of common experience in order to ensure the 'willing suspension of disbelief'. If there were not, communication would break down altogether. That in fact is what happens in a great deal of Surrealist art and explains why Buñuel took care to introduce a fairly strong element of verisimilitude into the near-Surrealist film *El angel exterminador*.

This amounts to saying that ordinarily there must be some degree of verisimilitude in most works except music, but that it must be transformed by the artist's visionary quality, which is the dominating factor in all creative work. The error begins when verisimilitude is regarded as a virtue in itself instead of the artist's vision. That no doubt is why Flaubert protested vigorously against being labelled a 'realist' and said, in a letter to George Sand in 1876, that he hated 'what is conventionally called *realism*'.

In so far as an artist aims at complete verisimilitude he ceases

[1] In an interview by Gideon Bachmann, *Sight and Sound*, Vol. 33, No. 2, Spring 1964, p. 85.

to be an artist. Happily, there are times when he is defeated by his own genius. Zola is the obvious example. The *Rougon-Macquart,* to be sure, is a fascinating documentary on the Second Empire which is more readable than it was a few years ago because its has acquired a period flavour but, as we have seen, the essential element is its visionary power. Nor should it be forgotten (as the letter to Bonnet shows) that he learnt a good deal from Flaubert and that in some respects the *Rougon-Macquart* is not less cinematic than *Madame Bovary.*

When we turn to other arts, we can see that in portrait painting the subject is recognisable, but that the picture's outstanding merit depends on the painter's interpretation of the subject. Among the most remarkable examples are Goya's portraits of the Spanish royal family. No doubt everyone recognised the individuals, but Goya's insight into their character and mentality can only be described as devastating. It means that whatever his intentions, a portrait of the royal family contains a self-portrait of the painter, who emerges as a person with a supreme contempt for the royal family and its world.[1]

Something of the same is true of landscape paintings, with Impressionism as the best illustration. Ordinary landscapes, which might almost be described in Pudovkin's words as 'dead objects', are transformed into scenes which are startlingly new. We may even think that there is an element of montage in the way in which colours and parts of the scene are related to one another. One of the outstanding examples is Monet's series of paintings of Rouen Cathedral in different lights at different times of the day or night.

The truth, as Fellini implies, is that an exact copy of reality is something which no sensitive person wants and is anyway almost impossible to achieve. Few accounts are more misleading than comparisons based on photography. The good photographer—the art photographer—does not aim at an exact copy of reality any more than a painter. He does not possess, or rather his medium does not possess, the same powers as that of a Goya or a Monet, but he is engaged in a constant struggle to find correctives to the excessive verisimilitudes of his medium. He arranges people, objects and, on occasion, colours in a way

[1] This reminds us of Winston Churchill's refusal to let people see Graham Sutherland's painting of him.

that corresponds as nearly as possible to the picture or pattern in his own mind and imagination.

This applies with particular force to film. What is not always appreciated and what is rightly stressed by Fellini is that in film there is from the first an element of modification of the visible world. We go, or should go, to the cinema among other things to see the pictures. It is precisely because there is an inherent element of modification, which prevents them from being true to life in an exclusively literal sense, that the pleasure they offer becomes an aesthetic one. Fellini's views on the differences between the camera and the human eye are of course correct, but Pudovkin described the position in a much more stimulating fashion when he said:

> Every object must, by editing, be brought upon the screen so that it shall have not a *photographic,* but a *cinematographic* essence.[1]

This is true of what appears to be a simple 'shot': the landscapes in Renoir's *La Règle du jeu,* in Heifit's *The Lady with a Little Dog,* or in what has been called Robert Bresson's 'breathtaking' shot of the *bâteau mouche* in *Quatre nuits d'un rêveur.* I have chosen these three films more or less at random because I have seen or re-seen them recently and because of the particular charm of the landscapes. It must be emphasised, however, that in a good film no landscape is merely decorative; it is an important element in the experience that the director is expressing. In spite of their beauty, the scenes remain 'dead objects' until 'editing' begins which makes them 'cinematographic'. It is possible then to take strips or fragments of 'reality' and arrange them in an order which conforms to the director's vision. It is the movement away from superficial verisimilitude towards the inner truth.

It follows that in Renoir's *La Règle du jeu* the engaging daylight landscape with its characters' happy shooting game only gains its full effectiveness when we move eventually to the night scene outside the mansion, where through some blunder the hero is not dead, which clearly looks back ironically to the game hunting during the sunny part of the day. One must go

1 *On Film Technique, Eng. tr.,* 1933, p. xv.

on to say that the contrast between the engaging daylight scene and the confusing night scene is much more important than it may first appear to be. The fact that the distinguished protagonist is staying as a guest with a woman friend in the splendid home belonging to herself and her husband and is shot outside in the dark by mistake by one of their servants, who apparently intends to shoot someone quite different, is an important reflection of the curious contrasts between different aspects of life which are dealt with in one way or another in many of Renoir's films as in those of his contemporaries. Changes in *The Lady with a Little Dog,* particularly the lovers' return from the seaside, where they met, to the two separate and uninteresting towns where they live, reflects their emotional problems. In *Les Quatre nuits d'un rêveur* the great white pleasure boat, with its mass of light and glass, gliding slowly under the Seine bridge and gradually disappearing in the darkness, stands for the collapse of the hero's romantic dreams, which fade out when his rival returns to Paris after being away for a considerable period on business and takes back the girl friend who was the subject of the hero's romantic dreams.

The immense effectiveness of scenery is also brought home to us by two other directors. The scenes from Monument Valley in John Ford's great film, *Stagecoach,* are not only tremendous in themselves; they are matched both with the powerful specially composed music and with the intensely exciting pursuit of the stagecoach by Indians. Ford achieved a similar success in a good many other films, particularly in *The Searchers,* which unlike *Stagecoach* is a colour film. A rather different, but nevertheless highly impressive effect can be seen in Antonioni's *L'Eclisse.* For here shots in the closing sequences of deserted streets, empty buildings and lamp posts, which are in no sense attractive in themselves and could very well be described as 'dead objects', point to 'the end of the affair' between a man and a girl, and acquire in their context an emotional significance which in the ordinary way does not belong to deserted places or objects.

Although the contrasts between landscapes and between living places are very effective in bringing out the problems and misfortunes of life in the films discussed, a remarkable way of elaborating them has been discovered in Werner Herzog's latest film. Although the middle scenes of his *Stroszek* are disappointing, the final scenes are fascinating and decidedly novel. In the beginning Stroszek, the main protagonist, who has spent years in orphanages and mental homes, is released from prison, where he was confined several times for drunkenness. He moves with his woman lover from Germany to Canada. The lover soon abandons him and departs with a different and much less engaging man to another country. In the last scenes Stroszek, who is a very decidedly robust eccentric, runs amuck in a amusement park in his lorry, then sets fire to it, and in the last scene of all rides round and round on an unstoppable scenic railway. What is really remarkable, however, is that these scenes alternate with the sight of two chickens, one a dancer, the other a piano player, each giving its show on their own in two tiny separate performance quarters. It is clearly a highly striking way in which the chickens summarise the protagonist's extraordinary eccentricity.

We have seen that unlike other famous directors Bergman is convinced that 'film has nothing to do with literature'. In spite of what has already been said, his views invite further discussion:

> It is mainly because of the difference between film and literature [he says], that we should avoid making films out of books. The irrational dimensions of a literary work, the germ of its existence, is often untranslatable into visual terms—and it in turn, destroys the special irrational dimensions of the film.[1]

There can be no doubt that the 'dimensions' of a novel are often a serious difficulty for a film director. A novel is frequently too long to be turned into a film without serious omissions which impoverish the novelist's own experience, or like some contemporary films lasting several hours would be too long for the spectator to follow them in their entirety. Although I shall naturally argue that *Madame Bovary* was the first great novel that is highly cinematic and though I naturally admire Jean Renoir, I was disappointed by his film of *Madame Bovary*. It was made during one of his supposedly 'realistic' pe-

[1] *Four Screen Plays of Ingmar Bergman*, p. xviii.

riods and he eliminated many of those features which strike us as cinematic or made them less cinematic than they seem to be in the novel, with the result that the film compares unfavourably with his admirable film of Maupassant's story *Une Partie de campagne*. Gerhard Lamprecht's film of *Madame Bovary* is even more disappointing. It begins with the Bovarys' arrival at Yonville l'Abbaye. This means that the whole of Part I of the novel, which is an essential part of Flaubert's experience, is simply omitted so that the director could concentrate on Emma's emotional and financial misfortunes. This is not all. The third film of *Madame Bovary* by Vincente Minnelli, is also a failure, and has been described as 'so tame' because the director toned it down as being unwilling or possibly not daring to reproduce the cruelty and immorality of the characters, which led to Flaubert's prosecution.[1]

G. W. Pabst's and Grigori Kozintsev's two films of *Don Quixote* also deserve mention. Although they are clearly more impressive than the films of *Madame Bovary*, it is evident that the immense length of the novel makes it impossible to turn it into a really successful film.[2] The result is that the two films are no more than entertaining tastes of the novel, with the omission of Don Quixote's dreams as one of the outstanding gaps. Stendhal has fared even worse than the authors of *Madame Bovary* and *Don Quixote*. It may have been the directors' fault, but after seeing the films of *Le Rouge et le noir* and *La Chartreuse de Parme*, I was left with the feeling that my favourite novelist is indeed unfilmable.

What emerges from all this is that length is a general problem for filmmaking. It is known that Renoir originally intended the film of *Madame Bovary* to be nearly twice as long as it is, but was compelled to make drastic cuts to reduce the length, which was no doubt the reason for omitting features which strike us in the novel as particularly cinematic. The result of all this is that films based on novels often suffer because the director cannot use as much of his material as he wishes or tries to use so much that the film would last too long for an audience's pleasure. This explains the special use of

---

[1] See Geoffrey Wagner, *The Novel and the Cinema*, 1975, p. 257.
[2] See Sigfried Kracauer, *Nature of Film*, 1961, p. 244.

short novels and long-short stories, reminding us of Renoir's success with Maupassant's *Une Partie de campagne*. The problem, however, is not confined to directors making films directly based on novels. One of the most curious examples is the work of Jacques Rivette. In *Out 1: Noli me tangere* and *Out 1: Spectre* we are told that he was prompted by Balzac's *Histoires des treize*, which consists in fact of three separate stories which are in no way identical. The first of the two films ran for twelve and a quarter hours and has only been shown once. In *Out 1: Spectre*, which runs for four and a quarter hours and has apparently been fairly widely shown, he tries to make something like a shorter version of *Out 1: Noli me tangere*. Compared with Balzac's work consisting of three separate stories, he produced four separate stories, running to and from one another, which are in no sense a copy of Balzac's work. Although there is plenty of ingenuity in the technique—I am reminded by black-and-white flash-backs in a colour film—it is extremely difficult, as I found, to follow the four stories at a single showing.[1]

Yet the failures mentioned above and Bergman's strictures cannot blind us to the fact that there are great films which are the fruit of major novels. Although I am inclined to the view that *Au hasard, Balthazar,* for which he wrote the script himself, is possibly Bresson's greatest film, his films of Bernanos's *Journal d'un curé de campagne* and *Mouchette* are also great films which do not detract from the novelist's own experience. I once took the view that *Une Femme douce* was inferior to the last two films because Dostoevsky was a greater novelist than Bernanos and placed too great a difficulty on film directors. This was probably unfair to both Bernanos and Bresson. In spite of its poor reception at two of the 1971 film festivals, Bresson's *Quatre nuits d'un rêveur,* based on Dostoevsky's *White Nights,* but with a modern setting and a change from St. Petersburg to Paris, is a great film and is immensely superior to a Russian film of the same novel by Ivan Pyriev without any change in the novelist's period or country.

The reasons are evident. A film director may use a novel for his film, but it acts as a catalyst rather than something which

---

[1] See Jonathan Rosenbaud (editor): *Rivette: Texts and Interviews,* 1977, pp. 95–96, and the editor's article in *Sight and Sound,* Autumn 1974, pp. 191–94.

has to be carefully copied. For what matters is not the exact fidelity of representation, but the way in which the director while avoiding distortion or impoverishment of the novelist's experience also uses it as a vehicle for his own particular vision. David Robinson put it admirably when he said of Bresson, 'with *Quatre nuits d'un rêveur* he again transposed a Dostoevsky story into a Bressonian world'; which is a good illustration of Cocteau's view that a 'film, whatever it might be, is always its director's portrait'.[1] Something of the same is true of Buñuel's *Tristana*, which is vastly superior to the work on which it is based, which is one of Galdos's less successful novels.

A particularly interesting case is Rohmer's *Die Marquise von O.* It is based on Heinrich von Kleist's long-short story of that name and is highly impressive, partly because the choice of a long-short story avoids the insoluble problems which arise from filming very long novels and partly because Rohmer makes skilful use of dialogue in most of his films.

The use of novels for many highly successful films naturally makes it a little difficult to understand Bergman's insistence on the gulf, or what he regards as the gulf, between film and literature. The answer is probably to be found in other statements in his introduction: the statement that literary work 'is often untranslatable into visual terms'; the importance that he attaches to 'illusion' and 'imagination', and the claim that 'the sequence of pictures plays directly on our feelings'. It suggests that the objection is really a personal one, that he simply prefers the visual image to the written word, the film to the novel or, to put it in another way: he prefers the actual visual image to the description of visual events however effective the description. It must, however, be said in fairness that it brings out some of the films' most important qualities. We must all recognise that there are some things which are much more effective in films than in literature: changes of angle, sudden cuts from one figure or one scene to another, even revolving images in a world turned upside down in the eyes of a character and so on. The most important factor of all is that even if we enjoy both the film and the novel, we have to admit that the cinemato-

---

[1] David Robinson, *World Cinema*, 1973, p. 262. *Cocteau on the Film*, 1954, p. 77.

graphic image always has a much greater immediate effect on us, or rather on our 'feeling', than the written word, or as Lindgren put it:

> It is the visual part of the film which leaves the deepest and most lasting impression on the majority of people, and those films are the most effective which apply primarily to the eye and only secondarily to the ear.[1]

This suggests, for example, that certain scenes in Racine's plays like Phèdre's first confession and Joad's prophecy would be more effective in a well-directed film than in a stage production. For while listening to the speakers and instead of watching them we could be shown the pictures of Phèdre's first meeting with Hippolyte, the sacrifices of the animals and the sight of the imaginary Venus pursuing her, which would be specially effective on the screen, or with Joad the sight of the immense past and future disasters that he describes.[2] We should also remember that the first showing of the Lumière brothers' *Arrivée d'un train,* a simple little film of a train coming into a station, caused panic because for a moment the spectators had the illusion that a train was actually running them down! Nor can anyone feel unmoved by the terrifying events in Rossellini's *Roma, città aperta* even when it is shown on a small television screen. But perhaps the most striking thing of all is that though colour is an immensely important development which adds greatly to the fascination of the cinema, black-and-white films—*Roma, città aperta* is a good example—can still retain their total effect on us and do nothing to disturb illusion.

It follows that what should be described as *impact* is, indeed, one of the film's most important qualities. We can always re-read a novel or look up those parts which particularly interest

[1] *Op. cit.,* p. 109.

[2] I have never been able to understand the enthusiasm of some critics for Jean-Marie Straub's film of Corneille's neglected masterpiece *Othon.* The characters wear Roman costumes, but filming took place on a hill near the centre of contemporary Rome. Most of the artists are Italians who speak French with a marked foreign accent. Speeches are often difficult to follow on account of the roar of traffic in the highly public setting chosen by the director. When the setting changes—another departure from the original—to the inside of a garden, we find that we are close to a noisy fountain which has the same effect as the traffic in the earlier scenes!

us and gradually appreciate the experience to the full. The great difficulty of the cinema is that it is often impossible to re-see a film in which we have a special interest, and even if a published scenario happens to be available it cannot be compared for utility purposes to the text of a play. The result is that though many modern films cannot be appreciated to the full at a single showing, the impact does at least convey the essentials of the imaginative experience.

What emerges from all this is that most of the main arts have elements in common, and that the cinema in varying degrees has similarities with music, the theatre, painting, and above all with the novel. M. Pierre Danger puts it well:

> The whole of Flaubert is in fact exactly conceived like a cinematographic work, that is to say that everything in it is expressed by the image, sound and the perception of the movement without any psychological analysis, without any commentary from the author ever coming to impose itself on the simple vision of the scene described, unless on rare occasions a few rapid lights appear on the inner discourse that unfolds itself in the clear conscience of the character.[1]

When we examine *Madame Bovary* in detail, we shall find that—in spite of the fact that it has so far proved too long to be turned into a successful film—there are plenty of examples of montage, close-ups, cuts and flashbacks. The most important of them is naturally montage. It is common knowledge that Eisenstein regarded Flaubert as one of the most impressive of those writers whom he regarded as the inventors of montage. He defined it as 'the need for connected and sequential exposition of the theme, the material, the plot, the action, the movement within the film sequence and within the film drama as a whole'.[2] Montage is most apparent in Flaubert from the immense care with which images are related to one another all

---

[1] *Sensations et objets dans le roman de Flaubert*, 1973, p. 186. It reminds us of a pronouncement of Robert Bresson's: 'What I see is not so much expression by gesture, word or mime, as expression by the rhythm and combination of images, by their position relationship and number'. (Quoted in *The Films of Robert Bresson*, 1969, p. 30.)

[2] *Film Sense*, p. 15.

through the novel and are responsible for its unity as a work of art. It is clearly related to symbolism and in discussing the cinematic elements in it I shall give the largest part of the space to the way in which images are related to one another in both directions, forward and backward.

II *MADAME BOVARY*

THE NINETEENTH-CENTURY novelists were splendid starters. Not
for them the eighteenth-century device of a manuscript found
in a bottle or a drawer. In *Madame Bovary* we are plunged
straight into the midst of things:

> We were in Big School when the Head came in, followed by a
> new boy in ordinary day-clothes, and by one of the juniors carry-
> ing a large desk.

The arrival of Charles Bovary as a new boy at school, the
uproar caused by his hat and his accent, a furious master dealing out *pensums* are related by an anonymous eyewitness, who
is one of the pupils, makes a solitary appearance and then van-
ishes for good. On the second page we come across the description of Charles's extraordinary hat:

> It was one of those composite head-dresses combining a number
> of different features—part busby, part lancer's cap, part pillbox,
> part otterskin cap, part cotton nightcap, one of those shoddy ob-
> jects in short whose dumb ugliness has depths of expression like
> the face of an idiot. Its general shape was that of an egg and the
> upper part, stiffened with whalebone, rose from a base consisting
> of three bulging, circular protuberances. Above them was a pat-
> tern consisting of alternating lozenges of rabbit fur and velvet
> separated from one another by strips of some red material. Higher
> still was a species of bag ending in a polygon of cardboard covered
> with a complicated design in braid, and finished off with a long
> and excessively thin cord from which hung a small cross of gold
> thread in place of a tassel. The whole contraption was new; the
> peak glittered.

Although the extraordinary hat is described by an anonymous pupil, it is clearly a 'close-up'. We must go on to say that
the whole novel grows out of this one image as surely as the
twenty volumes of Zola's *Rougon-Macquart* grow out of the
image of the disused cemetery of Saint-Mitre on the first page

of *La Fortune des Rougons* or, as we have seen, the whole of
Fellini's *La Dolce Vita* out of the film's opening sequences of
the helicopter carrying the statue of Christ the Worker.

Flaubert's novel is not, as it is sometimes said to be, a study
of the twin themes of stupidity and romantic illusion. Stupidity
is the main theme and romantic illusion simply one of its
forms. For the essence of stupidity is an inability to make a correct assessment of reality and to adapt oneself to it. The 'close-
up' of the hat is therefore a compelling statement of the main
theme. It is clear from the words 'dumb ugliness', 'the face of
an idiot', the burst of laughter from the other pupils when
Charles drops his hat, that it is a dunce's cap and that Charles
is the dunce. On top of this the undeserved punishment inflicted on him by the schoolmaster, who makes him write out
twenty times the verb *ridicule sum,* points to the disasters which
will overtake him and which in spite of his stupidity are as
undeserved as his school punishment.

It is naturally an altogether extraordinary dunce's cap which
becomes a symbol of the society to which the wearer belongs.
The position is clarified in the second sentence:

> Its general shape was that of an egg and the upper part, stiff-
> ened with whalebone, rose from a base consisting of three bulging,
> circular protuberances.

Although Charles is the kindest and gentlest character in the
novel, this somehow suggests that he stands for the birth of
stupidity, which makes him the centre of the circle, the source
from which stupidity seems to emanate, the prototye of all
other examples of stupidity who surround him.

The words 'composite' and 'circular', the construction of the
hat in layers or tiers, are the important part of Flaubert's
image. Stupidity is not the monopoly of any one class; it runs
all through society from top to bottom, goes round each of
them in 'circles'. The layers of the hat, with their mixture of
aristocratic, middle-class and proletarian trappings, emphasise
that the stupidity to which all of them are reduced has no
frontiers, social or otherwise. It is clearly indicated in the
words:

Above them was a pattern consisting of alternating lozenges of rabbit fur separated from one another by strips of some red material.

In the top layer of the hat there is complete confusion, showing that different classes do not understand one another. No part seems to have any relation to or to match any other part. This points to the rise and spread of stupidity, which leads to disaster. 'Red material' seems to look forward in advance to Emma's adultery and the 'small cross of gold thread' to the decline of her sentimental religion. The reference to 'red material' is important. We shall find that the colours, or rather the 'shots' of red, blue and black that will turn up on various occasions in Emma's love affairs, are clearly important, which means that parts of the novel could not be successfully filmed in black and white.

We should not overlook the last cryptic sentence. In spite of the oddity of the hat, the newness of the 'contraption' seems to confirm what I said of the 'birth' of stupidity. The novel is naturally the story of the way in which 'glitter', or rather imagined 'glitter', is repeatedly obliterated by stupidity.

Confusion of styles is a recurrent theme. It can be said of Flaubert's characters: By their dress ye shall know them. Charles's hat is not simply the model of all other strange hats worn in the book from Homais' pretentious 'bonnet grec' to Rodolphe's rakish 'boater'; there is a connection between the hat and the medley of clothes worn by the country bumpkins, the vehicles that they drive and the geography of the country. At the beginning of Part II we read:

On est sur les confins de la Normandie, de la Picardie et de l'Ile-de-France, contrée bâtarde où le langage est sans accentuation comme le paysage sans caractère.

[One is on the borders of Normandy, Picardy and the Ile-de-France, a bastard land where the language is without accentuation like the countryside without character.]

The 'bâtarde' of this passage matches the 'composite' of the earlier one. It is a nondescript, characterless area, a waste land lying on the borders of three different provinces and apparently belonging to none of them. It comes to stand for the deadly dreariness of everyday life, that 'bastard' reality which is much worse at Yonville than at Tostes and which will eventually bring the Bovarys down.

The three parts of the novel are strongly symmetrical. They are all organized round a central incident which is related to an effective image. The incidents are the marriage in Part I, of which the unsatisfactoriness leads to the move to Yonville-l'Abbaye, and the seductions in Parts II and III. The images belong to the visit to La Vaubyessard, the Comices Agricoles and the meeting between Emma and Léon in Rouen Cathedral. The images are not merely related; they could best be described as 'shots' leading to one another. They are reinforced by a series of supporting 'shots' which emphasise and prolong their psychological repercussions. It is characteristic of both the main and supporting images that they are images of destruction. They are directed against the marriage, which begins to founder in Part I, and is finally ruined by the seductions in the second and third parts, which are themselves the source of additional suffering.

The tightness of the novel's construction is illustrated by the events leading to marriage. Charles first meets Emma when he goes to the Bertaux to set her father's broken leg. At that time he is married to a woman older than himself who is comfortably off. Soon afterwards her lawyer decamps with her savings —it is the first mention of financial disaster, which plays a large part in the book—and she dies of chagrin.

The widowed Charles becomes a personal friend of the Rouaults and begins to court Emma. When his horse shies violently, as he arrives at the farm on his first visit to set the broken leg of Emma's father, the 'grand écart' is at once a caricature of the knight on horseback and a form of oracle: a premonition of what will happen, a mysterious and unheeded warning against a disastrous marriage. The time comes when he asks the father for his daughter in marriage. He is told to wait outside while the father consults Emma inside the house. If she accepts him, it would be too disturbing for her to meet him in the house on the same day. The sign of acceptance is therefore to be shown by the father opening the shutter of the window against the outside wall, which will mean that he must leave quietly. Charles stands on the ground beside his tethered horse and waits nineteen minutes for the result of his proposal of marriage. Suddenly there is a loud crash as the window shutter hits the wall. The loud crash is a sign not only that his proposal has been accepted, but that the obscure warning signified by the 'shot' of his horse shying violently at the time of his first visit to the farm has gone unheeded and that his doom is sealed.

One must go on to say that Charles standing on the ground waiting for the result of his proposal looks forward to a series of 'shots' of Emma constantly looking out of her bedroom window at Yonville-l'Abbaye. She begins with a friendly look down at her husband starting off on his rounds as a doctor. It is followed by the sight of the first of her two future lovers, but when she becomes completely disillusioned with marriage her window is seen to stand for a hope of escape from a house which has become like a prison for her.

Although marriage is the outstanding event of Part I, we must not overlook the great importance of the couple's invitation to the aristocrats' party at La Vaubyessard. We are told of Emma's visit that 'her journey to La Vaubyessard had made a hole in her life in the manner of those great crevasses that a storm sometimes causes in a single night'. It is not a particularly happy way of putting it, but we can easily imagine the way in which in a film a picture could be introduced in the form of an imaginary happening in her mind after the journey to La Vaubyessard and her return home. The implications in any case are plain. The contrast betwen the aristocrats' party and Emma's wedding party or the party that follows the Comices Agricoles is a clear sign of the gulf between two worlds. The visit, which provided Emma with a glimpse of a world of luxury and romance—the sort of world of which she dreams and which is completely beyond her reach—shatters her married life forever. We notice, too, that while she enters wholeheartedly into the pleasures of the party and dances twice with a cavalier, her husband is a complete non-dancer and stands about mooning and doing nothing, reminding us incidentally (as we shall see) of his lack of action during the wedding procession. It is all underlined by another 'close-up'—Emma's discovery, on the way home, of a cigar case belonging to one of the party's aristocrats lying in the road. She keeps it as a relic of one of the most fascinating events of her life, or rather that was her intention, but we find from later 'shots' that the cigar case becomes a reminder of her loss.

The disillusionment which follows the great ball leads to a prolonged illness and to the decision to move from Tostes to Yonville-l'Abbaye, which was to be the scene of the real disasters.

Emma has come to dislike Tostes and is anxious to leave it, but for Charles this 'meant a sad wrench'. He had been there for four years and his practice as a doctor was solidly established, but being a generous and responsible husband he feels that if it is necessary they must move however unwelcome it is for him. He takes her to Rouen to be examined by a doctor who was his former master and who sees that she is suffering from a nervous ailment which calls for a 'change of air'. As her health does not improve and Charles finds that there is a vacancy for a doctor at Yonville, he decides on departure.

This leads to three important 'shots' which are a reflection of past, present and future, are also an important contribution to the novel's structure and carry over from Part I to Part II. They are the destruction of Emma's wedding bouquet, the loss of the pet greyhound and the statue of the *curé*. Shortly before the departure we are told of Emma:

> One day when she was rearranging a drawer in anticipation of their departure, she pricked her finger on something. It was the wire which bound her wedding bouquet. The orange blossom was yellow with dust, and the satin ribbon with its silver fringe was frayed at the edges. She threw it on the fire, where it flared up quicker than dry straw. Soon it was no more than a glowing twig on the cinders, slowly falling to ash. She watched it burn. The little pasteboard berries crackled, the wire thread twisted, the tinsel melted. The paper leaves shrivelled, hung like black butterflies upon the fire-back, and, in a few moments, flew up the chimney.

When Emma is pricked by a wire from the wedding bouquet and sees that 'the orange blossom was yellow with dust', we remember being told in a previous observation about her feel-

ings that 'in the days before her marriage she had fancied that
she was in love, but the happiness that such love should bring
had passed her by'. It is this reminder which prompts her to
fling the wedding bouquet into the fire. The detailed description of the way in which it is burnt to pieces, ending with the
statement that the shrivelled paper leaves 'hung like black butterflies upon the fire-back and, in a few moments, flew up the
chimney' is a sign that morally and psychologically her marriage will come to an end through the loss of all marital feelings for her husband, the wrecking of life by two disastrous
love affairs, while the last sentence points to the way in which
her home will be theoretically 'burnt up' by her financial ex-
travagance and that a dead Emma will disappear into a grave,
which is the equivalent of the fragments of the wedding bouquet flying up the chimney.

Part I ends with the destruction of the wedding bouquet and
Part II begins with the journey to Yonville. The pet greyhound
was a gift from a gamekeeper whom Charles had cured of an
inflamation of the lungs. Emma used to take it out with her on
her walks, which she used 'to escape her everlasting solitude'
while her husband was away working and to have something
on which to rest her eyes. She bursts into tears and works herself into a temper with her husband when the pet suddenly
jumps off the van on the way to Yonville, but in spite of a hunt
by the driver, it is never seen again, which clearly foreshadows
the way in which Emma herself will 'go off the rails'.

The plaster statue of the *curé* reading his breviary, which
stood in Emma's and Charles's garden at Tostes, represents the
piety and respectability of the first years of Emma's married
life. The plaster, however, is a symbol of the brittleness of
both her religion and her virtue. When we find towards the
end of Part I that the *curé*'s face has become weather-stained
and that he has lost a foot, we know that deterioration has set
in. The fact that the statue fell off the van on the way to Yonville and was smashed to pieces completes, as it were, the first
two cases of damage and is another sign of Emma's own impending fall. The plaster *curé* also points the way to the living
though wooden Abbé Bournisien, who proves completely inef-
fectual when Emma appeals to him for help after her first
temptation, but before her first fall. The failure of religion is

emphasised by the contrast between the 'shots' of the *curé* falling and the statue of Cupid standing in the garden of the local solicitor at Yonville in Part III. The Christian religion sinks as the cult of Eros begins to rise. The Cupid suggests the secret propensities of the lawyer. It looks back to the innocent Cupid on Emma's wedding cake, and forward to the moment when we see the amorous lawyer at the feet of Emma, who has come to seek financial assistance. It leads to nothing because she refuses his attempt to 'buy' her. Religion and love are clearly both caricatured in this book. One is reduced to a broken plaster statue, the other to an 'old goat' grovelling on the floor.

We must take another look at the description of the *curé*'s foot. In an early chapter we are told that Charles's boot made him look as though he had a 'wooden foot'. Charles's imaginary 'wooden foot' is relayed by the *curé*'s missing foot. The two together look backwards and forwards to two social cases. Charles's successful stetting of Emma's father's broken leg clearly led to the marriage, but his mishandling of the damaged leg of a servant named Hippolyte meant that two other doctors had to come in and found that they were compelled by Charles's mishandling to amputate the wretched Hippolyte's leg. The unfortunate operation shows that the sound of the leg in real wood not only reminds us of Charles's imaginary 'wooden foot', but reverberates all through the rest of the novel, and will increase Emma's hostility to her husband.

The Comices Agricoles, as Eisenstein indicated, is the novel's most cinematic scene of all. It is arranged in tiers recalling the tiers of Charles's hat in the 'close-up' at the beginning of the novel. Emma and Rodolphe watch from the window on the first floor of the mayor's house. They look down on the prefect's representative and the president of the jury (which chooses the prize-winners among the peasants who produce the most impressive animals) in the middle distance, and on the crowd including the peasants and their animals on the lowest plane of all. The camera eye, for that is what the movement resembles, is continually tracking from one group to another. The effect is heightened by the alternation of different voices. The platitudes about love coming from the top layer echo and

mingle, or perhaps we should say with Eisenstein are in 'collision', with the platitudes about patriotism and agriculture
which float upwards from the middle layer and are punctuated
by the sounds of the crowd and the animals on the bottom
layer, admirably described by Flaubert in his letter to Louise
Colet when he says that the whole collection 'should bawl together'.

I have analysed the scene in greater length in another place,
but two of the echoes are particularly relevant here where the
emphasis falls on the scene's cinematic qualities.[1] When Rodolphe says: 'Did I know that I should accompany you?' the
mocking voice which chimes in cinematically from below with
'Seventy francs' becomes the imaginary voice of a courtesan an-
nouncing the price of her favours. When Rodolphe says: 'I
shall count for something in your life, shan't I?' the voice re-
torts, brutally, 'Race porcine *ex aequo*', which in the present
context means something like 'Pigs, the pair of you'.

Eisenstein was particularly intrigued by the alternation of
platitudes and his comments deserve to be quoted:

> As we can see, this is an interweaving of two lines, thematically
> identical, equally trivial. The matter is sublimated to a monu-
> mental triviality, whose climax is reached through a continuation
> of this cross-cutting and word-play, with the significance always
> dependent on the juxtaposition of the two lines.[2]

The Comices Agricoles, in which all the inhabitants of Yonville participate in some degree, is the epitome of the whole
novel. It is a Fête de la Bêtise whose echoes are heard in the
platitudes which pour out when any of the characters open
their mouths. Its intention is completely destructive. Everything—love, patriotism, agriculture—is reduced to babble. It is
supported by the images of height and distances. Height stands
for the exaltation of love and the falls which follow its satisfaction. Emma's first sight of Rodolphe from her bedroom window is an ironical comment on the romantic image of the lady
waiting on a tower or a balcony for the arrival of the knight
with a white plume riding a black steed which haunts Emma's
imagination. It recalls once again Charles's first clumsy ride to

---

[1] *The Novel in France*, pp. 270–72.   [2] *Film Form*, p. 13

her home, but looks forward to something very different when her love affair with him comes to an end. We must also observe that though the declaration of love was made on the first floor of the mayor's house, the lovers will turn out like animals on the lowest plane by rolling on the ground in the wood, which is the goal of their first ride together.

It is not until some six weeks after the Comices Agricoles that Rodolphe turns up to invite Emma to go out riding with him. Emma felt rather doubtful about the proposal, but Charles approved and advises his wife to get herself a riding suit. As soon as she has done it, he writes to Rodolphe, telling him in all innocence that Emma is 'at his disposition' and that 'he counts on his good offer', not realising for a moment in what direction things will go.

Rodolphe arrives the following day with two horses. When they are about to start another character advises them with the same innocence as Charles to be careful because 'Accidents can happen so quickly'. In the same innocent and friendly tone Homais wishes 'A pleasant ride' for them and advises them to 'be careful', meaning the way in which they handle their horses and not themselves.

The couple arrive at a wood which is at the top of a hill and turns out to be Rodolphe's goal or rather the setting which will lead to his particular goal. We ourselves see that it displays Flaubert's ingenuity in the use of images. In his account of the wedding procession we read:

> Emma's dress was too long and just touched the ground. Now and then she stopped to raise it, and daintily, with her gloved hands, to pick off the wild grasses and prickly thistles, which Charles, empty handed, waited for her to finish.

These shots look forward to what happens on the hill top:

> The high bracken on the edge of the path kept getting entangled in Emma's stirrups. Rodolphe, without slowing down, leaned across whenever it happened, and pulled it loose. At other times, when there were branches to be pushed aside, he edged close to her, and she could feel his knee against her leg. The sky turned blue . . . They dismounted and Rodolphe tethered the horses. She walked ahead of him on the mossy turf between the

ruts. But her long dress got in her way, though she was holding up
the train, and Rodolphe, following behind, kept his eyes fixed on
the strip of thin white stocking which showed between the black
cloth of her riding costume and her black bootlets. It had for him
something of the quality of her bare flesh.

It is no accident that we are told on both these occasions that
Emma's long dress 'got in her way' or that she was hindered by
'wild grasses', 'prickly thistles' and 'high bracken' sticking to
her clothes and stirrups. They are both forms of 'close-ups'. The
dress and the various growths which cling to her stand for the
obstacles which she repeatedly encounters in her married life,
which come between her and happiness and which she sets out
to remove—an action which points to her downfall. There is a
contrast between her husband standing on one side 'empty
handed' and incapable of helping her, and the more practical
Rodolphe who 'without slowing down' leaned across and freed
her from the bracken which caught in her stirrups and threat-
ened to hold her back, meaning that he removed obstacles
which in a purely metaphorical sense were keeping her from
him. She herself raises her dress when they are dismounted, recalling what she had done in the marriage procession, but Rodolphe does nothing because he is busy speculating about the
'bare flesh' which is to be seen underneath and this time reminds us of the non-activity for very different reasons on the
part of Charles during the wedding procession. This last phase
points to the way in which things are to turn out. Emma begins
by making nervous resistance, but in the end gives in and the
love-making provides Rodolphe what he was looking for. It
leads to the conclusion that the husband standing by 'empty
handed' looks forward to the way in which he will fail her by
doing nothing and that the lover will help to destroy her by
being too enterprising and then giving up.

It is worth noticing that Flaubert makes an important use of
colour. When Rodolphe arrives to take Emma out for a ride,
we are told that he was wearing a 'velvet suit' like the apparently imaginary husband in one of her daydreams which will be
examined later. She herself was wearing a large 'blue veil' which
stood for the virtue which was about to fall and looked forward
to the statement that 'The sky turned blue', which happened

shortly before they got off their horses and showed that they were on the verge of the 'fall'. Although Rodolphe was obliged to use considerable pressure to persuade her to make love with him, we find that on her return home Emma is filled with love for him and that another variation of the use of colour is employed to describe the exciting effects of the 'fall':

> Elle se répétait: 'J'ai un amant! un amant!' . . .
> Elle allait donc posséder enfin ces joies de l'amour, cette fièvre du bonheur dont elle avait désespéré. Elle entrait dans quelque chose de merveilleux où tout serait passion, extase, délire: une immensité bleuâtre l'entourait . . .

> [She repeated to herself: 'I have a lover! a lover!' . . .
> She was therefore going to possess the joys of love, the fever of love which she had despaired of finding. She was on the verge of something marvellous where passion, ecstacy, delirium would be everything: a blue immensity was surrounding her . . .]

It is easy to imagine the way in which a film director of a colour film would show the woman who imagined that in love 'une immensité bleuâtre l'entourait'.

We remember that on the night of the Bovarys' arrival at Yonville, Homais told Charles, as usual in all innocence, that one of the advantages of the house which he was about to occupy was the side door which would enable a doctor like himself to come and go without being seen. It turns out to be the door that Emma will use after the first ride for many clandestine meetings with Rodolphe which will not be seen by Charles. The enthusiasm for him which follows the first 'fall' continues without a break. She then persuades him that she wishes them to elope together. He agrees, but on the day of the expected elopement Emma receives a letter from him, delivered by hand by one of his servants and hidden in a basket of fruit, calling it off. It brings us to a scene in which she only just escapes suicide. She hastens to the top of the house with the letter in hand:

> Beyond the roofs opposite spread the open country as far as eye could reach. Below was the village square. There was not a soul about. The pebbles of the footpath glittered; the weathercocks on the houses were motionless. At the corner of the street a sort of

moaning sound, with occasional strident modulations, was coming from one of the lower floors. It was Binet working at his lathe.

She leaned against the embrasure of the window and read the letter with little harsh bursts of angry laughter. But the more she concentrated her attention on its contents, the more muddled her mind became. She felt as though she could see his face, hear his voice, hold him in her arms. The irregular beating of her heart, which was like a battering-ram inside her chest, grew quicker. She stared about her wishing that the earth would open. Why not have done with it all? Who could stop her? She was free.

She went closer to the window and stared down at the paved roadway.

'I'll do it!' She said to herself.

The light striking up at her from below seemed to draw the weight of her body down into the great empty space. She felt as though the surface of the square was spinning before her eyes, climbing up the walls to meet her. The floor of the room was tilting like the deck of a pitching ship. She stood there almost hanging over its edge. All round her was nothing but empty space. The blue of the sky enveloped her, the air eddied in her empty skull. She had only to let herself go, only to let that nothingness receive her body. The whirring of the lathe went on and on, like a furious voice calling to her:

'Emma!' cried Charles. 'Emma!' She stopped.

'Where on earth are you? come down!'

The thought that she had just escaped death made her almost faint with terror. She closed her eyes. Then, at the touch of a hand on her sleeve, she gave a start.

'Master's waiting for you, ma'am. The soup's on the table!'

This is one of the most spectacularly impressive scenes that Flaubert ever wrote. The irony is there once more. It reminds us not only of Emma's unsuccessful attempt to locate her house when she and Rodolphe arrived at the top of the hill on the first ride, but of her first sight of Rodolphe himself from the window of her house. Instead of the lady waiting on the tower to greet her lover arriving on horseback, Emma is the abandoned mistress looking down on the street where in a few minutes she will see the faithless lover disappearing from view. Flaubert succeeds marvellously in conveying an extraordinary

sense of hallucination—the silent, deserted street, the remorse-
less reflection of sunlight striking up at Emma, the sudden
sense that she has lost her bearings, that reality is disintegrating,
that street and room are rocking like a pitching ship, the insistent whirring of Binet's lathe, of which there will be more
to be said later and which in the midst of the unnatural silence
seems to her disordered imagination to be a furious voice bid-
ding her to throw herself down. Then, very suddenly, the hallucination is dissipated and she is brought back to reality with
a shock by the sound of Charles's voice, the hand laid on her
shoulder, the servant's matter-of-fact remark about the soup.

We can see that on the screen the scene would be conveyed
by a series of 'cuts' or rapidly changing images from the window
down to the street—with a long shot to bring out Emma's
fears—and back again, possibly with a series of blurs, blackouts
or even a glimpse of a ship tossing in a storm to convey Emma's
giddiness and above all what is happening inside her mind, all
followed by a sober, almost realistic sequence showing the servant making her way into the room.

Although Emma has been saved from suicide by the unsuspecting servant and brought down to lunch, there is still another shock coming to her. She looks out of the window and
suddenly catches sight of Rodolphe's tilbury dashing away from
the town:

> Tout à coup un tilbury bleu passa au grand trot sur la place.
> Emma poussa un cri et tomba par terre à la renverse.
>
> [Suddenly a blue tilbury drove across the square at a brisk trot.
> Emma uttered a cry and fell to the floor on her back.]

The fact that Rodolphe is driving a 'blue' tilbury naturally
does not mean a return to virtue on his part. He has had many
mistresses and his sudden departure after promising to elope
with Emma simply shows that a singularly heartless and unsympathetic individual has grown tired of his latest mistress and is
doing a bolt for his own convenience. The colour of the tilbury
also has another significance. Although 'blue' normally stands
for virtue of one kind or another, we know that in the case of

Emma it had become the symbol of an illicit, but very happy love affair which is disappearing into the void.

Emma's illness which follows Rodolphe's abandonment of her is a long one. There are visits by the Abbé Bournisien. She starts to feel religious again, suddenly thinks that she is about to die, asks for Holy Communion and receives it in bed.[1] It produces a form of ecstasy which recalls the way she felt when she returned from her first love-making with Rodolphe:

> Alors elle laissa retomber sa tête, croyant entendre dans les espaces le chant des harpes séraphiques et apercevoir en un ciel d'azur, sur un trône d'or, au millieu des saints tenant des palmes vertes, Dieu le Père tout éclatant de majesté, et qui d'un signe faisant descendre vers la terre des anges aux ailes de flamme pour l'emporter dans leurs bras.

> [Then she let her head fall back, believing that the space was filled with the music of angelic harps, and that she could see, mounted on a golden throne within a sky of blue, and surrounded by saints with green palms in their hands, God the Father shining in majesty, at a sign from Whom angels would wing to earth on flaming pinions to carry her away in their arms.]

We know that Emma's moods are continually changing from one extreme to another. One of the most striking examples is the thrill that followed her return from the first ride with Rodolphe and the return to religion that follows the collapse of her love affair with him. We saw that on the return from the ride she felt that 'she was on the verge of something marvellous where passion, ecstasy, delirium would be everything'. When they all vanish we find that she imagines that she can see 'mounted on a golden throne . . . God the Father shining in majesty' and apparently on the point of having her brought to Heaven by his angels. It is summed up in the contrast between the '*blue* immensity surrounding her' which was no more than the imaginary result of successful adultery, and the imaginary vision of God 'on a golden throne within a sky of *blue*'.

The effect of her reconversion, or rather temporary recon-

---

[1] Flaubert seems to have overlooked the fact that the adultress could not, or should not, have received Holy Communion before making her confession, which is the one thing that he never mentions.

version as it will turn out to be, has considerable effects on her mood:

> Amid the illusions of her hope she caught a glimpse of a state of purity which floated above the earth and merged with that of Heaven where she aspired to be. She wanted to become a saint.

In spite of her desire to become a saint, we are told shortly afterwards:

> When she knelt at her gothic prie-Dieu, she addressed the Lord in the same words which she had murmured to her lover in the ecstatic transports of adultery. This she did in the hope of finding faith, but no delectation of the soul descended on her from high, and she would get to her feet with a sense of physical exhaustion, and a vague feeling that she had been cheated.

We see that she is adopting the same attitude to God that she had already adopted to her first lover. It shows that her imagined vision of God and angels was no more than a very feeble illusion though it will not prevent her from trying to do something of the same kind immediately before her next act of adultery.

The alternation of religion and adultery therefore illustrates what I said at the outset. It is largely a sentimental religion which on occasion provides a temporary refuge against the dullness of Emma's marriage, her guilty feelings over love and the shattering effects of the abandonment of her by her first lover, but remains without any real or lasting effect against her problems, as we shall see when Rodolphe is replaced by Léon.

When Emma has recovered from her illness and is moving to really sound health again, Homais persuades husband and wife to go to Rouen to hear a famous opera which is only to be performed there once. At the opera they meet Léon. It must be remembered that as soon as Emma arrived at Yonville, she met Léon. They fell in love with one another, but there was no seduction. The first break in the innocent love affair took place when Léon had to leave Yonville and continue his law studies in Paris. The result is that the couple have not seen him for three years, but learn that he has settled in Rouen on account of his work. Charles, who knows nothing about the love affairs, persuades Emma to spend a couple of days by herself at Rouen, which will have the same result as her husband encouraging the first ride with Rodolphe.

Part III begins with Emma's meeting next day with Léon, who has been careful to find out at which hotel she is staying. It is clear from the start that he is completely in love with her. He asks for another meeting the following day and she suggests Rouen cathedral as the meeting place. For Léon the cathedral, where he is waiting for Emma to join him, is the image of a 'gigantic boudoir'. Although Emma is aware that Léon is wildly in love with her, she feels that she cannot go in for any more love affairs. She prepares a *lettre de rupture* (which reminds us of Rodolphe's letter, but will be dealt with in a very different way), arrives at the cathedral intending to break with him and hurries into the Lady chapel in order to pray for help. This produces not merely a conflict of mood, but a conflict of imagery. The chapel is pitted against the imagined 'boudoir', the image of Virtue Resisting against Léon's image of Virtue Succumbing. He is exasperated by the length of her prayers, but they are both exasperated by the intrusion on their privacy by the beadle, who on week days acts as a guide. His platitudes about the cathedral correspond to the platitudes about agriculture at the Comices Agricoles, but the deference to the tomb of Diane de Poitiers—the celebrated adultress lying buried among the saintly and the worthy—is no more accidental than the guide's parting words: 'At least leave by the north door . . . in order to see the Resurrection, the Last Judgement, Paradise, King David, and the damned in the fires of hell', which shows ingeniously what is going to happen.

Léon, who seems to be rather tougher than he was when Emma first knew him three years ago, bundles her into a cab and tells the driver to go where he likes as long as he keeps going. The cab with drawn blinds not only repeats the image of the boudoir; it registers its triumph over the image of the chapel. The 'shot' of the 'naked' hand which emerges and throws away the pieces of the torn up *lettre de rupture* is an ironical reference to the hands in prayer in the chapel which in a film might well be brought out by a 'flashback'. The fragments of the letter are a sign that the increase in piety, which followed the break with Rodolphe and was reflected by apparently long prayers in the cathedral chapel, has faded away again and that marriage vows have been torn up like the letter for the second time. The 'white butterflies' falling on the field of 'scarlet clover'—a sign presumably that virtue is actually being destroyed in the boudoir-cab—look back to the 'black butterflies' formed by the charred remains of Emma's wedding bouquet flying up the chimney in Part I and provide an excellent example of the importance of colour in any successful film of the novel, which could not leave out this particular cab ride which is highly cinematic all round.

What emerges from all this is that the destruction of the *lettre de rupture*—presumably carried out by Emma herself—is a sign that all disagreement between the pair has been removed. They plunge into an intense love affair which is made possible by Emma's supposed music lessons at Rouen. It comes to an end in what might be called the usual way. It is mutual. They simply begin to grow tired of one another. One of the first signs is Emma's hallucinatory impression of the lover shrinking in size and vanishing into the distance: 'Et Léon lui parut soudain dans le même éloignement que les autres'.

Then we learn:

> Elle était aussi dégoûtée de lui qu'il était fatigué d'elle. Emma retrouvait dans l'adultère toutes les platitudes du mariage.

> [She was wholeheartedly sick of him as he was weary of her. Emma found in adultery all the commonplaces of marriage.]

The affair is finally brought to a complete end through Léon's failure to do anything to help her over the family's financial disaster, for which she was to blame.

We know that travel often plays an important part in fiction. We have already seen that travel whether by individuals or couples has led to some of the outstanding incidents of the present novel. We must go on to observe that the various kinds of travel are woven into a chain which plays an important part in welding the three parts of the novel into a whole. We shall also find that after producing temporary triumphs and misfortunes, they will lead to the final destruction of the principal characters.

Flaubert's characters travel on horseback, in horse-drawn vehicles and on foot. The first rides on horseback, as we have seen, take the unsuspecting Charles to Bertaux, where through misfortune and the lack of insight he meets and marries an unsuitable wife. These rides look forward to the tragic rides of servants galloping frantically to fetch specialists to the dying Emma, the doctors arriving too late, the father reaching Yonville to find his daughter's house draped in mourning. The rides of Charles and Emma cancel out. His are errands of mercy; hers escapades which waste the money that he has so laboriously earned on his rounds, and they bring them both to ruin.

The horse-drawn vehicles are a deliberately varied collection: the aristocratic tilbury, Charles's unromantic *boc* and the diligence known, significantly, as *L'Hirondelle.* The last is the most important in the book. It is the vehicle which carries the Bovarys from Tostes to Yonville, and the reader out of Part I into Part II. It takes them to Rouen, where they meet the returning Léon. Emma's overnight stay, as we have seen, covers the transition from Part II to Part III, which begins with the ride in a cab and the return journey to Yonville in *L'Hirondelle.* Its shuttle service between Yonville and Rouen, which follows, is a reflection of Emma's alternation between dream and reality. For most of her journeys, whether real or imaginary, are searches for the *pays bleu,* the land of romantic love. It is characteristic of all of them that they end in disillusionment and disaster. The first carriage drive takes Emma to the disappointments of married life at Tostes. The second is the imaginary journey in the post-chaise, which will be examined in detail later on. The move from Tostes takes her to the 'contrée bâtarde'; the outings to Rouen lose their charm as her love for Léon turns to disgust.

The journeys on foot mingle with, repeat and sometimes mock the other journeys—the visits to Rodolphe's château early in the morning or the brief sorties to the arbour in the garden on a winter's night. In the closing pages there are journeys which cover the same ground, but which ironically have a different aim: the last journey to Rouen in the vain effort to raise money to save herself from being sold up, the last visit to Rodolphe's château in the hope of borrowing money, the des-

perate appeals to the solicitor, the tax-gatherer, the visit to
Homais' shop, where she steals the arsenic that kills her.

Although the immediate goal of the journeys may vary, the
ultimate goal is either flight into an unreal world or flight from
the very real world of menacing creditors. At this point the jig-
saw begins to fit together. The central image in each part is in
reality a double image of destruction and flight. La Vaubyessard leads to the 'flight' to Yonville, which is the scene of Emma's downfall; the Comices Agricoles to the fatal ride with
Rodolphe and to Rodolphe's flight from Emma; the meeting
in the cathedral to the ride in the cab; the ride in the cab to
the journeys to Rouen and the last catastrophic round of visits.
Destruction is inevitable, escape impossible for a person with
Emma's mentality; flight from destruction therefore leads back
to destruction.

Although Binet only makes a few appearances, he is an important figure. His lathe is significant and reminds us of the
importance of the use of sound in film. When we first hear it,
its sound seems unimportant, but its effect on Emma turns out
to be frightening. Its monotonous droning, which can be heard
all over the village, is a reflection of the monotony and frustration of her life. It also makes her feel that she is somehow being
pursued, that a loud voice is reproaching her for the way that
she is behaving. The tax-gatherer is in fact the one man of integrity among the villagers. He has been described as Emma's
conscience. He does in fact 'catch' her one morning when she
is on her way back from a visit to Rodolphe and he himself is
engaged in some harmless poaching expedition. His gun is
pointing in Emma's direction before he is able to see who she is
and suggests a finger pointing accusingly at the adultress on her
way home. Emma at once looses her head and tells him a wildly
improbable story about visiting her daughter. What is remarkable is that though Binet has been described as her conscience
and though the lathe sounds like a voice reproaching her, the
actual effect, as we have seen, is nearly to drive her to suicide
and that she is only saved by her husband calling her down to
lunch.

This is not the last that we hear of Binet or his lathe. Emma's
frantic round of visits to try to borrow money locally after the
failure with Léon at Rouen in order to prevent the house from

being sold up is another series of highly cinematic scenes. We go with her first to the solicitor's house, then to Binet's, and finally to Rodolphe's château. Although all the three unsuccessful appeals are impressive, the visit to Binet is in some respects the most striking. She walks into the building where Binet's lathe is working and disappears. Two local women have caught sight of her and rush to the upper room of one of their houses. It is through their eyes that we see what happens and listen to their commentaries. Emma appears in front of the window in Binet's attic. The lathe stops. We see her pacing up and down, see the tax-collector blushing as she grips his hands. We do not hear what she is saying: we only hear the unsympathetic comments and speculations of the women spectators. Then Binet suddenly recoils 'as though he had seen a snake' and we catch two words, 'Madame! You can't be serious!' When she calls later on her daughter's nurse, the sound of the spinning wheel not only makes her think for a moment that she is hearing Binet's lathe; it almost certainly recreates horrifyingly in her mind the scene when she was on the verge of suicide and in a sense seems to provoke the real suicide.

This brings us to another remarkable example of Flaubert's cinematic scenes. It is the relations between Binet's lathe and the singing of a poor battered tramp. There is a strong contrast between the respectable tax-collector and the tramp, but in spite of that the sound of the lathe and the tramp's singing are made very ingeniously to work in the same direction. The description of the tramp is decidedly startling in its way and has prompted a commentator to describe him as standing for Death:

> There was a well-known local figure, a poor tramp, who used to wander with his stick amidst the traffic on the road. His body was a mass of rags, and an old, shapeless beaver, which he wore down over his brow like an inverted basin, hid his face. When he took it off he revealed, where the eyes should have been, two gaping, bleeding holes. The flesh was flaking away in scarlet tatters . . . Whenever he spoke to anybody he threw back his head with a sort of imbecile giggle, exhibiting bluish pupils which rolled continually with an outward movement which brought them in contact with the open sore.

He sang a little song as he followed along behind the carriages:
> Souvent la chaleur d'un beau jour
> Fait rêver fillette à l'amour.

What is remarkable is the contrast between the tramp's physical state and the gay song. It reflects not only the contrast in Emma's life between her love affairs, which began romantically and led in the end to disaster, but the disastrous picture of the contemporary world as Flaubert saw it.

The disturbing impression given by the tramp is clearly reflected in Emma's reactions whenever he makes an appearance:

> Sometimes he appeared suddenly behind Emma with a naked head. She started backwards with a cry . . . His voice was feeble at first and whining, rose to a shriller note and trailed off into the night like a wordless lamentation of some vague distress. Heard through the tinkling of bells, the whispering of trees and the rumbling of empty vehicles, it held a far-away suggestion which Emma found very unsettling. It went down to the bottom of her soul like a whirlwind in an abyss and carried her into the setting of a melancholy without limits . . . Emma in a frenzy of sadness, sat shivering in her clothes, feeling her feet growing colder, and the touch of death in her heart.

Although this is a description of what happened to Emma on a return from Rouen before the affair with Léon had begun to collapse, the reference to 'the touch of death in her heart' suggests that she feels that the tramp's singing has something in common with Binet's lathe. It is underlined by her final return from Rouen when the affair with Léon has collapsed. She sees the tramp, is filled with disgust and flings a five-franc coin over her shoulder to him. We are told that 'It was the whole of her fortune. It seemed to her fine to throw it like that'. It looks forward in fact to the last moments of her life. She is lying in bed suffering from the poison that she has given herself:

> Suddenly one heard on the pavement the sound of heavy clogs and the tapping of a stick. A voice rose, a hoarse voice singing:
> > Souvent la chaleur d'un beau jour
> > Fait rêver fillette à l'amour.

Emma raised herself like a galvanized corpse, her hair in disorder, her eyes fixed and staring.

> Pour amasser diligemment
> Les épis que la faux moissonne,
> Ma Nanette va s'inclinant
> Vers le sillon qui nous les donne.

'The blind man!' she cried.

And Emma began to laugh with an appalling, frantic, desperate laugh, believing that she was seeing the hideous face of the wretch standing out from eternal darkness like the figure of terror.

> Il souffla bien fort ce jour-là
> Et le jupon court s'envola!

A convulsion brought her down on the mattress. Everyone came towards her. She had ceased to live.

It is a highly ingenious ending of her life which once more emphasises the remarkable unity of all the major happenings in the novel. Nor should we overlook the fact that 'le jupon court s'envola' seems to look back to what happened with Emma's skirts during the wedding procession and the ride with Rodolphe.

There is one other technique which deserves attention. Dreams and daydreams are a device that we often find in contemporary films like Bergman's *Cries and Whispers* and Losey's *Accident*. When watching a film, it is sometimes a little difficult to distinguish between the dream or daydream and reality. One of the ways of avoiding the difficulty for the spectator is a change of scene, colour, focus or the use of a blackout. Although Flaubert does not face the same problems as a film director, he uses something of the same kind of method in the first of Emma's two impressive daydreams.

She is beginning to feel disillusioned with her married life. 'She could not imagine', we are told at the end of a chapter, 'that the calm in which she was living was the happiness of which she had dreamt'. There is a move or rather a 'cut' to a new chapter. The daydream begins at once:

Elle songeait quelquefois que c'étaient là pourtant les plus beaux jours de sa vie, la lune de miel, comme on disait. Pour en goûter la douceur, il eût fallu, sans doute, s'en aller vers ces pays à noms sonores où les lendemains de mariage ont de plus suaves paresses! Dans des chaises de poste, sous des stores de soie bleue, on monte au pas des routes escarpées, écoutant la chanson du postillon qui se répète dans la montagne avec les clochettes des chèvres et le bruit sourd de la cascade.. Quand le soleil se couche, on respire au bord des golfes le parfum des citronniers; puis, le soir, sur la terrasse des villas, seuls et les doigts confondus, on regarde les étoiles en faisant des projets. Il lui semblait que certains lieux sur la terre devaient produire du bonheur, comme une plante particulière au sol et qui pousse mal toute autre part. Que ne pouvait-elle s'accouder sur le balcon des chalets suisses ou enfermer sa tristesse dans un cottage écossais, avec un mari vêtu d'un habit de velours noir à longues basques, et qui porte des bottes molles, un chapeau pointu et des machettes!

[She thought, at times, that these days of what people called the honeymoon, were the most beautiful that she had ever known. To savour their sweetness to the full, she should, of course, have travelled to those lands with sounding names where newly wedded bliss is spent in exquisite languor. Seated in a post-chaise behind curtains of blue silk, she should have climbed, at a foot's pace, precipitous mountain roads, listening to the postillion's song echoing from the rocks to the accompaniment of goats's bells and the muted sound of falling water. She should have breathed at sunset, on the shores of sea bays in the south, the scent of lemon trees, and at night, alone with her husband on a villa terrace, have stood hand in hand, watching the stars and planning for the future. It seemed to her that certain places on the earth must produce happiness like a particular plant in the sun which grows badly everywhere else. Why was it not her fate to lean upon the balcony of a Swiss chalet or hide her melancholy in some Highland cottage, with a husband dressed in a black, long-skirted velvet coat, soft leather boots, a pointed hat, and ruffles at his wrist!]

The beauty, the colour of the scene and the lyrical element in the prose convey admirably the imagined change from a prosaic to a romantic life and are exactly the sort of change of representation that we might see in a film. We have the impression that she imagines that she is travelling alone, that she is detached from her marriage and is searching for a very different type of husband. It is brought out by the words 'with a husband dressed in a black, long-skirted velvet coat': an imaginary and no doubt ideal husband whose face naturally cannot be seen and who is wearing a suit which would have been appropriate to the aristocrats whom she will see at La Vaubyessard—particularly the cavalier 'en habit bleu'—but is unimaginable for Charles, as the 'bottes molles' are an ingenious contrast with his usual boot, which makes him look as though he has a 'wooden foot'. The daydream is not confined to an imagined husband; the scenery is important. It refers to countries which she has never seen and the way in which they are described is a clear indication that her daydream is essentially romantic—the hunt for a perfect husband in perfect surroundings.

The scene is not only impressive in itself; its links with other scenes are another sign of Flaubert's 'montage'. We know that blue is one of Emma's favourite colours. She is still a virtuous woman who has not yet fallen in love with anyone fresh because she is still at Tostes. The 'blue silk blind' therefore seems to stand for chastity in spite of her daydream of a different husband, but we know that the chaste imaginary ride leads to something very different.

Another method used by film directors to show a character moving into a dream world is to introduce some special sound. This is what Flaubert does with Emma's second daydream, in which religion plays a part. Although she is still virtuous, at any rate in practice, she has fallen in love with Léon for the first time and is beginning to feel guilty about it. It is a fine evening in spring. She is sitting in front of an open window watching the local sexton doing garden work and suddenly hears the Angelus:

> On était au commencement d'avril, quand les primevères sont écloses; un vent tiède se roule sur les plates-bandes labourées, et les jardins, comme des femmes, semblent faire leur toilette pour les fêtes de l'été . . . La vapeur du soir passait entre les peupliers sans feuilles, estompant leurs contours d'une teinte violette, plus pâle et plus transparente qu'une gaze subtile arrêtée sur leurs branchages. Au loin, des bestiaux marchaient, on n'entendait ni leurs pas ni leurs mugissements; et la cloche, sonnant toujours, continuait dans les airs lamentation pacifique.
>
> A ce tintement répété, la pensée de la jeune femme s'égarait dans ses vieux souvenirs de jeunesse et de pension. Elle se rappela les grands chandeliers, qui dépassaient sur l'autel les vases pleins

de fleurs et le tabernacle à colonnettes. Elle aurait voulu, comme
autrefois, être encore confondue dans la longue ligne des voiles
blancs, que marquaient de noir çà et là les capuchons raides des
bonnes soeurs inclinées sur leur prie-Dieu; le dimanche à la messe,
quand elle relevait sa tête, elle apercevait le doux visage de la
Vierge, parmi les tourbillons bleuâtres de l'encens qui montait.
Alors un attendrissement la saisit; elle se sentit molle et tout aban-
donnée . . . ce fut sans en avoir conscience qu'elle s'achemina vers
l'église, disposée à n'importe quelle dévotion, pourvu qu'elle y
absorbât son âme et que l'existence entière y disparût.

[It was the beginning of April, when the primroses are in bloom.
A warm wind was blowing over the dug flower-beds, and the gardens, like women, seemed to be furbishing their finery for the
gaieties of summer . . . The mist of evening was drifting between
the leafless poplars, blurring their outline with a violet haze, paler
and more transparent than a fine gauze hung upon their branches.
Cattle were moving in the distance, but her ear could catch neither
the noise of their hooves nor the sound of their lowing. The bell,
continuously ringing, struck upon the air with its note of peaceful
lamentation.

The repeated tolling took the young woman's mind back to the
memories of childhood and of her school. She remembered the
branched candlesticks which used to stand upon the altar, over-
topping the flower-filled vases and the tabernacle with its little
columns. She would have liked, as then, to be an unnoticed unit
in the long line of white veils in which, here and there, the stiff
coils of the good sisters kneeling at their prie-Dieu, showed as
accents of black. At Mass, on Sundays, whenever she raised her
head, she could see the sweet face of the Virgin in a blue cloud of
eddying incense. At such moments she had been conscious of deep
emotion, had felt alone and immaterial . . . It was almost without
knowing what she was doing, that she set out towards the church,
ready to enter into any act of devotion provided only that her
feelings might be wholly absorbed, and the outer world forgotten.]

We can see at once that this is a decidedly impressive passage
which is dominated significantly by the insistent ringing of the
Angelus. When we are told that 'the gardens, like women,
seemed to be furbishing their finery for the gaieties of summer',
we see that women are being neatly linked to their everyday
setting, but that the ordinary pleasures of the coming summer
are about to change to a different sight.

The Angelus is so dominant that it stifles the sounds of the
hooves and lowing of the distant cattle and 'struck upon the
air with its notes of peaceful lamentation', while the evening
mist 'drifting between the leafless poplars [blurred] their outline with a violet haze'. The result is that the perpetual sound
of the Angelus helped by the blurring of the trees by mist
works on Emma's mind and produces a 'flashback' to the young
girl attending Mass at her school chapel, which recalls an earlier description of her youth.[1] She sees herself in front of the
altar of the chapel looking at its 'flower-filled vases' in place of
the garden trees and wishes that she was once again 'an unnoticed unit in the long line of white veils . . . of the good sisters kneeling at their prie-Dieu'. The sudden difference between
the two worlds is emphasised by the statement that at Mass on
Sundays whenever she raised her head 'she could see the sweet
face of the Virgin in a blue cloud of eddying incense'.

'At such moments', we are told, 'she had been conscious of
deep emotion, had felt alone and immaterial'. The result of the
daydream is therefore 'almost without knowing what she was
doing, that she set out towards the church, ready to enter into
any act of devotion provided only that her feelings might be
wholly absorbed, and the outer world forgotten'.

Although this attempt to leave 'the outer world forgotten'
obviously looks forward to her move in a similar state of mind
in Rouen cathedral, it leads to a different kind of failure. On
the way to the village church she mets the Abbé Bournisien.
He is chiefly concerned at the moment of meeting with the
children who are being taught their catechism, with the result,
as on other occasions, we see his complete inability to grasp and
understand her problems.

Flaubert was naturally a great writer who possessed many admirable qualities, but psychological originality was not among
them.[2] We have seen that his way of dealing with his characters
was highly able, but they do not deepen our knowledge of human nature in the same way as, for example, those of a Stendhal
or a Proust, for the simple reason that they are basically com-

---

[1] The glimpse of her youth is given in Part I, chapter VI.

[2] It is emphasised by M. Pierre Danger's reference to 'the perception of
the movement without any psychological analysis' (see p. 186).

monplace people whose love affairs resemble the private lives of a good many French nineteenth-century writers. The result is that the unity of the novel does not depend on psychological development and discoveries about human nature. That is why the success of the novel is largely the result of what I have called 'cinematic' handling, meaning that the experience communicated to us comes from the ingenious use of related images, close-ups, flashbacks, daydreams, colour and sound. It follows from this that the characters are figures in a pattern rather than individuals in the fullest sense. The novelist manipulates them not merely with the same skill, but in the same way that he manipulates his images.

This is strikingly demonstrated as soon as we turn from the principal to the secondary characters. They not only have considerably less psychology than Emma; they are both simplified and stylized, and resemble the characters in primitive comedy or in allegory. They are sufficiently individualised for the novelist's purpose, but their individuality derives from repetition—from the same repetition of the same foolish things in slightly different terms. The primitive-allegorical element is also apparent in Flaubert's choice of names, which is not confined to those of the minor characters. I once suggested that if Bovary fits Charles like a label, it is probably because it contains an allusion to the words *boeuf* or *bovin* and thought that the supposition was strengthened when we remember that after Emma's death Léon marries a Mlle Leboeuf. I have, however, since come across a very different view in the Harrap dictionary which applies to Emma instead of to Charles. It appears that the name has led to the invention of the verb 'bovaryser' meaning 'to live in a romantic dream divorced from reality; (from Madame Bovary, the heroine of Flaubert's famous novel)'.[1] On the other hand, there seems to be little doubt that the name of the Abbé Bournisien is intended to suggest *borné*. Homais, as we know from Flaubert's notes, is a pejorative form of *homme*. The owner is 'the little man', the product of the brash enlightenment of the nineteenth century which was as abhorrent to Flaubert as to any *dévot*. Lheureux is the happy or fortunate man, and in this context the successful swindler.

[1] It reflects Emma's own pronouncement: 'Je déteste les héros communs et les sentiments tempérés, comme il y a dans la nature (Part II, chapter II).

It is not difficult to see how the characters fit into the allegorical framework. In spite of his shortcomings, Charles is a sympathetic figure, but he is not merely the dumb ox; he is the stock figure of the dupe, the *cocu,* the *mari trompé,* who has been handed down from primitive comedy through the Molière of *George Dandin ou le Mari confondu.* Bournisien is the Priest, Rodolphe and Lèon the Faithless Swains, Lheureux the Usurer, Homais the Quack.

These are the people who form the society which is slowly choking Emma and into whose hands she plays. She is tricked by her enemies and let down by her friends. Her husband fails her because he cannot understand her romantic *élans,* and in any case does not possess the character which would enable him to help her to make proper use of them; the priest because her emotional religion is beyond his comprehension. Her lovers turn against her and walk out on her. She plays Homais' game by egging her husband on to make the experiment on Hippolyte's clubfoot because the quack can only rise if the qualified doctor comes to grief. She plays into the hands of Lheureux by her extravagances; and her signature to his bills—that peculiarly nineteenth-century instrument of disaster which looms so large in Balzac—brings ruin to her husband and herself.

Although Emma's romanticism is a species of *bêtise,* Flaubert felt a tenderness for her which he did not feel for any of his other characters. She may be foolish and deceitful, but she is more sympathetic and more sensitive than them, is in the last resort superior to them all. There were personal reasons for Flaubert's preference. Her predicament was his own. It was the predicament of the romantic individualist trapped in a hostile civilisation which provided no outlet for his natural aspirations. This brings us back to Charles's hat and the image of the circle. Emma is imprisoned in a double circle which is at once physical and psychological. It is the physical circle formed by the nondescript country, the 'contrée bâtarde où le langage est sans accentuation comme le paysage sans caractère'; and the psychological circle formed by the people with their maddeningly stupid remarks. In addition to everything else the journeys are attempts to break out of the double circle. One can go further still. Emma is not only imprisoned in a double circle; she is imprisoned in a shrinking circle reflected by Binet's lathe and the tramp's song. What makes the climax so dramatic is the spectacle of her going round and round in an ever-narrowing circle as Lheureux and his pack of bankers, bailiffs and process-servers close in on her. The victim's death does not put an end to the chase; it swells the pack which turns on the husband, recalling in an odd way the opening scene of the book. Once again the poor foolish Charles finds himself the centre of a jeering hostile throng. The music mistress demands payment for lessons that Emma never had; the lending library for books which she never borrowed. The trusted maid elopes with a lover and steals the remainder of her dead mistress's wardrobe. We are even told that Emma 'corrupted' the widower from beyond the grave. It is, indeed, the discovery of her correspondence with her lovers which puts the finishing touch on the handiwork of Lheureux and the rest; the husband is hounded to death as surely as the wife.

'The world described in *Madame Bovary*', said Thibaudet, 'is a world falling apart . . . But in every society when something is destroyed, another thing takes its place'.[1] It is not confined to Flaubert. The same thing occurs in the work of other novelists, particularly in Zola, as well as in films by Eisenstein, Pudovkin and in our own time in Fellini's *La Dolce Vita*. In *Madame Bovary* the disasters of Emma and Charles are followed by the triumphs of Homais and Lheureux, and the novel closes with an ironical twist of the Quack receiving a medal for political services after getting rid of three more doctors as well as having the unhappy tramp shut up in the name of Progress because he cannot cure him with his dubious potions. We must, however, be clear about the meaning of these events. In Flaubert's Yonville, as surely as in Stendhal's Parme, we are watching a world in microcosm. However shabby its reprensentatives, the world which is falling apart is the traditional world, the world of the liberal professions: the world which is taking its place, which is rising in the persons of Homais and Lheureux, is a world of 'spivs'. The exchanges between Bournisien and Homais when they spend a night beside Emma's deathbed are something more than the bickerings of the village priest

1 *Gustave Flaubert*, 1935, pp. 115, 116.

and the village rationalist. They reflect the conflict between religion and science which rent France in the nineteenth century. There is, indeed, something prophetic about the pair Homais-Lheureux. It was the ascent of men like these which brought France to the brink of destruction. We cannot contemplate the activities of the small-time usurer without thinking of what was happening in Paris on a huge scale during the Second Empire, and was chronicled by Zola in a novel like *L'Argent*. We cannot forget that it was the triumph of the free-thinking lower middle class, which emerged from the Revolution, that later produced the split between right and left in France—a split which completed in the moral sphere the damage done by speculation in the material sphere.

ALAIN-FOURNIER

LE GRAND MEAULNES

1

On Ascension Day, 1905, an eighteen-year-old schoolboy went to visit an art exhibition in Paris. The exhibition was at the Grand Palais, which lies between the Champs-Elysées and the Seine. When he was leaving in the late afternoon, he saw an elderly lady with a slim blonde girl going down the steps in front of him. As he caught up with them, the girl lifted her head slightly and looked at him. Her eyes were so intensely blue that for a few seconds he stopped dead in his tracks. He felt obscurely that this was a moment of destiny, that the girl was not simply the most beautiful person he had ever seen, but was the girl for whom he had been waiting. He followed the couple along the Cours-la-Reine and boarded the same river steamer. He continued to follow them on the other bank until he saw them go into a house in the Boulevard Saint-Germain. He now had the girl's address. On Saturdays, Sundays and Thursday afternoons he was free. He took to posting himself near the house in the Boulevard Saint-Germain, hoping for another glimpse of the girl. On Whitsun Eve he was rewarded: she came to the window and looked out. Alain-Fournier, for he was the schoolboy, thought that she saw him and smiled.

On Whit Sunday he was at his post in good time, feeling sure that she would go to Mass at Saint-Germain-des-Prés. He was right. As soon as she appeared, he set off in pursuit. They both mounted the same tramcar. He spoke to her as she was about to enter the church and got a chilly reply. He followed her into the church and out again. He managed to get into conversation with her in the street. She was somewhat put out, but thawed a little during the walk. He told her who he was and talked about his ambition to become a writer. She gave him her name, explained that she was only in Paris on a visit and would be leaving the following day. The impact was not entirely one-sided. In the notes that he made after the meeting, Alain-

Fournier records that in reply to some question about the future the girl said: 'What's the good?' The conversation ended by her declaring: 'We're children. We've been silly'. She asked him to leave her, stopped and looked back for a long moment, either to discourage any further pursuit or because she herself had been touched by the meeting.

Alain-Fournier did not see her again until 1913, when she was married and the mother of two children, but the meeting of 1905 was indeed a moment of destiny for him. She was the model for the heroine of his only novel. The anniversary of their encounter was kept year after year almost as a day of mourning and was the source of anguished outpourings in his letters to his family or friends, providing in real life an almost classic example of a hopeless passion. Although he used her Christian name for his heroine, her full name was a closely guarded secret and was not revealed to the public until March, 1964, a few weeks after her death. It was Yvonne de Quiévre-court.

Henri Alban Fournier, as he was christened, was born on October 3, 1886, at La Chapelle d'Angillon in the department of Cher in the Berry country. He was the elder child of a village schoolmaster, and the rural surroundings in which he spent his early years played a vital part in his formation. In his make-up there were two conflicting impulses. One was a restless desire for adventure and discovery which he seems to have inherited from his father's family. The other was a profound attachment to his native province. The first of these impulses became transformed into a desire to discover and explore an inner world: the mysterious childhood paradise which is evoked in the novel. The attachment to his native Berry remained with him all his life. He was seldom happy when he was away from it, and he used it as the setting of his novel. It is, as we shall see, the skill with which he blends these two impulses, so that the childhood paradise seems an extension of the life of the peaceful and remote corner of France in which the story unfolds, that gives the book its strange haunting charm.

He left home for the first time at the age of twelve when he was sent to the Lycée Voltaire in Paris. Three years later he transferred to the lycée of Brest, where he intended to study for

the entrance examination to the training ship *Borda*, which
was the naval equivalent of the famous Saint-Cyr military academy. At the end of sixteen months, he abandoned his naval
ambitions and began to think of a career as a teacher. He went
to the lycée of Bourges, a few miles from his birthplace, and
then in 1903 he moved to the Lycée Lakanal in Paris in order
to study for the entrance examination to the Ecole Normale. At
Lakanal he met Jacques Rivière, his future brother-in-law
and the future editor of the *Nouvelle Revue Française*. The
shattering effect of his meeting with Yvonne in 1905 became
apparent the following year. He failed hopelessly in his examination, and though he managed to pass the written part in
1907 he was rejected at the oral. The same year he was called
up for two years military service, and in October reported at
the barracks of Vincennes for training with the 23rd Regiment
of Dragoons. He eventually transferred to the infantry, and
more successful in his army than in his civilian examinations
graduated as an army officer.

He was released from the army in September, 1909, and began to earn his living as the writer of a literary gossip column
in the *Paris-Journal*. In December, 1912, *Le Grand Meaulnes,*
which he had begun as long ago as 1905, was completed. It was
serialised in the *NRF* from July to November, 1913, appeared
in book form in October of the same year, and nearly won the
Prix Goncourt.

At the outbreak of war in August, 1914, Alain-Fournier and
Rivière, who had married Isabelle Fournier in August, 1909,
were both mobilised and sent to the front. Rivière was taken
prisoner on August 24. On September 22, a few days before his
twenty-eighth birthday, Alain-Fournier was reported missing
when a French patrol was ambushed at Saint-Rémy, and was
never heard of again.

2

Le Grand Meaulnes is a unique novel which has been more
widely, more intensely and more passionately studied than the
works of a number of other famous one-book novelists. It has
been variously interpreted as a religious allegory, as a 'morality', as fantasy and as a modern version of the medieval 'quests'.

It is plainly much more than a straightforward love story with a disastrous ending, but it is difficult to believe that it can be described as a religious novel in any useful or positive sense. The other elements that I have mentioned are undoubtedly there in some degree. The dominant feature is the theme of the 'quest', but we shall find that this alone is far from resolving all the problems of interpretation.

There is another factor which deserves special emphasis. Although its description as an autobiographical novel has been vigorously challenged, it is clear from the characters and the setting that it does contain an important autobiographical element which calls for careful examination.[1] Alain-Fournier's meeting with Yvonne was his moment of destiny in the sense that it provided him with exactly the kind of inspiration that he needed in order to make the right use of his creative genius, but though he used her as a model for his heroine the meeting was far too brief for him to produce anything like a portrait of her. The result is that though we are given for psychological reasons something like a dual view of her, Yvonne de Galais owes a good deal to the transforming power of literature. The novelist was clearly influenced by the *princesse lointaine* of the Symbolists, who in turn derives from the untouchable idol of the romantic myth: the woman who is beautiful, mysterious, inaccessible and pure. The idea of purity plays a large part both in Alain-Fournier's correspondence and in the novel. 'Purity', he wrote in a letter to the painter, André Lhote, 'is the great question, the great torment of the impure in heart'. It is evident, however, from his sister's latest account of his life that he himself was not exactly the chaste knight waiting for an ethereal union with the beloved. He was extremely susceptible to women. It is true that he tried to transform the women whom he met into fresh incarnations of the ideal and could be decidedly cruel when he failed, but in these encounters purity was invariably a casualty. Four of them became his mistresses, two of whom were married women.[2]

Although a good deal of attention has been given to the affair with the actress-novelist Mme Simone, who deals with him

---

[1] See Michel Guiomar: *Inconscient et imaginaire dans Le Grand Meaulnes*, 1964, pp. 7–11.

[2] Isabelle Rivière: *Vie et passion d'Alain-Fournier*, 1963, *passim*.

in a volume of reminiscences which appeared in 1957 under the title of *Sous de nouveaux soleils,* it is of no importance in literary terms because it did not take place until after the publication of *Le Grand Meaulnes.* What is important is that soon after the completion of his military service in 1909 he plunged into a tempestuous affair with a youthful milliner known to us as Jeanne. It was as different as could be from his ethereal devotion to Yvonne and seems to have been the liaison which cost him his innocence. 'She had nearly all the best qualities', he said in a letter, 'except purity'. There is no doubt that as a result of his own fall she paid dearly for the exception, but in spite of his own fall the true beneficiary was the novelist. Jeanne unwittingly provided him with the model for Valentine, Meaulnes's second love, which brings out the resemblance between the novelist and his protagonist.

This throws further light on the autobiographical element in the novel. It has become fashionable among critics with psychoanalytical leanings to discover 'doubles' among the characters of novelists and dramatists. The term may be new: the practice to which it refers is not. Novelists, as we know, generally put something of themselves into a number of different characters. 'Doubles' or 'pairs' are to be found in many literatures in many ages, even in the work of French classic dramatists, as Charles Mauron has demonstrated in his ingenious psychoanalytical study of Racine.[1]

That is the difference between an autobiographical novel like Radiguet's *Le Diable au corps,* in which the novelist identifies himself with the protagonist, and *Le Grand Meaulnes,* in which the autobiographical elements are divided between the two principal male characters. François Seurel, the narrator, and Augustin Meaulnes are 'doubles' in the sense that they are both partial portraits of the artist.[2] Although the novelist is careful to make the couple look different in a number of ways, Meaulnes is a reflection of some of his own failings and Seurel a reflection of the man of integrity that he wished to be. They are

---

[1] *L'Inconscient dans l'oeuvre et la vie de Racine,* 1957.

[2] Fournier's father was the village schoolmaster at La Chapelle-d'Angillon until 1891 and then became the schoolmaster at Epineuille-Fleuriel. Meaulnes's name was a borrowing from the neighbouring village of Meaulne.

both projections of tendencies which belonged not merely to
the novelist, but to other members of the family on his father's
side: a sober, down-to-earth realism and the spirit of adventure.
Seurel is the countryman attached to the soil; the representative of the everyday world, the voice of sanity, a mixture of
Greek chorus and confidant from French classical tragedy, trying to control Meaulnes's more reckless impulses and to preserve an equilibrium. One of the most striking features of his
style as narrator is its concreteness: the presentation of the sights
and sounds of the countryside, the way in which a gesture is
caught and fixed, whether it is a countrywoman battling against
the wind and the rain or a peasant standing speechless, finger-
ing his hat and wondering what to do next. This is in no sense
a matter of background; it is an essential element in the pattern of the book which places in perspective Meaulnes's adventures, his extraordinary experience during his first visit to
the *domaine mystérieux* and what can only be called the quest
for an earthly paradise.

Nor is that all. We find in the novel what the French call a
dédoublement, which means that we are looking at life simultaneously under two different and usually conflicting aspects.
It is the story of a great adventure in which we move at times
in what seems like an enchanted world, but we are conscious
all the time of a sense of fragility, an underlying menace. Once
a peak has been passed the atmosphere becomes more and more
threatening as the magic is gradually dissipated by a sense
of disenchantment, the fading of dreams and hopes, the sudden plunge from an earthly paradise into something like an
earthly hell. François Seurel is the instrument by which the
sense of disenchantment seeps in. The word 'quest' is never
used in the novel: the word 'adventure' occurs constantly. It is
clear, however, as I have already suggested, that the core of the
novel is a number of related 'quests' in which the protagonists,
with one exception, are frustrated by every kind of mistake and
misunderstanding, with the result that they are continually
setting out on a false trail which carries them away from their
goal or brings them to a goal which is not the one they were
hoping for. It is naturally underlined by continual travelling
in various ways: in carriages, on horseback, on bicycles and on
foot, usually in search of a woman.

3

The novel opens with a simple matter-of-fact statement of Meaulnes's arrival at Sainte-Agathe without actually mentioning his name:

He arrived at our place one Sunday in November 189 . . .[1]

There follows a deliberately prosaic account of the family's life in the country, the father's work as a village schoolmaster and a description of the school buildings. The intention is to bring out a very ordinary world to which François belongs, to prepare the way for the violent disruption introduced by Meaulnes, and the contrast with the *domaine mystérieux*.

M. Guiomar has suggested that in the novel images are more important than events.[2] The pattern is, indeed, formed by a series of interrelated images. The images of the sea and ship-wreck, which were probably inspired by the novelist's early naval training, are outstanding and are strategically placed. Stephen Ullmann has pointed out that there are altogether eighteen sea images and that they represent one third of the total number of images in the novel.[3] We should add that they divide into two groups which can be described as major and minor. The small number of major images are a direct and dramatic reflexion of the central theme: the continued changes in the protagonists' fortunes, the oscillation between them, between the real world and something, as we shall see, like a dream world. The remainder, which look at first like a series of casual references to sea, boats and even fishermen, are an ingenious and disturbing way of ensuring that the reader never for a moment loses sight of the main theme or is released from its impact.

The first major sea image comes on page one or two, immediately after the description of the school buildings:

[1] We are told that Mme Meaulnes and her son 'had come by carriage from La Ferté-d'Angillon, which was fourteen kilometers from Sainte-Agathe'.

[2] *Op. cit.*, p. 18.

[3] *The Image in the Modern French Novel*, 1960, p. 102.

... tel est le plan sommaire de cette demeure où s'écoulèrent les
jours les plus tourmentés et les plus chers de ma vie—demeure d'où
partirent et où revinrent se briser, comme des vagues sur un rocher,
nos aventures.

[... such is the brief account of the house where I spent the most
painful and the most beloved days of my life—the house from
which set out and to which returned, like waves breaking on a
barren rock, our adventures.]

The first thing that strikes us about the passage is its gram-
matical oddity. We may set out on an adventure and return to
our starting point; an adventure may begin and end in the
same place, but an adventure cannot itself 'set out' or 'return'
or 'break' on a 'barren rock'. The construction reveals the novelist's determination to introduce the marine image at this
early stage even if it means doing violence to logic. Its incor-
rectness is not without relevance. The novelist means that it
was the adventure rather than the adventurers which was
wrecked.

The order of the words deserves attention. 'Les jours les plus
tourmentés et les plus chers de ma vie' suggest at once a blend
of contrary feelings, with the accent on pain and the extremes
between which the emotional life of the characters moves. It is
underlined by the double movement of the waves surging forward only to fling themselves back on the barren rock. For this,
indeed, is what happens to the adventurers setting out full of
hope, then returning frustrated to their starting point. The
construction of the phrase with the crucial word thrust to the
end clearly places immense emphasis on 'adventures', which
means the 'quest'.

The impact of the chief adventurer on the simple community is described two pages later:

Tout ce paysage paisible . . . est à jamais, dans ma mémoire,
agité, transformé par la présence de celui qui bouleversa toute
notre adolescence et dont la fuite même ne nous a pas laissé de
repos.

[The whole of this peaceful countryside . . . is fixed forever in
my memory, disturbed, transformed by the presence of the person

who turned our adolescence upside down and whose flight even did not leave us in repose.]

When Meaulnes enters the scene he appears as a large youth with his hair cropped like a peasant's. There is in fact more in him of the countryman—the practical countryman versed in country lore—than in François Seurel. As soon as he arrives, he proceeds to explore the building on his own, unearths some of last year's fireworks and lets them off, which points already to his independence and his individualism. The ominous nature of the 'presence' is emphasised at an early stage in Chapter 2:

> But someone came who took me away from all these peaceful childish pleasures. Someone blew out the candle which lighted up for me the gentle motherly face bent over the evening meal. Someone put out the lamp around which our happy family gathered.

The contrasted images of 'home' and 'world', 'interior' and 'exterior', 'security' and 'danger' are part of the pattern of the novel and add to the effect of the marine images. Meaulnes is seen here as an intruder, the stranger who coming from outside, from the world beyond the village, disrupts the peace and security symbolised by the home with the gentle motherly face and the inmates gathered round the lamp, which metaphorically he 'put out'.

The 'quest' does not begin as a quest. It begins as a schoolboy prank when Meaulnes decides secretly that he will drive to the station to meet the narrator's grandparents instead of the narrator himself and one of his schoolfellows, who have been chosen by M. Seurel, because they know the way, which Meaulnes significantly does not. This is François' comment:

> . . . I was afraid that my companion was going to deprive me of the modest pleasure of going to the Station in a carriage; and yet, without daring to admit it to myself, I expected from him some extraordinary enterprise which turned everything upside down.

The sense of impending disaster or 'shipwreck' underlies all these early chapters, but we see from this passage that it is a prospect of disaster which paradoxically is both feared and desired.

The prank takes place in Chapter 3. François' mixed feelings clearly look back to a remarkable factor described at the start of Chapter 2. The child had been handicapped by coxalgia. The malady made it difficult for him to walk and he was seldom allowed out on his own. He concludes:

> Augustin Meaulnes's arrival, which coincided with my recovery, was the beginning of a new life.

In other words, the recovery of the ability to walk made life seem pleasanter and prepared the way for his own part in the 'quest'.

Although the 'adventure' begins as a schoolboy prank, the difficulties and physical hardships that Meaulnes encounters when he loses his way have obvious affinities with the ordeals of the knights in medieval stories. The discovery that he has missed his way is brought home to him when the penetrating cold awakens him from the doze into which he had fallen in the cart and he notices that 'the landscape had changed'. 'Anyone but Meaulnes', we are told, 'would have at once retraced his steps. It was the only way of not going still further astray'. He obstinately pushes on. 'He felt growing within him an exasperated desire to achieve something and get somewhere in spite of all the obstacles'. He is brought to a halt when his horse stops at the edge of water. He finds a poor cottage belonging to a peasant who agrees to put him up for the night. He goes out to place a rug on the horse, turns down a path which appears to lead directly back to the cottage, only to find he is lost again. When the horse and cart return to Saint-Agathe without Meaulnes, it produces another major marine image on the part of François Seurel which looks forward to what will happen:

> Je m'étais approché jusqu'au premier rang et je regardais avec les autres cet attelage qui nous revenait, telle une épave qu'eût ramenée la haute mer—la première et la dernière, peut-être, de l'aventure de Meaulnes.

> [I had moved as far as the front rank and with the others I looked at the lost horse and cart which had come back to us, like

a piece of flotsam washed up by the high sea—the first piece of
flotsam and, perhaps, the last of Meaulnes's adventure.]

Meaulnes spends a cold night in a hut and next day, in spite
of the discomfort brought on by the cold night, he pushes on:

> Au coin du bois débouchait, entre deux poteaux blancs, une
> allée où Meaulnes s'engagea. Il y fit quelques pas et s'arrêta, plein
> de surprise, troublé d'une émotion inexplicable. Il marchait pour-
> tant du même pas fatigué, le vent glacé lui gerçait les lèvres, le
> suffoquait par instants; et pourtant un contentement extraordi-
> naire le soulevait, une tranquillité parfaite et presque enivrante,
> la certitude que son but était atteint et qu'il n'y avait plus main-
> tenant que du bonheur à espérer.

[At the corner of the wood, there emerged from between two
white posts, a lane which Meaulnes entered. After a few steps he
came to a stop, filled with surprise, disturbed by a feeling that he
could not explain. He went on, however, with the same weary
gait; the icy wind made his lips sore, at moments made him feel
suffocated. And yet he was filled with an extraordinary sense of
contentment, a perfect and almost intoxicating feeling of peace,
the certainty that his goal was reached and that now only happiness awaited him.]

The passage is the prelude to Meaulnes's discovery of what
he was to call the *domaine mystérieux* and the *domaine sans
nom*. It is also the first occasion on which we hear of a 'goal'.
The sense of euphoria is a sign that he is about to enter what
must be described as a dream world and will culminate in the
meeting with Yvonne de Galais—the central incident in the
novel as it was in Alain-Fournier's life. It is a psychological experience which brings about a profound change in Meaulnes.
The feeling that he is in a dream world is heightened by the
fact that though there are plenty of adults, the setting is a
children's fancy-dress party or a children's carnival, and we
are told expressly that everything had been planned in accord-
ance with the wishes of the infant guests.

This is the stage at which we first become vividly aware of
the *dédoublement*. The sense of enchantment is psychological,
but the psychological effect is largely the result of material fac-

tors.[1] The period clothing of the guests, the period décors of
the room where Meaulnes sleeps, the grotesque figure of the
clown who lights the lanterns make us feel that we are indeed
in a 'mysterious domain', but in a curious way the link with the
everyday world is never completely severed. It is a carnival, a
temporary departure from the everyday world into a world of
make-believe. Strange things may happen, but the presence of
the children and the fact that Meaulnes wears his school uni-
form under the period costume that he puts on can hardly be
unintentional. They emphasise that the break *is* temporary,
that underneath Meaulnes remains a schoolboy, that he will
take off the fancy dress and return to reality, that in some respects he himself is little more than a child who will try to
perpetuate his experience and that in spite of François' assistance everything will come to grief.

This brings us back to the description of François and
Meaulnes as 'doubles'. Meaulnes describes his experience at the
'mysterious domain' to François, who reproduces it in the third
person, but it is clear that what we are really hearing is the
novelist's own experience translated into highly imaginative
terms. He emphasises one point which Meaulnes himself would
have been less likely to notice. When he walks through the different parts of the building for the first time, we are told:

> Everything there seemed old and ruined. The openings at the
> bottom of the staircases were gaping because long ago the doors
> had been taken away; nor had the window panes been replaced,
> which made black holes in the walls. And yet all these buildings
> had a mysterious air of fête. A sort of coloured reflection floated
> in the lower rooms where lanterns must have been lighted in
> those facing the country side of the buildings. The paths had
> been rolled; and the grass which had been invading it had been
> removed.

The contrast between the 'old and ruined' state of the buildings and 'the mysterious air of fête' brings out once again the

[1] In the engaging film of the novel which he made in 1967 with the
valuable help of Isabelle Rivière and which was particularly popular with
the young, J. G. Albicocco tried ingeniously to bring out the dreamlike
feeling by the unusual lighting effects that he used in some of the sequences
of the visit to the 'mysterious domain'.

dual vision of life and underlines the illusory element in the fête. It also looks forward to the misfortunes which will overtake the Galais family.

Meaulnes's entry into the dream world and his meeting with Yvonne had been prepared by a dream which he had long ago and which he suddenly remembered in the hut where he spent the first night away from Sainte-Agathe:

> Glacé jusqu'aux moelles, il se rappela un rêve—une vision plutôt, qu'il avait eue tout enfant, et dont il n'avait jamais parlé à personne: un matin, au lieu de s'éveiller dans sa chambre, où pendaient ses culottes et ses paletots, il s'était trouvé dans une longue pièce verte, aux tentures pareilles à des feuillages. En ce lieu coulait une lumière si douce qu'on eût cru pouvoir la goûter. Près de la première fenêtre, une jeune fille cousait, le dos tourné, semblant attendre son réveil . . . Il n'avait pas eu la force de se glisser hors de son lit pour marcher dans cette demeure enchantée. Il s'était rendormi . . . Mais la prochaine fois, il jurait de se lever. Demain matin, peut-être! . . .

> [Frozen to the marrow, he recalled a dream, or rather a vision, that he had had as a little child and had never mentioned to anybody. One morning, instead of waking up in his own room, where his trousers and overcoats were hanging, he had found himself in a long green room with wallpaper like the foliage of trees. The place was bathed in a light which was so soft that he had the impression that he could taste it. Near the first window, a girl was sewing with her back to him and seemed to be waiting for him to wake . . . He had not had the strength to slip out of bed and walk into this enchanted dwelling; he had gone to sleep again . . . But next time he swore firmly that he would get up. Tomorrow morning, perhaps! . . .]

This highly engaging passage not only looks forward to his entry into the dream world; it explains the excitement that he felt just before he caught sight of the 'mysterious domain' for the first time and the sense that he had somehow reached his 'goal'. Nor is that all. One has the impression that something of the same kind had happened to the novelist when he was a child, which explains why he was completely carried away by his first glimpse of Yvonne de Quiévrecourt and supports M. Guiomar's contention that Alain-Fournier was psychologically conditioned for such a meeting, that given his disposition and emotional history, a crystallisation of this nature was almost bound to occur.[1]

Meaulnes sees Yvonne de Galais for the first time after supper on the evening of his arrival at the domain:

> . . . a woman or a girl, with a large maroon cloak thrown over her shoulders, with her back to him, was playing very softly on a piano some tune from roundelays or old songs. On a divan, close beside her, were six or seven little boys and girls placed as though in a picture, well-behaved as children are when it is late, who were listening . . .

His reaction is exactly what we might expect:

> It was a dream like his old dream. For moments on end he could imagine that he was in his own home, married, on a fine evening, and that the charming, unknown being who was playing the piano was his wife . . .

It shows the way in which the memory of the dream creates a daydream and underlines once again the idea of a refuge from reality and its temporary nature.

It is picked up by a scene in the garden next day before he has actually come face to face with Yvonne and produces another highly engaging passage:

> Un instant, dans le jardin, Meaulnes se pencha sur la branlante barrière de bois qui entourait le vivier; vers les bords il restait un peu de glace mince et plissée come une écume. Il s'aperçut lui-même, reflété dans l'eau, comme incliné sur le ciel, dans son costume d'étudiant romantique. Et il crut voir un autre Meaulnes; non plus l'écolier qui s'était évadé dans une carriole de paysan, mais un être charmant et romanesque, au milieu d'un beau livre de prix . . .

> [For a moment, in the garden, Meaulnes leaned against the rickety wooden barrier surrounding the fish pond; near the sides there remained a little thin, wrinkled sheet of ice like foam . . . He saw himself reflected in the water as though he were leaning against the sky, in the dress of a student of the romantic age. And

[1] *Op. cit.*, pp. 9–10.

he thought he saw another Meaulnes; no longer the schoolboy who had run away in a peasant's cart, but a charming and romantic being in the middle of a beautiful and expensive book...]

Although he is standing by nothing more than a 'fish pond', the references to his reflection in 'water' and 'foam' strike me as one of those passing reminders of the sea image. It is perhaps because a fish pond is a harmless piece of water that he has a romantic vision of a romantic Meaulnes 'leaning against the sky'.

The meeting with Yvonne in the novel has a good deal in common with the meeting in real life. The similarity applies to what they do and what they say. In this respect one of the most important events at the *fête* is the boat trip on the second day. The guests are divided between three boats. For the outward trip Meaulnes manages to find a place for himself in the same boat as Yvonne, which clearly recalls the crossing of the Seine in the river steamer: the real life 'quest' that came to nothing, but fortunately did not lead to tragedy. When they land at the end of the outward trip, Meaulnes manages to link up with Yvonne. They give their names to one another. Meaulnes asks whether he can come and see her again. 'I shall expect you', she replies simply. Then there is a change. When they arrive at the place of embarkment for the return journey, we are told

> She stopped suddenly and said thoughtfully:
> 'We're two children; we've been silly. We musn't go back on the same boat this time. Good-bye. Don't follow me.'

We are told next:

> Meaulnes remained speechless for a moment, as he watched her depart. Then he started walking again. And then the young girl in the distance, the moment before losing herself again among the crowd of guests, stopped and turning in his direction, for the first time stood and gazed at him. Was it the last sign of a goodbye? Was it to forbid him to accompany her? Or had she perhaps something more to say to him?

We can see at once that the references to 'two children' and

'silly' as well as the way in which she looked back at him are
clearly based on what happened to Alain-Fournier at the second meeting with Yvonne de Quiévrecourt on Whit Sunday.

The other point that deserves emphasis is that we begin to see
the differences between Meaulnes and Yvonne, which are apparent in the references to what happened on Whit Sunday. The
best opportunity of examining Yvonne's differences in some
detail will occur later when she has had her first meeting with
François. What needs observing here is that Meaulnes himself
has clearly become aware that something irrevocable has happened to him, that he is somehow a changed person. It is
brought out by his reflexions when he finds himself back in the
bedroom where he had spent his first night:

> He was there, mysterious, a stranger, in the midst of an un-
> known world, in the room he had chosen. What he had obtained
> was beyond his wildest hopes. It was sufficient now to fill him
> with joy to recall the face of the young girl turning in the high
> wind towards him.

'High wind' during the river party is another reminder of
'sea', but once again it is safe.

Much later in the novel, when Meaulnes is on the verge of
wrecking his own happiness and Yvonne's, he remarks to François Seurel:

> But how could a man who has once made the leap into Para-
> dise later adapt himself to everyday life? ... For I am convinced
> now that when I discovered the Domain without a Name, I had
> reached a height, a degree of perfection and purity that I shall
> never attain again. Only when I am dead, as I once wrote to you,
> I may perhaps recover the beauty of that time ...

The rest of the novel is, indeed, taken up with the dissipation of the 'dream'. Although it took the form of a childrens'
party, the *fête* was intended as a welcome to Yvonne's brother,
Frantz de Galais, and his fiancée. There has of course been a
breach between them and Frantz's return alone brings the *fête*
to an abrupt end. In view of what is to come, it is important to
observe that Meaulnes meets Frantz at the end of the party,
learns who he is and what has happened to him. He discovers

his presence by chance in the next room to the one in which he spent the first night. Frantz is in a miserable state, but adopts a friendly attitude towards Meaulnes and invites him to go downstairs and tell everybody that the *fête* is over. Meaulnes finds that people already know what is happening and seem to be disappointed by it. We are told that the carefree atmosphere has vanished; instead of hearing their chatter and their laughter, we see the 'figures inquiètes' of the children huddled silently together in the vehicles that are taking them home. The ending, as we shall find, will turn out to be something like a fore-taste of the next party to take place at the 'domain'.

As Meaulnes is leaving the 'domain' in a carriage whose owner is giving him a lift part of the way home he hears the sound of a pistol shot and catches another glimpse of the pierrot, which evokes again the damaging forces at work beneath the surface:

> And while he was shaking the window with his face pressed against the pane, [Meaulnes] saw owing to a bend in the road a white form running. It was the tall pierrot of the *fête*, looking haggard and almost out of his mind, the bohemian wearing the clothes of the masquerade, who was carrying a human body in his arms clutched against his chest. Then everything disappeared.

The 'human body' is Frantz, who has just tried to shoot himself. Yet in spite of the meeting between them and the fact that Meaulnes has not only heard a pistol shot, but had noticed a pistol among his belongings, he never suspects for a moment that the 'human body' is Frantz's.

4

The account of Meaulnes's return to Sainte-Agathe (which incidentally precedes the account of his adventure which comes to us through François) throws a curious light on his experience which has been insufficiently remarked. When he enters the schoolroom, we are told:

> ... et surtout son air de voyageur fatigué, affamé, mais émerveillé, tout cela fit passer un étrange sentiment de plaisir et de curiosité.

[...and above all his appearance of a tired, hungry, but enraptured traveller gave us a strange feeling of pleasure and curiosity.]

The key-word is 'émerveillé'. The literary antecedents are very ancient, but it does show that the experience was so intense and so novel that it is still visible in the expression on Meaulnes's face. The sequel is even more interesting:

> There was nothing to remind us of Meaulnes's adventure [says the narrator] except the strange fact that since the afternoon of his return, we no longer had any friends.

The experience of the 'earthly paradise' has somehow removed not only Meaulnes, but his friend François Seurel from the ordinary world; they have become outsiders, almost enemies, among their schoolfellows.

Frantz de Galais is in some respects the oddest character in the novel. He appears to represent a perpetual adolescent, but though he is the only character in the book whose adventures end up happily, he is by no means one of the most convincing characters. He suddenly turns up as a temporary pupil at the school. There is nothing to show that he gave any name, real or invented, to M. Seurel. He is wearing the bandage that was put on after his attempted suicide at the end of the *fête*. It serves as a disguise. In spite of the fact that they had met, that Meaulnes knew his name and who he was, it is not until just before his departure when he takes off his disguise that Meaulnes discovers who he is. He is accompanied by his pierrot, whose name becomes known. They are both described as 'bohemians' and live together in the carriage in which they have come to Saint-Agathe. Their activities are varied. Before Frantz appears in the school they organize a riot during which Frantz captures the map which Meaulnes has been trying, quite unsuccessfully, to draw in order to find his way back to the 'domain'. In order to provide food for themselves, the pierrot indulges in stealing fowls and rabbits belonging to local inhabitants. The visit ends with a performance by the couple in a tent, which they put up by their carriage, consisting of 'pantomimes . . . chansons . . . fantaisies équestres', and also compared to a 'circus'.

Frantz, the temporary pupil, begins by adopting a hostile

attitude to Meaulnes whom he recognises from the first, but rather oddly is not recognised by him. In addition to the premature riot, he organises for no explained reason at attack on Meaulnes and François at the school, ousts Meaulnes as the schoolboys' leader and adopts the position himself. It is followed by a sudden switch. In spite of his continued disguise, Frantz becomes their friend. He returns the map, pretending that he has completed it to the best of his ability. Although he mentions that he was at the *fête,* which somewhat oddly reveals nothing of his personality to Meaulnes, he pretends that he does not know the name of the 'domain' or its exact whereabouts. Instead, he gives Meaulnes an address in Paris where Yvonne sometimes stays, which is responsible for throwing him completely off the track. This is the start, as we shall see, of the disastrous series of misunderstandings, mistakes and pursuits down the blind alleys which follow. In spite of this, we must not overlook the fact that it is at the close of the 'circus' that Frantz's identity is at last disclosed to Meaulnes. This makes him feel that notwithstanding Frantz's pretended doubts about the whereabouts of the 'domain', the two of them will be able to go back to it together. He rises early in the next morning, makes his way to the place where the carriage was, only to find that the 'bohemian' couple have departed.

Although the 'domain' was only a comparatively short distance from Sainte-Agathe and turns out to be well-known to local inhabitants, Meaulnes never makes any enquiries on his own. The result of his failure to do so and Frantz's unexplained failure to come clean on the matter is that Meaulnes persuades his mother to remove him from the school so that he can follow Frantz's suggestion and try to find Yvonne in Paris.

This leads to the conclusion that the apparent impossibility of locating the 'domain' is one of the most serious technical weaknesses of the novel. If Meaulnes had made enquiries, he would undoubtedly have found his way back to the 'domain' at once, which would presumably have made the rest of the novel, as we know it, impossible. In spite, however, of the technical weakness that goes with it, there is another point which deserves emphasis. We have the impression—an impression that could only have come after completing the reading of the novel—that *unconsciously* Meaulnes was ceasing to be mesmerized by Yvonne, which will turn out to be the cause of the novel's tragedy.

François's comment on Meaulnes's departure is illuminating:

> I noticed a strange thing mingling with the sadness that swept over me. It was like a feeling of liberation. Now that Meaulnes had gone and the whole adventure was over and done with, it seemed as though I had been delivered from that peculiar anxiety, that mysterious concern which had prevented me from behaving like a normal person.

His comment is illuminating in the sense that though a sound, well-balanced young man, François becomes in spite of it involved in something like changes and conflicts of feeling which are the result of the very different attitude of Meaulnes. The passage is, indeed, something like the breaking of a spell. The moment that Meaulnes has gone, François is accepted again by the other pupils as one of themselves and the riddle of 'the mysterious domain' is solved. When he hears the story, Jasmin Delouche at once recognises the 'domain' not as a 'domain without a name', but as Sablonnières and knows exactly where it is. It transpires that Yvonne de Galais is a customer at a shop kept by one of François' uncles, that another uncle and aunt were actually present at the *fête* when Meaulnes met Yvonne, and that Frantz's lost fiancée had spent some months with them after the break with him.

We then hear of François' first meeting with Yvonne, which takes place in the shop belonging to his uncle. He is deeply moved by her from the start, but there are a series of subtle comments which look forward to what is to come. Although François will describe her at the end of the novel as the person 'who had been the fairy, the princess and the mysterious love for the whole of our adolescence' and though he himself will fall passionately though innocently in love with her, his reactions at the first meeting are very different from Meaulnes's or from those that he himself has caught from Meaulnes. He thinks that she is 'perhaps the most beautiful girl who has ever lived in this world', but he is no longer an adolescent and does not imagine for a moment that she belongs to a mysterious world. On the contrary, it is evident that she belongs to the ordinary world, that she is the daughter of a local landowner or, as we shall see, a former landowner, and a normal member of the village community. It is emphasised by her own comments. When she hears that François is about to become a schoolmaster, she observes that if her father would allow her to become a schoolmistress, 'I wouldn't encourage school children to go wandering all over the world, as you probably will, M. Seurel, when you are an assistant schoolmaster. I should teach them to discover the happiness which is under their noses even if it doesn't look like happiness . . .'

This is clearly a plea for ordinary everyday life instead of a life of romantic adventure. It also suggests that without knowing it, Yvonne is referring to Meaulnes's stay in Paris and his forthcoming visit to Germany—incidentally, a country celebrated for its legendary romantic pursuits—with Frantz in search of the lost fiancée, which François will try unsuccessfully to prevent. It prepares the way for an even more striking remark. 'She felt our embarrassment', we are told, 'stopped, bit her lip, lowered her head and then smiled as though she was teasing us' and said: 'There is perhaps some big mad young man who is looking for me at the end of the world while I am here, in Madame Florentin's shop, under this lamp, and while my old horse is waiting for me at the door'. It suggests that she is making a deliberately comic reference to her first meeting with Meaulnes. It makes François say: 'Perhaps this big young man is someone whom I know?' The conversation is then interrupted (intentionally from the novelist's point of view) by the arrival of fresh people in the shop, which brings the meeting to an end. It is, however, a clear indication that in spite of Yvonne's affection for him, Meaulnes's strange attitude was confined to himself, and that though François had been influenced by it in spite of the fact that he had not then seen Yvonne, he freed himself as soon as Meaulnes left the school or, as he himself put it: 'I had the impression that my adolescence had disappeared for ever'.

One of the merits of the novel, as already suggested, is its symbols, which seem to look backwards and forwards to one another. Although François' first meeting with Yvonne is a prelude to the local 'picnic', which is one of the most important events in the novel, it is desirable to look back to an ap-

parently minor event. It occurs in a chapter called, significantly,
'A la Recherche du Sentier Perdu', which immediately precedes
the chapter describing Meaulnes's departure from the school.
In spite of his coming departure, Meaulnes had gone off on his
own to look once again for the way to the 'domain'. François
abandoned the party of schoolboys who were in charge of his
father and who seemed to be looking for shells washed up by
stream water and the like, and gave himself up to the following
reflexions:

> Je cherche quelque chose de plus mystérieux encore. C'est le
> passage dont il est question dans les livres, l'ancien chemin ob-
> strué, celui dont le prince harassé de fatigue n'a pu trouver
> l'entrée ... Et soudain, en écartant, dans le feuillage profond,
> les branches, avec ce geste hésitant des mains à hauteur du visage
> inégalement écartées, on l'aperçoit comme une longue avenue
> sombre dont la sortie est un rond de lumière tout petit.

> [I was looking for something still more mysterious. It was the
> path that we read about in books, the ancient blocked path, the
> one to which the prince, overcome by fatigue, has not been able
> to find the entrance ... And suddenly, as you push aside the
> bushes and hold them, with a hesitating movement of the hands,
> stretched out unequally at the height of your face, you see what
> looks like a dark avenue whose exit was a tiny circle of light.]

The reference to 'books' suggests that François has in mind
the legendary story of a prince (presumably on horseback) engaged in a 'quest' not for the Holy Grail, but for a 'princess'
who is hidden in a building to which he is trying unsuccessfully to find his way. His description of the 'blocked path' and
the 'dark avenue' seems to refer to the fact that Meaulnes found
his way by chance to the 'domain' where his own legend started,
while the 'tiny circle of light' may well refer to the feeling of
uncertainty provoked on François' part by Meaulnes's departure from school in order to go on prying round in the same
obscurity in Paris.

This looks forward to the way in which the zealous François
brings Yvonne and Meaulnes together again, but shows that in
spite of his generosity it will lead to disaster. The picnic is
arranged by François' uncle, who tells Yvonne in advance:

'Mademoiselle, you will be coming on horseback; it has been agreed with M. de Galais.'

He evidently thinks that the sight of her arriving on horseback will show that she is one of the outstanding figures at the 'picnic', but we see at once from François' description of her arrival that it has the opposite effect:

> Et au premier détour j'aperçus Yvonne de Galais, montée en amazone sur son vieux cheval blanc, si fringant ce matin-là qu'elle était obligée de tirer sur les rênes pour l'empêcher de trotter. A la tête du cheval, péniblement, en silence, marchait M. de Galais. Sans doute ils avaient dû se relayer sur la route, chacun à tour de rôle se servant de la vieille monture.

> [And at the first turning I caught sight of Yvonne de Galais riding side-saddle on her old white horse, which was so lively that morning that she was obliged to tug at the reins to stop it from breaking into a trot. At the horse's head M. de Galais was walking painfully and silently. No doubt they had had to help one another on the way by taking it in turns to make use of the old mount.]

The description of Yvonne's arrival is evidently a reference to the fable of the prince and the lost princess, but with a significant change. Instead of the man riding, it is the non-princess mounted not on an impressive steed, but riding side-saddle on a broken-down old cart horse, the only survivor of the stables of the family which has fallen on evil days, and she has to share it with her father. This disposes of the flattering view of François' uncle and emphasises the fact, as we have already seen, that there is nothing romantic about Yvonne, who though highly attractive is a normal and thoroughly respectable member of the village community.

The fable of the prince goes still further. It is evident that Meaulnes's visit to Paris, which we do not hear about until far too late, has demolished his romantic outlook. The conclusion that one reaches therefore is that the fable of the prince looking unsuccessfully for the 'princess' and Yvonne riding side-saddle on a broken-down old cart horse point to the tragedy which in different ways will overtake both of them. Yvonne's coming tragedy is already suggested by the fact that the father and daughter are so ashamed of the horse's appearance that they take care to separate it from the horses of other guests by tying it to a tree by itself. Yvonne enlarges on the position when she says to François:

> 'I only want you to see old Bélissaire, and not to put him with the other horses. First of all he is too ugly and too old, and on top of that I am afraid of his being injured by one of the others. It is the only horse I have to ride, and when he dies I shall not ride a horse any more.'

We can see that the sight of the broken-down old horse and Yvonne's decision to give up riding when he dies are signs of the fundamental change in the very heart of the novel. The *fête,* as we already know, created a series of illusions. What we are now going to find is that the 'picnic' works in the opposite direction and is something like complete disillusionment. The worst thing about it is the extraordinary behaviour of Meaulnes. François' devotion to his friend has brought him back to the beloved, or supposed beloved, but instead of being carried away by joy he is sullen, boorish and even gives the impression of being a stranger:

> Why [asks François] did the big Meaulnes seem like a stranger, like someone who had failed to find what he was seeking and whom nothing else interested? Three years before he would have been unable to face the happiness in front of him without being afraid, without going out of his mind perhaps with joy. Where had this emptiness, this sense of distance, this incapacity for happiness come from that one sensed in him at this time?

There is clearly a difference between the use of the word 'stranger' in the account of the *fête* and its use in the present context. At the *fête* Meaulnes had the impression that he had escaped from the everyday world and had entered as a 'stranger' into a new and mysterious world. At the 'picnic' he turns out to be a 'stranger' who is completely out of place in the ordinary world, not because there is anything remarkable about him, but because he is a clumsy, unsociable character who simply doesn't fit in. It must be remembered that Meaulnes's feeling at the *fête* was purely *personal,* that in spite of Yvonne's charm nobody except Meaulnes had the impression, or rather the illusion, that she was a 'fairy' or a 'princess'. This and the physical destruction of the supposedly 'mysterious domain', already hinted at earlier, as we saw, explains at least in part Meaulnes's disillusionment and his extraordinary behaviour. For this is the point at which the curve of the book dips steeply. Meaulnes seems determined to wreck everything. He presses the unhappy girl with questions about the destruction of the 'domain', which to her are simply embarrassing questions about purely family misfortunes:

> And every time the girl, who was in a state of agony, had to repeat that everything had disappeared: the old house, so strange and complicated, demolished; the big pool, dried up and filled in; the children with their costumes, gone away.

Again:

> 'Already M. de Galais was ruined without our knowing it . . . Mme de Galais is dead and we lost all our friends in the matter of a day'.

It is the fading of a dream: the house where it had all happened, gone; the pool in which Maulnes had once admired his own reflexion, significantly 'dried up and filled in'.

It is matched by a minor or rather a semi-image:

> On the other side of the river the banks were formed by grey, abrupt rocky hills; and on the most distant of them one discovered among the pines, some romantic little châteaux with turrets.

This suggests that romanticism is moving away into the distance.

The worst incident comes at the end of the 'picnic'. It is suddenly discovered that owing to faulty tying up the old horse has fallen and hurt itself. Meaulnes, the countryman who is expert in such things, rushes to the rescue and releases it, but not without some stinging comments on the way that it has been tied up. He learns that it was done by Yvonne's father:

I thought that he would change his tone and apologise [says the narrator]. He breathed for a moment. Then I saw that he was taking a savage pleasure in making things worse, wrecking everything for ever by saying:

'Well, I can hardly congratulate you on the job'.

Nevertheless, the same evening he asks, 'in tears', as we are told, for Yvonne's hand and is accepted.

'In tears', as used here, seems to be a sign of Maulnes's disillusionment and loss of love. It looks forward to his changed behaviour towards Yvonne, beginning with the unexciting engagement.

5

The engagement lasted five months. We hear, significantly, that it was 'peaceful, as peaceful as the first meeting was animated'. Meaulnes turned up, either on a bicycle or in a carriage, 'more than twice a week' to visit his fiancée, but we hear nothing about the meetings except that he took the same path that he had done at the time of his visit to the *fête.* The comment that 'happiness seems to have put his strange state of torment to sleep' only suggests that he was making some sort of attempt to overcome the disillusionment and loss of love reflected by his proposal of marriage made 'in tears'.

The marriage took place on a cold, windy day in February in the ancient chapel of Sablonnières. Once again there are no details. We simply hear that the family had lunch together and that the married couple retired by themselves to the drawing-room of the surviving part of the mansion.

In his handling of the wedding, the novelist uses two of his sea images. The first appears in Part III, Chapter 7, which is called 'Le Jour des Noces':

Pour celui qui ne veut pas être heureux, il n'a qu'à monter dans son grenier et entendre, jusqu'au soir, siffler les naufrages; il n'a qu'à s'en aller dehors, sur la route, et le vent lui rabattra son foulard sur la bouche comme un chaud baiser soudain qui le fera pleurer. Mais pour celui qui aime le bonheur, il y a, au bord d'un chemin boueux, la maison des Sablonnières, où mon ami est rentré avec Yvonne de Galais, qui est sa femme depuis midi.

[The person who does not wish to be happy has only to go up to his attic and he will hear, until the evening, the whistling of shipwrecks; he has only to go out of doors, along the path, and the wind will blow his scarf on to his mouth like a sudden warm kiss which will make him weep. But for one who is fond of his happiness, there is, on the edge of the muddy road, the house of the Sablonnières, where my friend Meaulnes has returned with Yvonne de Galais, who is his wife since midday.]

The second image appears in Chapter 9, called ironically, as it turns out, 'Les Gens Heureux':

Comme deux passagers dans un bâteau à la dérive, ils sont, dans le grand vent d'hiver, deux amants enfermés avec le bonheur.

[Like two passengers in a drifting vessel, they are, in the high winter wind, two lovers closed in with their happiness.]

The first image seems to hint that 'the person who does not wish to be happy' is Meaulnes, that the marriage will not give him what he wants, or has come to want, and suggests that after hiding away in an 'attic' the sound of 'shipwrecks' will draw him out and that once again he will face a hard life, ingeniously expressed by the contrast between 'chaud baiser' and 'pleurer'. The second sentence does not mean that Meaulnes is really the man 'qui aime le bonheur', but that if he had been, then the 'maison des Sablonnières' would have satisfied him completely.

The most important words in the second image are 'un bâteau à la dérive' and 'le grand vent d'hiver'. They mean that for the moment, but only for the moment, the lovers are cut off from reality, imagine that they are apparently 'enfermés avec le bonheur'. What is going to happen is that metaphorically, 'the high wind' will drive the 'drifting' vessel on to the rocks.

Seen together, the two images are in fact a clear indication of what is to come. When the married couple retired by themselves, François went for a stroll in the grounds with his friend Jasmin Delouch. He suddenly hears a strange whistle. He realises that it must have come from Frantz de Galais, who has not been seen for a long time, and that it must be the appeal to which he and Meaulnes once promised to respond. He meets Frantz and his clown, learns that in three days' time they will be leaving for Germany in search of Frantz's lost fiancée and that they hoped to reach Sablonnières before the marriage in order to persuade Meaulnes to join them. François does his best to persuade Frantz to keep away for a year and to go on the search with his clown in order to avoid upsetting the marriage. Frantz agrees and moves off. François thinks that he has been successful. It is left to Meaulnes to spoil the generous arrangement. He, too, has heard the whistle, realises that it comes from Frantz, and without Yvonne slips out of the house like 'the person who does not wish to be happy'. François takes him in hand, tells him that Frantz has agreed to stay away for a year and is trying to convince him that what he calls a 'childish' vow must not be allowed to trouble the marriage, when one of the most harrowing incidents in the novel takes place. Yvonne like the others has recognised her brother's whistle and guesses that Meaulnes has gone to join him. For her it is an alarm. She rushes out into the wood in the vain hope of averting what she suspects is a mortal threat to her happiness:

Il [Meaulnes] allait répondre, lorsqu'une figure échevelée, déchirée, hagarde, se dressa entre nous. C'était Mlle de Galais.[1] Elle avait dû courir, car elle avait le visage baigné de sueur. Elle avait dû tomber et se blesser, car elle avait le front écorché au-dessus de l'oeil droit et du sang figé dans les chevaux.

[He was about to answer when a dishevelled, scratched, haggard face rose between us. It was Mlle de Galais. She must have been running for her face was bathed in perspiration. She must have fallen and hurt herself because her forehead was grazed above the right eye and there was congealed blood in her hair.]

The spectacle of 'the dishevelled, scratched, haggard face' somehow looks back to the sight of her riding the broken-down old cart horse and the destruction of much of the estate, as it clearly looks forward to her death. The fact that Frantz has agreed to stay away and has actually left before the pair meet

---

[1] The narrator tells us that in spite of the marriage he intends to go on speaking of her as 'Mlle de Galais'—a sign of the husband's forthcoming abandonment of her.

does nothing to deter Meaulnes. After what will turn out to be the only night the married couple spend together, he sets out to join Frantz.

After the flight François becomes the devoted companion of the abandoned wife, himself the victim of a hopeless, unspoken love. The loved one is a poor, gentle, broken, suffering creature, as far removed as possible from any conception of a *princesse lointaine*. There is not a single letter or message from Meaulnes. Yvonne dies after the birth of her daughter. Her death is soon followed by that of her father. The outcome is that the only successful 'quest' is that of Frantz who, with the help of Meaulnes, finds his fiancée, marries her and returns with her to the security of the cottage known to the family as 'Frantz's house'. Meaulnes has won only to lose again. He collects his daughter and abandons the Sablonnières, possibly to become involved in more unfortunate adventures. François, the model of integrity, generosity and compassion for the misfortunes of his fellows, gets nothing. His is the grim task of reversing what should have been the happy situation of the bridegroom carrying the bride into the marriage home by carrying the body of the dead Yvonne downstairs in his arms because the house, or what is left of it, is too narrow for the coffin to be brought upstairs into the chamber of death. He writes his own epitaph:

> The taste of earth and death in my mouth, the weight of your body on my heart are all that remain for me of the great adventure and of you, Yvonne de Galais, young wife so greatly sought after and so loved . . .

6

One of the technical faults of the novel, as already indicated, is that it is not until after Yvonne's death that François discovers a diary that Meaulnes left behind him and we learn what he has been doing during the three years between leaving school and the 'picnic'. The result is that though it provides an explanation of his extraordinary behaviour when he rejoins Yvonne, its late appearance makes it less effective than it should have been.

The adventure began, 'the mysterious domain' was discovered, as we saw, by a schoolboy taking the wrong turning and
losing his way. Another wrong turning, which was the result of
Frantz's advice to move from the area of the Sablonnières to
Paris, plunges him into a very different kind of adventure.

He goes to the Paris address given him by Frantz and day
after day stations himself outside the house where Yvonne
sometimes stays in the hope of seeing her again—an obvious
recollection of Alain-Fournier's vigils outside the house in the
Boulevard Saint-Germain. It is there that, without knowing it
until a good deal later, he meets Frantz's ex-fiancée, Valentine,
who seems to have come there in the hope of finding Frantz.
She is living with her sister, and like her works as a seamstress.
Frantz was not her first love and there is a suggestion that in
the past she had not earned her living so innocently and might
even cease to do so in the future. Meaulnes and Valentine gradually form an attachment for one another. Although the attraction appears to be genuine, it was clearly the result of
chance. It could only have happened because they were both
waiting in the same place for their former lovers, neither of
whom turned up. It must also be added that in the case of
Meaulnes it was encouraged by Valentine's mistaken announcement that Yvonne was married, which is mentioned in the
second of Meaulnes's three letters to François which appear at
the end of Part II and is not given the emphasis that it deserves.

Valentine was first mentioned when her arrival was expected
at the *fête*. One of the children remarked:

> Mummy told me that she was wearing a black dress and a mus-
> lin collar and looked like a pretty pierrot.

This seems to link her distinctly to the pierrot at the *fête*,
particularly when two hundred and fifty pages later Meaulnes,
too, compares her to a somewhat different kind of pierrot:

> Delicate and grave, dressed in black with powder on her face
> and a muslin collar which made her look like a *guilty pierrot*.[1]
> An expression which was at once unhappy and malicious.

We know that the novelist used one of his own mistresses

[1] Italics mine.

called Jeanne as a model for Valentine. He goes out of his way to emphasise that, compared with Yvonne de Galais, Valentine is not 'innocent' or 'pure', which clearly reflects what he took to be the difference between Yvonne de Quiévrecourt and Jeanne. His treatment of the pair in the novel gives the impression that the two of them somehow represent sacred and profane love. In spite of Meaulnes's critical attitude, he and Valentine become engaged. Then there is a bitter quarrel which leads to the break-up of the engagement and the separation of the pair. In the novel it is provoked by Valentine's disclosure that she is Frantz's ex-fiancée, but in life it is evidently a vivid memory of Alain-Fournier's quarrels with his mistresses, whom he tried carefully to turn into copies of Yvonne de Quiévrecourt.

The relations between Meaulnes and Valentine are one of the most controversial incidents in the novel. Some critics have suggested that Meaulnes not only became engaged to Valentine, but was her lover. This has been denied by Isabelle Rivière.[1] It is evident, however, from the discarded fragment of one of the drafts included in *Miracles,* a posthumous collection of Alain-Fournier's miscellaneous writings, under the title of 'The Quarrel and the Night in the Cell', that Alain-Fournier did at one time intend Meaulnes unwittingly to seduce his friend's ex-fiancée, but changed his mind because he was determined to preserve his protagonist's 'purity', determined to preserve in the work of fiction what he had himself failed to preserve in life. Although it can be argued that the change improved the novel morally, there can be no doubt that it damaged it artistically and gave the latter part an unnecessary ambiguity. For Meaulnes's remorse and the intense emphasis on what he describes as his 'faute' are only comprehensible if he did in fact seduce Valentine or, what seems more probable in view of her past, was seduced by her. This applies equally to his extraordinary decision to abandon his wife the day after the wedding in order to help Frantz to find his ex-fiancée and make things up with her. For it is clear that neither Meaulnes's changed attitude to life, to be discussed presently, nor his schoolboy promise of help would have made him abandon his wife the day after marriage if he had not been Valentine's

[1] *Op. cit.,* pp. 118, 124.

lover, particularly as even if the search had ended with Valentine preferring her second ex-fiancée to Frantz it would have merely been an embarrassment to a married man!

Although there is an element of ambiguity in the novel, the last stages nevertheless throw remarkable light on both the novelist and his protagonist. François' statement that Valentine 'was the companion that, before his mysterious adventure, the "huntsman and peasant" who was the big Meaulnes, must have desired' shows that the *fête* must have been an illusion, that the intense attraction that he felt for Yvonne was a romantic impulse which belonged to the adolescent. Valentine would have made a much more suitable wife for the 'huntsman and peasant' precisely because though less beautiful than Yvonne she had considerably greater physical appeal. It is enlarged by another observation of François', who says that 'for Meaulnes, at that time, there remained only one love, the ill-satisfied love whom he had so cruelly rebuffed'. It explains his extraordinary behaviour at the 'picnic', which he was obliged to attend at the moment when he was apparently about to set out on his own accord to find Valentine not for himself, but for Frantz, though as he was still unmarried it could not have prevented Valentine from choosing him instead of Frantz if she had wished!

The resemblances between the novelist and his protagonist are clear. Alain-Fournier's passion for Yvonne de Quiévrecourt was as much an illusion or an adolescent dream as Meaulnes's for Yvonne de Galais. The girl, indeed, seems to have shown a greater insight into psychology than the young man when she said: 'We're children. We've been silly'. There is no evidence that he ever abandoned his devotion, or at any rate not to the extent of Meaulnes, but though he tried to turn mistresses into copies of Yvonne de Quiévrecourt and insisted on the necessity in life of 'purity', it did nothing to prevent his fall and he seems to have treated Jeanne nearly as cruelly as Meaulnes treated Yvonne de Galais.

7

Although Alain-Fournier had the misfortune not to win the Prix Goncourt, *Le Grand Meaulnes* has since become one of the most greatly and widely admired novels of the age. 'It has been translated into thirty-three different languages; it has been the subject of theses in such diverse universities as Montpellier, Neuchâtel, Brussels, Hamburg, Paris, London, Cambridge, Indiana and Melbourne'.[1] Thousands of copies have been sold in a paperback edition of the English translation. It not only inspired Albicocco's very popular film, but has been turned into a ballet now in the repertoire of the Royal Ballet Company of Sadler's Wells and has had several broadcasts as a radio play by the BBC.

What emerges from this is that though there are a number of technical faults in the novel, to which I have drawn attention and which have been admitted by many admirers, including Isabelle Rivière, they are only the kind of faults that one finds in a young writer and do nothing to undermine the compelling experience conveyed by the novel. Naturally this has not prevented a number of critics—usually academics—from launching an onslaught on the work as a whole. The most sustained attack of all comes from Léon Cellier in a short work called *'Le Grand Meaulnes' ou l'initiation manquée*. The essence of the attack is indicated by the subtitle. M. Cellier goes very thoroughly into the image of the 'quest', decides that Meaulnes is a 'nihilist' who through fear and lack of understanding wrecks everything, and concludes that because it is the story of a 'failed initiation', or failed 'quest', it is therefore a 'failed novel'. An unexpected answer to this approach is provided by Jessie Weston in *The Quest of the Holy Grail*, which was published in 1913, the year of publication of *Le Grand Meaulnes* (which was evidently unknown to her) and exactly fifty years before M. Cellier's attack on it:

Regarded, then, from a ritual point of view [she wrote], it seems clear that the Grail Quest should be reviewed primarily as an initiation story, as a search into the secret mystery of life; it is the record of an initiation *manqué(e)*.

What Jessie Weston is saying is that in the medieval stories the 'quest' always ended in failure, which in itself is a useful contribution to an understanding of this particular novel, which

[1] Robert Gibson: *The Land without a Name*, 1975, p. 283.

might be described as a modernised version of the legend with a secular goal.

We have seen that the 'quest' is the central theme of the novel and that it reminds us of the medieval 'quests'. We must now look again not only at their resemblances, but at their differences.

The medieval 'quests' were clearly religious in inspiration. The Grail was 'holy'. The knights were convinced that if they succeeded in finding it, its effect on the community would be in some way miraculous. We find something of the same kind in Meaulnes's conception. His 'quest', too, was an 'initiation story', a 'search into the secret of life'. In a passage already quoted he declared that he had already made a 'leap into Paradise', to which he gave a capital letter. 'I am convinced now', he went on, 'that when I had discovered the Domain without a Name, I had reached a height, a degree of perfection and purity that I shall never attain again.'

The differences lie largely in the application of the concept to modern life. The 'goal' is a girl who for all her virtues and her beauty has little in common with Dante's Beatrice and turns out, as we saw, to be 'ordinary'. This shows that it is the child's or adolescent's enthusiasm for romantic legends about mysterious sleeping beauties, captive princesses or *princesses lointaines* which created the illusion that there was something magical about the meeting with Yvonne, that the place was a *domaine mystérieux* which was really a childhood paradise like Baudelaire's 'vert paradis des amours enfantines'—a point emphasised incidentally by the mass of children at the *fête*.

'How', asked Meaulnes, 'could a man who has once made the leap into Paradise later adapt himself to everyday life?' The answer is that it was not a failure to reach the 'goal', but the return to 'everyday life' which dissipated the dream, showing that Meaulnes either had no vocation for discovering 'the secret mystery of life' or had once again taken the wrong turning. It was this that turned his 'quest' into a failure like that of medieval knights or, as both Jessie Weston and M. Cellier put it, an 'initiation manquée'. Indeed, Meaulnes himself speaks of 'mon aventure manquée', describes what was once 'le Domaine mystérieux' as 'le Domaine perdu' and concludes:

The frightful thought comes to me that I have renounced paradise and am in the process of marking time on the verge of hell.

It is an important statement. There can be no real doubt that at one time Valentine became Meaulnes's mistress as well as his fiancée, which was one of the main reasons for the failure of his 'quest'. It explains the return to 'everyday life' and the suggestion that he had 'renounced paradise' and was 'marking time on the verge of hell'. This makes it particularly unfortunate that a full account of his relations with Valentine was suppressed, possibly as a result of pressure from Isabelle Rivière.

Childhood or adolescence calls for a further comment. When François is trying to persuade Meaulnes not to abandon his bride—it is one of the moments when his role most strongly suggests the classical dramatist's confidant—he speaks of 'the terrible temptation of smashing on the spot the marvel that he had won'.

Childhood, as the poets have suggested, is a time when we may catch a fleeting glimpse of another and mysterious world beyond our own which is closed to us for ever once childhood has really ended. But childhood is also a time of senseless destruction when we are capable of throwing away our chances, our certainty of happiness from the same impulse that drives us to smash our toys. Whatever the nature of Meaulnes's *faute* and the feeling of guilt (as explained above) which makes him fly to Frantz's assistance at the expense of his wife's happiness, there is an element of wilful destruction behind the tragedy of *Le Grand Meaulnes*.

It can be summed up by a glance at the structure, divided into three parts. Part I deals with enchantment; Part II with frustration; Part III with disaster leading to the tragedy of the three protagonists and, ironically, to the success of the 'quest' of Frantz, who might be described as a child who preserves his toys instead of smashing them, but is unlikely ever to grow up into a mature man. We also see that the unsatisfactory placing of the account of Meaulnes's adventures in Paris at the end of Part III simply tells us belatedly of the way in which frustration of a double kind came to pass in Part II.

It is the glimpse, or imagined glimpse of an earthly paradise

and its agonising loss, expressed in the terms of a youthful love
affair, that makes *Le Grand Meaulnes* a unique novel. It has
been described as a 'minor masterpiece'. The formula is exact
provided that we realise that 'minor' is not in this case a de-
precatory word. It was the first novel of a young man and compared with the great masterpieces of European fiction it must
in a special sense rank as 'minor'. The great masterpieces bring
a new vision to literature which changes the pattern of experience: the minor masterpiece simply introduces a variation into
an existing pattern and uncovers a fresh corner of experience.
Yet they have one thing in common. It is the *finality* of their
vision. *Le Grand Meaulnes* gives final expression to what
Robert Gibson has well called 'that fleeting period of life...
between the end of youth and the beginning of full manhood'.[1]
For this reason its sensitiveness, its remarkable psychological insight and its poetry have exercised a subtle and pervasive influence on the work of the French novelists who followed
Alain-Fournier.

[1] *The Quest of Alain-Fournier*, 1953, p. 271.

RAYMOND RADIGUET

I. THE INFANT PRODIGY

'RAYMOND RADIGUET', said Jean Cocteau, 'shares with Arthur Rimbaud the terrible privilege of being a phenomenon of French literature. He is a sort of talking plant. In *Le Diable au corps* the plant describes the mystery of its roots. In *Le Bal du comte d'Orgel* the plant produces its flower. And its perfume is words.'[1]

It is in many ways a typical Cocteau pronouncement: an engaging mixture of exaggeration and acuteness. It brings out the remarkable qualities of Radiguet's first novel, is right in suggesting that it forms a pair with the second novel, but is mistaken in claiming that the second novel is superior to the first on account of the gentleness which is supposed to be the result of a contrast between 'roots' and 'flowers'. The reference to 'the terrible privilege of being a phenomenon of French literature' is a reflection of the extravagant atmosphere of the 1920s, the noisy meetings of writers at the *Boeuf sur le Toit* in the Rue Boissy d'Anglas and the performance of some of them at Proust's less reputable establishment in the same historic street.

The beginnings of the 'phenomenon' were inauspicious. Radiguet was born at Parc-Saint-Maur on the banks of the Marne on June 18, 1903, was the son of a cartoonist and the eldest of ten children, three of whom seem to have been born after his early death. At the age of six he went to a local primary school where he distinguished himself at everything except drawing and singing, and won a scholarship to the Lycée Charlemagne in Paris in 1914. At the Lycée his masters thought poorly of him and he frequently played truant like the hero of his first novel. In 1917 his father decided to take him away from school and educate him, or rather finish his education himself at home. During the war Radiguet read omnivorously and laid the foundations of a literary career.

He also collected the raw material for his first novel. It is

[1] In his preface to Keith Goesch's *Radiguet avec des textes inédits*, 1955, p. vii.

unlikely that we shall ever have a completely accurate version of the love story, but a good many of the facts were uncovered by relentlessly inquisitive journalists and served up to readers of *Le Figaro Littéraire, Paris-Match* and *Arts-Spectacles* in a collection of articles published in 1953-54 to mark the fiftieth anniversary of the novelist's birth. This does not mean that they were flattering. The titles of some of them were deliberately provocative: 'From *Le Diable au corps* was born a terrible family drama'; 'In the heroine of *Le Diable au corps* a man has recognised his wife'; '*Le Diable au corps* reveals its secret'.

It seems that as early as 1912, when he was only nine years old, Radiguet wrote something like a love letter to one of his teachers at the primary school, who became known to us as Alice S. and who is believed to have had a flirtation with Radiguet's father before she took on the son. The liaison began in 1917, the year in which Alice like Marthe in the novel married a soldier who was home on leave from the front and who is known in the novel as Jacques, when she was nearly twenty-five and Radiguet only fourteen—ages changed to nineteen and fifteen in the novel. The parting seems to have taken place in 1918, a few months before the end of the war.

It was not the end of the trouble. The husband found out about the liaison, which cast a gloom over the marriage. He was inclined to beat up his wife and on one occasion actually broke her arm. In spite of his brutality, he tried to rehabilitate her after her death in 1952, which was only two years before his own death. He went to see Roland Dorgelès, but was unable to produce any evidence in her favour except a copy of *Le Diable au corps* with his own annotations, which indicate that he took part in a number of the minor incidents attributed to the narrator in the novel. This suggests that in spite of the absence of any proof, there may have been some truth in his allegation that a diary, which his wife kept during the war, was stolen by Radiguet and used by him in writing the novel.

One of the main reasons for Gaston S.'s ill-treatment of his wife was his doubts about the legitimacy of the son who was the elder of the couple's two children. It remains a complete mystery. Cocteau maintained stoutly that it was not Radiguet's child because the novelist had never mentioned it to him.

The wife herself spoke bitterly about Radiguet at one of the interviews with journalists shortly before her death. She described him as a 'very ordinary boy'. 'If he had lived', she went on, 'I would have kept a grip on him! I had already given him a dressing down. He was a boy who would have gone to any lengths to make a career for himself. He wasn't interesting'. Although she denied that they had had a love affair, there has never been any serious doubt about it and the bitterness of her words to the journalist sound very much like those of a woman who had been abandoned by her lover. We also know that at the time when the liaison came to an end she made André Salmon her confidant and that he had to spend a good deal of his time listening to her lamentations about Radiguet's abandonment of her. There was nothing that he could do about it, but though he was sympathetic to Radiguet at the start of his literary career, it did not prevent him from describing him, in his memoirs, as Alice's 'cruel little lover', or saying that he had gone out of his way to shock people by writing 'the story of a perverse child going to bed with the wife of a *pauvre con du front*'.

Radiguet himself denied that the novel was a 'confession' or anything more than a 'false autobiography'. We also know that one of his critics, who had no doubts about the love affair, went to the other extreme by expressing surprise that the novel ended with the death of Marthe because it was the reverse of what happened in life.[1] It is a fair inference that Radiguet's own position is best described by his mother. 'There was truth in the story', said Mme Maurice Radiguet, 'but many of the things are inventions'.

Radiguet's career as a writer began in 1918. He used to bring his father's cartoons to André Salmon, who after an early demobilisation in 1917 had become editor of *L'Intransigeant*. He shrewdly took advantage of his meetings with the then sympathetic editor by suggesting that he, too, might contribute drawings to the newspaper and also showed him some of his poems. André Salmon used a few of the drawings in spite of the fact that drawing was one of Radiguet's two weak subjects at the primary school, but did not feel able to publish his poems. He

[1] Clément Borgal: *Radiguet*, 1968, p. 73.

did, however, advise him to take up journalism and seems to have helped him to make contact with some minor reviews to which he contributed poems, stories and literary articles, and became editorial secretary of one of them for six months.

This was also the time, as already suggested, when he entered literary society. André Salmon claims to have introduced him to Max Jacob, who sent him to see Jean Cocteau, which was the beginning of a friendship which lasted for the rest of his life and was of the greatest importance to both of them.

His first volume of poetry was published under the title of *Les Joues en feu* in 1920 and was republished posthumously in an extensively revised edition in 1925. When he reviewed Radiguet's *Oeuvres complètes* in 1952, Robert Kemp declared that none of the early works deserved reprinting. This is a trifle hard. I do not myself think that *Les Joues en feu* or any of the other early writings are impressive, but Radiguet's particular handling of language—it might almost be described as ascetic in the age of Dada—reveals already the influence of classic poets and novelists which was to play an important part in the two novels.

Radiguet abandoned poetry in 1921. He had already made a start in another direction some time earlier. In a letter to Jacques Doucet on December 22, 1919, he explained that he was sending him a short chronicle by the same post because 'at the moment I am working on a novel'. The inference is that he was drafting the opening of *Le Diable au corps,* which still had a long way to go. Cocteau described Radiguet as being at once his master and his pupil. He was right. There can be little doubt that as a novelist he owed a good deal to him. What is clearer still is that Radiguet's debt to him was even more important. It is not merely that without Cocteau's help his two novels would have been less successful. It means that without the pressure that Cocteau brought to bear on him they might never have been finished. When they were on holiday in the summer of 1921 at Le Piquey, near Arcachon, Cocteau seems to have shut him up in a room and made him concentrate on writing. On their return to Paris, he became his agent. He was dissatisfied with his negotiations with the first publishing firm and went to Bernard Grasset, who was filled with enthusiasm for *Le Diable au corps,* accepted the novel at once, drew up a contract and arranged a monthly payment of fifteen hundred francs, which was a help to Radiguet's family as well as enabling him to enjoy life himself.

The arrangement did not lead to rapid publication. It was felt that the end of the novel needed some revision. We have no information about the changes, but the revision was made and the novel published on March 10, 1923. Grasset employed all the resources of modern publicity to launch his infant prodigy, but though the book caused a considerable stir the publisher seems to have gone too far and provoked reviewers who found it 'heartless', 'cynical' and 'immoral'. The references by an adolescent to the war and to the seduction of a soldier's wife, when the husband was fighting for France at the front, inevitably caused great offence in some quarters, and an association of ex-service men sent a telegram of protest when the novel won a minor literary prize.

Radiguet managed to complete his second novel before his death from typhoid fever on December 12, 1923. It was first published in *La Nouvelle Revue Française* in two instalments in June and July, 1924, with a commentary by Jacques Rivière, the review's most distinguished editor, who was himself to succumb to the same illness a little more than six months later in February, 1925. If the commentary did a little less than justice to Radiguet, it may have been because both his novels were in a different class from Rivière's *Aimée*, an autobiographical novel about a chaste triangular love affair for which the novelist, his wife and Yvonne Gallimard, who was the wife of Rivière's own publisher, served as models.

II. THE NOVELIST

1 *Le Diable au corps*

. . . ce drame de l'avant-saison du coeur.—Raymond Radiguet

'I SHALL be severely reproached for what I have done', runs the opening sentence of *Le Diable au corps*. 'But how can I help it? Was it my fault that I was twelve years old a few months before the war broke out? The difficulties that I encountered during that extraordinary period were no doubt of a kind which no one ever experienced at that age; but since there is nothing on earth which in spite of appearances is strong enough to age us, it was as a child that I behaved in an adventure which would have embarrassed a grown man. I am not the only one. And my friends will retain a memory of the period which is not the same as that of their elders. Let those who are already feeling angry with me realise that the war was for so many young boys a four-year holiday'.

It is an admirable start and touches on some of the main issues. Radiguet's achievement lies in the veracity and convincingness with which he presents a child's vision of the world and his refusal to allow the naked vision to be toned down or blurred by empty moralising or by literary tricks borrowed from the repertoire of other writers. He writes with a child's vividness and directness, and he reveals the child's ruthless disregard for other peoples' feelings. It follows that it is not sufficient to describe the novel, as has been done, as 'le seul livre *vrai* que nous ayons sur l'adolescence'. What is outstanding is that the story of an adolescent love affair is told by an adolescent with the power and psychological insight which belong to a gifted and mature novelist.

We must go on to say that too little attention has been paid to the setting and structure of the novel. Wartime France means that there will be a relaxation of discipline and that children will be able to behave more or less as they choose during what appears to them something like an exceptionally long holiday, but which may well end in disaster for them (as it does for the narrator) simply on account of the slackening of discipline.

Radiguet enlarges on the situation by the ingenious use of the images of the cat, which are particularly effective in a novel about adolescent love:

> Mes parents condamnaient plutôt la camaraderie mixte. La sensualité qui naît avec nous et se manifeste encore aveugle, y gagna au lieu d'y perdre.
>
> Je n'ai jamais été un rêveur. Ce qui semble rêve aux autres, plus crédules, me paraissait à moi aussi réel que le fromage au chat, malgré la cloche de verre. Pourtant la cloche existe.
>
> La cloche se cassant, le chat en profite, même si ce sont ses maîtres qui la cassent, et s'y coupent les mains.
>
> Les vraies vacances approchaient, et je m'en occupais fort peu puisque c'était pour moi le même régime. Le chat regardait toujours le fromage sous la cloche. Mais vint la guerre. Elle brisa la cloche. Les maîtres eurent d'autres chats à fouetter et le chat se réjouit.

> [My parents were more or less opposed to boys and girls going about together. Sensuality, which is in us from birth and makes its appearance while still blind, increases in us rather than diminishes.
>
> I have never been a dreamer. What seems like a dream to others, who are more credulous, seemed to me to be as real as the cheese is to a cat in spite of the glass dome over the cheese platter. Nevertheless the dome exists.
>
> When the dome breaks, the cat benefits, even if it is its masters who break it and cut their hands.
>
> The real holidays were approaching, and I paid little attention to them because for me it was the same régime. The cat went on looking at the cheese under the dome. Then came the war. She broke the dome. The masters had other cats to flog and the cat rejoiced.]

In what is really a piece of self-criticism, the narrator sees himself as a cat mischievously trying to find a way of extracting cheese from under the dome in order to have a pleasant little meal consisting, significantly in view of what is to come, of the masters' food. The second part of the first cat image is an indication of the way in which discipline will be neglected by masters whose clumsiness or blunders lead to the breaking of the dome for the benefit of the cat and damage to themselves. The last image shows that once war has broken out, it is the 'cat' who breaks the dome and can do so with impunity because the 'masters' are taken up with wartime activities and are treating the enemy as 'the other cats'.

The image of the cat looking hungrily at the cheese which it is prevented from reaching by the glass dome stands of course for an adolescent looking hungrily at a girl, even if his 'sensuality', which is inborn like a cat's taste for cheese, is still 'blind', but is unable to reach her because she is carefully protected under the 'dome' which is her parents' home. The war will have the same effect as the smashing of the 'dome', except that fortunately for the couple there will be no actual 'smashing'. After her marriage the girl will go to live in her husband's flat. She will naturally be alone because the husband will spend most of his time at the front, but she will take a major step in developing the love affair by inviting the 'cat' to visit her in the new 'dome'! Her family will know virtually nothing about the liaison even in its last stages and the narrator's own family will turn a blind eye and refuse to intervene.

There are two pre-war events which in different ways look forward to what is to come. The first of them is related, significantly, between the appearance of the two 'cat' images. The narrator is under twelve when he is scolded for writing a love letter to one of the little girls at his primary school, which is evidently a substitution for the early letter to Alice. His reactions are a mixture of boldness, embarrassment and deception. They show what sort of a person he is and what we can expect to happen when at the age of fifteen, he meets the soldier's nineteen-year-old fiancée.

The importance that Radiguet attaches to the preludes to war and their effect on peoples' inborn tendencies is apparent from an incident of a more general nature which occupies the whole of Chapter 2. On the evening of July 14, 1914, a local councillor's servant goes mad, climbs on to the roof of the house, wanders round it giving unearthly wailings and throwing slates at the crowd assembled below. When she throws herself down through the councillor's failure to rescue her and the narrator hears cries of 'She's still alive', he faints and falls off his father's shoulders, which looks forward to his fainting fit when he hears at the end of the novel his brothers shouting that Marthe is dead.

The narrator meets Marthe for the first time in 1917, when the two families are on a Sunday outing together. The couple discuss Baudelaire and Verlaine, the poets they admire, but of whom Marthe's fiancé and her parents disapprove. This prompts the observation:

> I was glad to find that we had a secret, and I, who am timid, began to feel tyrannical.

'Timid' and 'tyrannical' are keywords. They reflect the vacillations and doubts about the narrator's real feelings for Marthe and the aggressiveness which is characteristic of a child and will play an important part in the novel. He keeps on repeating to himself at the first meeting that Marthe does not 'intimidate' him and that he is only prevented from kissing her by the presence of her parents, then admits:

> What luck that I was not alone with her! For I still should not have dared to kiss her, and there would have been no excuse.
> That's how the timid person cheats.

He soon moves in the opposite direction and displays the 'tyrannical' element. He has seen some of Marthe's water colours before the meeting which her father had brought to his parents' house so that they could be used for a wartime charity. The attraction that he had come to feel for her does not prevent him from remarking candidly in recalling them:

> Ces aquarelles était sans nulle recherche; on y sentait la bonne élève du cours de dessin, tirant la langue, léchant les pinceaux.

> [These water colours were without any studied elegance; they gave the impression of a good pupil at a drawing class, sticking out her tongue, licking the brushes.]

When he happens to meet Marthe unexpectedly in Paris on

his way to school, decides to play truant and accepts her invitation to help her choose furniture for the marriage flat, he says:

> Cette obligation d'accompagner Marthe m'apparut comme une malchance. Il fallait donc l'aider à choisir une chambre pour elle et un autre! Puis, j'entrevis le moyen de choisir une chambre pour Marthe et pour moi . . .
> Son fiancé goûtáit le style Louis XV.
> Le mauvais goût de Marthe était autre; elle aurait plutôt versé dans le japonais. Il me fallut donc les combattre tous les deux . . .
> J'étais parvenu à transformer, meuble à meuble, ce mariage d'amour, ou plutôt d'amourette, en un mariage de raison, et lequel!

> [The obligation to accompany Marthe seemed to me unfortunate. It meant helping her to choose a room for herself and another! Then I saw the means of choosing a room for Marthe and for me . . .
> Her fiancé's taste was for the style Louis XV.
> Marthe's bad taste was of another kind; she was rather inclined to go in for the Japanese. It was therefore necessary for me to combat the pair of them . . .
> I succeeded in transforming, piece by piece, this love marriage, or rather this marriage of infatuation, into a marriage of reason—and what a one!]

The first thing that strikes us in this passage is the statement that 'I saw the means of choosing a room for Marthe and for me', which is exactly what happened. We can go on to observe that although his comments might be described as brazen, there is nothing that is really heartless about the narrator. We shall find that as his feeling for Marthe deepens, he will revoke his criticisms and will even regret his own taste for the furniture that he helped to choose, dismissing it as 'odious' and saying that it was not chosen for his pleasure, but simply in order to 'displease Jacques'. We also find that he is completely honest and never attempts to conceal from himself or excuse the harshness that he not infrequently displays towards Marthe. On one occasion during a visit to her at the husband's flat he is greatly shocked when he sees her fling some of her husband's letters into the fire unread. It looks forward to an incident on his side which among other things shows the ingenious construction of the novel. He is unable to see Marthe for the time being because she is with her husband, who is on leave. A letter arrives from her:

> Un jour, impatienté par ma faiblesse, et dans un mouvement de rage, je déchirai une lettre sans la lire. Dès que les morceaux de papier eurent jonché le jardin, je me précipitai à quatre pattes. La lettre contenait une photographie de Marthe. Moi si superstitieux et qui interprétais les faits les plus minces dans un sens tragique, j'avais déchiré ce visage. J'y vis un avertissement du Ciel. Mes transes ne se calmèrent qu'après avoir passé quatre heures à recoller la lettre et le portrait. Jamais je n'avais fourni un tel effort. La crainte qu'il arrivât un malheur à Marthe me soutint pendant ce travail absurde qui me brouillait les yeux et les nerfs.

> [One day, made impatient by my feebleness, and in a movement of rage, I tore up a letter without reading it. As soon as the bits of paper were scattered about the garden, I flung myself down on all fours. The letter contained a photograph of Marthe. I who was so superstitious and interpreted the tiniest facts in a tragic sense, had torn up this face. I saw in it a warning from Heaven. My trances did not calm themselves until I had spent four hours sticking the letter and the portrait together again. Never had I made such an effort. The fear that misfortune had fallen on Marthe kept me going during this absurd undertaking which jumbled my eyes and my nerves.]

It is a striking passage. Marthe had destroyed an unread letter from her husband, but was entirely unrepentant because she no longer loved him. She was merely glad to be persuaded by the narrator not to destroy a second letter, because it announced that the husband's leave had been postponed for a month, which pleased her. The narrator's love for Marthe puts him in a very different position. It was his practice to keep himself waiting for fifteen minutes between opening the envelope and reading the letter, which was something like a mild form of penance. On this occasion he is suddenly carried away by a feeling of impatience provoked by his own feebleness and is overcome with horror at what he has done. He spends four hours trying to put the letter and picture together again. It is the destruction of Marthe's portrait which makes the worst effect on him. The idea that it is a warning from Heaven is important: it clearly looks forward to the destruction of Marthe herself by her premature death.

The impact of the first meeting on the narrator is considerable, but his feelings are anything but clear to himself, or rather are blind. When he goes to school the day after his very first meeting with Marthe, he avoids his friend René:

> Feeling love for Marthe, I took it away from René, from my parents, from my sisters.

Nobody's feelings for the loved one can be the same as those for friends or relations. What is important about the statement is the way in which it shows that even the beginning of a love affair absorbs a person completely and isolates him or her from everybody else.

A change, or rather an apparent change, takes place the following day. He was supposed to go to Marthe's home on the Thursday to deliver a promised copy of Rimbaud's poetry. He is so impatient that he turns up on the Tuesday and finds that she is out with her fiancé. He jumps to the conclusion that he will never have a chance of seeing her again:

> ... I forced myself not to think about Marthe any more, with the result that I thought of no one but her.

It is an example of his particular form of insight, which shows that his real preoccupations are exactly the reverse of what he imagines them to be. In other words there is a marked contrast between the genuine inner and the misleading outer reactions.

It becomes still more radical during the period which follows the purchase of the furniture, and the couple are out of touch on account of the forthcoming marriage:

> ... if I believed that I no longer loved Marthe, at least I considered that she was the only love who would have been worthy of me. That is to say, I still loved her.

When the couple are married, the husband out of the way again at the front and Marthe living in the new flat, she takes the initiative by telling the narrator in a letter that she is surprised at his silence and inviting him to come and see her. The meetings do not lead to any immediate change in his imagined feelings:

> My mind gradually became sluggish when I was with her. I found her different. It meant that now that I felt sure that I no longer loved her, I was beginning to love her.

The way in which he says on two occasions that he believed that he 'no longer loved Marthe', but in reality 'still loved her' or was 'beginning to love her', is a typical illustration of the extreme complexity of his feelings. It shows that he is moving in the opposite direction to the one he imagines:

> Suddenly, I felt better. This sudden change would have opened the eyes of every other person: I did not see that I was in love Marthe. On the contrary, I regarded it as a proof that my love was dead, and that a beautiful friendship was replacing it. This long view of friendship made me admit suddenly how criminal another feeling would have been, wounding the man who loved her, to whom she had to belong and who could not see her.

The illusion that love has changed to 'beautiful friendship' promptly makes him believe that love would have made him guilty towards her husband, as he will naturally be when the husband's wife becomes his mistress.

Doubts about his own love for her lead to equally mistaken doubts about hers for him:

> For I often had doubts about her love. Sometimes I asked myself if I was not for her a pastime, a caprice from which she would detach herself at a day's notice when peace [brought war to an end] and recalled her to her duties.

What makes this novel virtually unique is the extraordinary insight that the novelist displays when he eventually came to reveal the complexity of the feelings of the adolescent lovers.

My clear-sightedness was only a more dangerous form of my ingenuousness... This pretended insight obscured everything from me, made me doubt Marthe. Or rather, I doubted myself, not finding myself worthy of her. Even if I had had a thousand more proofs of her love, I should not have been less unhappy.

We must go on to observe that the initial attraction, which seems to have been something like a youthful flirtation on the narrator's part, or so he believed for a time, gradually changes into a much deeper feeling which is both emotional and physical:

However, there was another thing which ought to have made me understand my true feelings. When I met Marthe a few months ago, my pretended love did not prevent me from judging her, from finding ugly most of the things that she found beautiful, and from thinking that most of the things she said were infantile. Now, if I did not think like her, I told myself that I was wrong. After the crudity of my first inclinations, it was the gentleness of a deeper feeling which deceived me . . . I began to feel respect for Marthe because I was beginning to love her.

His first view of Marthe's poor taste and childish talk was no doubt correct and a sign of the narrator's far greater intelligence, but it has been obscured by something like genuine love—genuine because of the respect that he feels for the loved one. The paradox lies in the fact that it is an illusion about her abilities which begins to reveal his real feelings to himself.

We observe that the word 'beginning' turns up again in the last sentence. The narrator's illusion that he does not love Marthe any longer or, in another place, that his love for her is 'dead', is only completely dissipated when they begin to make love, first by kisses provoked by Marthe, then by intercourse. I suggested that the use of the 'cat' image at the beginning of the novel was peculiarly suitable in a novel about adolescent love. The same is true of the images of the magnet and the alarm clock which are used to describe the last two stages of becoming lovers:

Un jour que je m'approchais trop sans pourtant que mon visage touchât le sien, je fus comme une aiguille qui dépasse d'un millimêtre la zone interdite et appartient à l'aimant.

J'embrassai Marthe sur l'épaule. Elle ne s'éveilla pas. Un second baiser, moins chaste, agit avec la violence d'un réveille-matin. Elle sursauta, et, se frottant les yeux, me couvrit de baisers, comme quelqu'un qu'on aime et qu'on retrouve dans son lit après avoir rêvé qu'il est mort.

[One day I moved too close, but without my face touching hers. I was like a needle which goes a fraction of an inch beyond the forbidden zone and is caught by the magnet.

I kissed Marthe on the shoulder, but she did not wake. A second and less chaste kiss acted with the violence of an alarm clock. She shot up and, wiping her eyes, covered me with kisses, like someone whom one loves and whom one finds in one's bed after dreaming that he is dead.]

It is characteristic of some of the great French novelists that their work often contains phrases which might have come from one of the seventeenth-century maxim writers. They are not abstract pronouncements; they spring directly from the contemplation of experience and are nearly always dramatically appropriate. The maturity which they distil contributes largely to the sense of maturity which belongs peculiarly to the French novel. Although, as already suggested, the images of the magnet and the alarm clock are peculiarly suitable to the account of two adolescents becoming lovers, later in the novel we shall come across what we are inclined to call mature maxims because they show that the adolescents have reached something like a state of maturity in their love.

The passage describing the way in which the narrator's kiss 'acted with the violence of an alarm clock' deals with something that happened on the morning after the night of love-making for the first time. In the middle of the night there had been a touch of something like black comedy. The narrator had turned up at Marthe's flat entirely unexpectedly:

I opened the door and whispered 'Marthe?'
'Rather than give me a fright like that', she answered, 'you could very well have put off coming till the morning. You've got your leave a week early then?'
She thought that I was Jacques.

The brutal way in which she addresses her imagined husband naturally reminds us of the occasion on which she shocked the narrator by flinging one of her husband's unread letters into the fire, which may in spite of himself have been responsible for his treatment of one of her letters which caused him so much emotion. It shows that the 'tyrannical' element was not confined to the male lover, though the woman only uses it with her husband. Although I observed earlier that there would be no smashing of a 'dome' to bring the two lovers together and that Marthe herself would invite the narrator into the new 'dome', his unexpected arrival on this occasion, which leads to love-making for the first time, reminds us not only of the 'cat' breaking the glass dome and presumably thoroughly enjoying the 'cheese', but also of the narrator's remark, when he was helping to choose the marriage furniture, that he saw 'the means of choosing a room for Marthe and me'. For it becomes of course the room where, in spite of what the narrator calls 'ma timidité maladive', love-making will take place on innumerable occasions.

The narrator's reactions to this first occasion are highly complex and brilliantly analysed. At one moment he is dazzled by the sight of Marthe:

> Her face was transfigured. I was even astonished at not being able to touch the halo which really shone round her face as in religious paintings.

The realisation that Marthe has enjoyed the love-making more than himself because she is more experienced and because he cannot get the maximum pleasure out of his first experience of love-making makes him jealous. The imagined 'halo' seems to fade away and is replaced by something different. 'I felt cross with Marthe because I understood from the look of gratitude on her face the great value of physical relationships. I cursed the man who had awakened her body before me. I considered that my stupidity was to have seen in Marthe a virgin'.

Then they weep together. 'It was the fault of happiness. Marthe reproached me for not having prevented her marriage'. Soon after this they weep together again, this time because they 'are only children with so little at their disposal'. He is secretly

angry when Marthe declares that she will give up everything
and everyone for him because he feels that his is not a 'nature
disposed to rebel'. Marthe dwells on the unfortunate difference
in their ages. He is cross with himself for not 'appearing sufficiently convinced of the contrary', but it prompts the most perceptive reflection of all:

> Alas! I was too conscious of youth not to foresee that I should
> detach myself from Marthe the day her youth faded and mine
> blossomed.

It looked forward to the novelist's treatment of Alice and
might well have applied to Marthe if it had not been for her
tragic death!

We have seen that something like borrowings of sevententh-
century maxims is part of Radiguet's inheritance. It makes his
comment on the first kiss far more pregnant than the corres-
ponding observation on love-making:

> La saveur du premier baiser m'avait déçu comme un fruit que
> l'on goûte pour la première fois. Ce n'est pas dans la nouveauté,
> c'est dans l'habitude que nous trouvons les plus grands plaisirs.

> [The taste of the first kiss disappointed me like a fruit that one
> tastes for the first time. It is not novelty, but habit which provides
> the greatest pleasure.]

'Habit' is an important word and will turn out to have a
dual meaning.

The temporary separation of the couple when the husband
is home on leave prompts the narrator to remark with another
use of homely comparisons:

> What worried me most was the fast imposed on my senses. My
> restlessness was the same as that of a pianist without a piano or a
> smoker without cigarettes.

The passage brings home the highly amorous nature of his
attraction for Marthe and the 'habit' it has become through
the husband's absence. His susceptibility is underlined by the
way in which he agrees, during one of these separations, to put

the fidelity of his friend René's mistress to the test and is promptly seduced by her. It is also underlined by his own unsuccessful attempt to seduce Marthe's Swedish girl friend, which produces another comment which is typical of the adolescent love-maker:

> Happily she was a glutton. My own gluttony took an unpublished form. I had no hunger for the tart, the rasberry ice-cream, but desired to be tart and ice-cream to which her mouth approached. With my own mouth I made involuntary grimaces.

The contacts with René's mistress and the Swedish girl friend are, incidentally, the only occasions on which the otherwise honest narrator deceives his mistress and does not condemn himself. He asserts roundly that his infidelity has no effect on his love for Marthe.[1] Nor does it curb his jealousy of her husband.

Marthe is as susceptible as the narrator, and the way in which they indulge themselves as soon as the husband is out of the way again leads to something on the part of the narrator which is like a temporary loss of appetite through over-eating and illustrates the other implications of 'habit':

> In bed beside her, the desire which seized me from moment to moment to be in bed alone, at my parents' home, made me see the unbearableness of life together. On the other hand, I could not imagine life without Marthe. I was beginning to know the chastisement of adultery.

It is another example of his insight and the remarkable clarity and brevity with which it is expressed. It is a reaction from which even adult lovers, whether married or not, do not always escape. What Radiguet does, as usual, is to emphasise the adolescent nature of the experience by references to the narrator's desire to escape, to be alone, and his nervousness at the prospect of 'life together'. It is capped by his inability even to 'imagine life without Marthe', which exposes or sums up the complexity of his feelings in a mere five lines.

What emerges is that the state of confusion which followed

---

[1] This reminds us a little oddly of the attitude adopted by the narrator in Crébillon *fil*'s *Les Egarements du coeur et de l'esprit*. (See page 100).

love-making becomes permanent. Love continues to grow; there are periods of happiness; but fears for the future, internal conflicts on the part of the narrator, the mixture of 'timid' and 'tyrannical' impulses persist. The discovery that Marthe is pregnant produces characteristic reactions:

> L'instinct est notre guide; un guide qui nous conduit à notre perte. Hier, Marthe redoutait que sa grossesse nous éloignât l'un de l'autre. Aujourd'hui, qu'elle ne m'avait tant aimé, elle croyait que mon amour grandissait comme le sien. Moi, hier, repoussant cet enfant, je commençais aujourd'hui à l'aimer et j'ôtais de l'amour à Marthe, de même qu'au début de notre liaison mon coeur lui donnait ce qu'il retirait aux autres.

> [Instinct is our guide; a guide which leads to our fall. Yesterday, Marthe feared that her pregnancy would separate us from one another. Today, when she had never loved me so much, she believed that my love was growing like hers. I, who after repelling the child yesterday, today was beginning to feel love for it and took away love from Marthe in the same way that at the beginning of our liaison my heart gave her what it had taken away from others.]

The first sentence is an admirable example of what I have described as 'mature maxims'. Whatever the intention, its appearance in the present context seems to indicate that pregnancy, which is undoubtedly the fruit of 'instinct', will lead to tragedy, and that is what will happen.

The narrator's change from 'repelling' to 'loving' the coming child, of which he is already convinced that he is the father, shows that on this occasion the novelist deliberately emphasises the closeness of the structure of his work by comparing the way in which at the beginning he took away love from other people to give it to Marthe and is now doing the opposite by taking away some of his love for her and giving it to the child. Nor should we overlook the reappearance of the word 'beginning', which reflects alternately movements towards and away from Marthe.

Although what has happened is paradoxically a reflection of the narrator's vacillations, in this case it is only temporary. When Marthe returns from another stay with her husband, he says to himself:

Sensual fatigue, the secret desire to sleep alone, had vanished.
. . . I wanted to make the most of Marthe before maternity ruined
her.

It is a brutal thought as he comes to realise shortly afterwards:

When Marthe was naked, I hardly dared look at her. Does this
mean that I am a monster? I was feeling remorse for the noblest
occupation of man. I considered myself a vandal for having
ruined Marthe's beauty, for having made her belly stick out.

We saw at the beginning of the novel that Radiguet attached
great importance to the setting and its effect on the behaviour
of the narrator. He enlarges on it, or rather develops it, with
his highly critical picture of French suburban life which emerges with the growth of the love affair: the small town with its
stuffy atmosphere and whispers about the strange goings-on of
the youthful couple; the gradual withdrawal of neighbours and
even acquaintances who no longer greet the erring wife; the
'terrible' smile of complicity on the face of the milkboy when
he meets the narrator, shoes in hand, creeping downstairs in
the early morning after the usual night with Marthe; the growing anguish of his parents, who have themselves connived at
their son's adultery. We know that a local councillor came out
badly over the mad servant's leap from the roof owing to his
failure to ensure her rescue. It is another councillor and his
wife who organize the 'surprise party' which is the one really
comic event in the novel and an extremely damaging criticism
of the bourgeoisie. Marthe's flat is on the first floor of the councillor's house:

Imagine my surprise when I discovered that the chief attraction
at the Marins was to stand under the bedroom towards the end of
the afternoon in the hope of hearing the sounds of our love-
making.

The narrator takes good care to ensure that there is not a
sound until he hears the guests departing, thoroughly disgusted
with the councillor and his wife over the joke which had failed

to come off. Then, in order to pay them out, the couple proceed
to give plenty of noisy evidence of their activities!

The last stages of the novel are the most moving and in some
respects the most striking:

> Maintenant Marthe ne m'était pas seulement la plus aimée, ce
> qui ne veut pas dire la mieux aimée des maîtresses, mais elle me
> tenait lieu de tout . . .
> L'amour anesthésiait en moi tout ce qui n'était pas Marthe.
>
> [Now Marthe was not only my most loved, which is not to say
> the best loved of mistresses, but she took the place of everything
> for me. . . .
> Love had anaesthetized in me everything that was not Marthe.]

The two passages may create the impression that their love
has become absolute, but it would be misleading. We have seen
that in spite of everything the narrator's vacillations, his internal conflicts, his fears of the future and his uncertainties
about his own feelings have never been eliminated. The important words are not 'the best loved of mistresses' in the first of
the two passages. It means that though the narrator is completely absorbed by his attitude to Marthe and is indifferent to
everything and everybody else, it is not the absolute love of a
mature man. It remains the powerful attraction of an adolescent, reminding us of the contradiction of the 'unbearableness
of life together' and the narrator's inability to 'imagine life
without Marthe'. For true love means the complete unity of
the couple, which depends on the internal unity of each of
them—something which is never achieved by the narrator.

'The storm is approaching', we are told elliptically. It will be
remembered that in the novel's opening passage the narrator
attached special importance to the effect of war, which meant
that children escaped normal discipline and found themselves
on a 'four-year holiday'. What emerges is that the realisation
that the free period was limited is responsible for the uncertainty about his future which continually haunts the narrator.
It is expressed with remarkable effectiveness a little over half-
way through the novel:

Notre union était donc à la merci de la paix, du retour définitif des troupes. Qu'il chasse sa femme, elle me resterait. Qu'il la garde, je me sentais incapable de la lui reprendre de force. Notre bonheur était un château de sable. Mais ici la marée n'étant pas à heure fixe, j'espérais qu'elle monterait le plus tard possible.

[Our union was therefore at the mercy of peace, the final return of the troops. Let him [Jacques] drive his wife away, she would remain with me. Let him keep her, I felt incapable of taking her from him by force. Our happiness was a castle of sand. But here the tide not having a fixed time, I hoped it would rise as late as possible.]

It is clear that the narrator sees no hope of Jacques abandoning his wife. This means that his own union will come to grief with 'the final return of the troops'. It is summed up brilliantly by the use of the sea image in the last two sentences, in which happiness is reduced to a 'castle of sand' which will obviously be washed away when the tide rises. The result is that the only consolation can be a delay in the rising of the tide, which fortunately for him has no 'fixed time'. In other words, the adolescent lover hopes that instead of victory and peace, war will go on!

The statement that 'The storm is approaching' refers to two factors: the knowledge that the armistice is very near (meaning that the 'tide' is about to 'rise' and wash away the 'castle') and the belated attempt of the narrator's father to stop the pair spending nights together. The narrator is prepared to defy his father, but Marthe opposes him and threatens to move to her parents' home. The narrator then proposes that they shall go to Paris and spend a night at an hotel, comparing the couple to 'children upright on a chair and proud to be a head and shoulders above the grown-up people'. Marthe does not like the idea of going to Paris, but gives way to her lover. The visit to Paris turns out to be another mixture of the 'timid' and the 'tyrannical' on the part of the narrator, but this time the order is reversed. He is 'tyrannical' in insisting that they should go together to Paris, but 'timid' in his repeated pretence that he was unable to obtain a room at any of the hotels, where he simply pretends to make enquiries on his own while Marthe remains in the street. The result is that they are obliged to abandon the

plan to stay the night, owing to the narrator's absurd 'timidity'
in not applying for a room at any of the hotels he visits, with
the result that they return home in a miserable state. 'Marthe',
we are told, 'in a corner of the carriage, exhausted, terrified,
her teeth rattling, *understood everything*'. She may, he adds,
have been able to see that 'there could be no other issue except
death'.

That is precisely what happened. 'This night of the hotels',
he says, 'was decisive'. The narrator finds her ill in bed the next
morning. The doctor has to be called in. She is moved to her
parents' house and eventually dies after the birth of her child
without her lover ever seeing her again.

The restraint with which the tragedy is described gives the
last pages their extreme impressiveness:

> Notre maison respirait le calme.
>
> Les vrais pressentiments se forment à des profondeurs que notre
> esprit ne visite pas. Aussi, parfois, nous font-ils accomplir des
> actes que nous interprétons tout de travers.
>
> Je me croyais plus tendre à cause de mon bonheur et je me
> félicitais de savoir Marthe dans une maison que mes souvenirs
> heureux transformaient en fétiche.
>
> Un homme désordonnè qui va mourir et ne s'en doute pas met
> soudain de l'ordre autour de lui. Sa vie change. Il classe des
> papiers. Il se lève tôt, il se couche de bonne heure. Il renonce à
> ses vices. Son entourage se félicite. Aussi sa mort brutale semble-
> t-elle d'autant plus injuste. *Il allait vivre heureux.*
>
> De même, le calme nouveau de mon existence était ma toilette
> du condamné. Je me croyais meilleur fils parce que j'en avais un.
> Or, ma tendresse me rapprochait de mon père, de ma mère parce
> que quelque chose savait en moi que j'aurais, sous peu, besoin de
> la leur.
>
> Un jour, à midi, mes frères revinrent de l'école en nous criant
> que Marthe était morte.
>
> [Our house breathed calm.
>
> True presentiments are formed at depths which our mind does
> not reach. At times therefore they make us perform acts which
> we interpret in a way that is all wrong.
>
> I thought that I had become more tender because of my happi-
> ness, and I rejoiced in the thought that Marthe was in a house
> that my happy memories transformed into a fetish.
>
> A disorderly man who is going to die and does not suspect it

suddenly puts everything that concerns him into order. His life
changes. He files his papers. He gets up early and goes to bed in
good time. He gives up his vices. Those around him rejoice. This
makes his brutal death seem all the more unjust. *He was about to
live happily.*

In the same way the new calm of my existence was my dress of
a condemned person. I thought myself a better son because I had
one. Now my tenderness brought me closer to my father, to my
mother because something in me knew that, in a short time, I
should need theirs.

One day at noon, my brothers came back from school crying out
to us that Marthe was dead.]

We can see that this is Radiguet's plain style at its best in its
extreme perceptiveness, in its simplicity, directness and vigour.

It is another sign of Radiguet's originality that he does not
leave off there. There is a short description of the narrator's
collapse and his long illness. Then we find that he is the same
tough child:

Marthe! With my jealousy following her right into the grave, I
hoped that there was nothing after death. It is intolerable that the
person whom we love should find herself in the midst of a large
company at a feast at which we ourselves are not present. My
heart was at an age at which one does not yet think of the future.
Yes, it was indeed oblivion that I desired for Marthe rather than
a new world where I should join her one day.

They are not his last words, which are a little happier. He
catches his only sight of the widower at his father's house where
he has come to look at Marthe's watercolours, which are still
there. The narrator hears him mention his own Christian name,
which Marthe had given to the son and which remains unknown to us, as her last word—showing that the last word was
addressed to her lover and not, as the husband imagined, to her
son.

Although Radiguet was 'severely reproached for what he had
done' by some of his first critics and though the narrator might
fairly be called an *enfant terrible,* there is nothing 'heartless' or
'cynical' or 'immoral' about the novel itself. Its great originality lies in the contrast between the immaturity of the child's

reactions, with the jealous hope that there is no after-life for his mistress as the outstanding example, and the absolute maturity with which they are presented. If the novel makes a painful impression it is because of the frankness and the veracity with which it describes the child's behaviour, the refusal to allow it to be blurred or toned down by sentimentality or empty moralising, and the honesty with which the child admits his faults. It is, indeed, the mastery with which Radiguet presents a picture of adolescent love in a way in which it had never been done before that makes *Le Diable au corps* a unique work.

2 *Le Bal du comte d'Orgel*

Roman d'amour chaste, aussi *scabreux* que le roman le moins chaste.
—RAYMOND RADIGUET

For a writer whose first novel is outstanding, the second presents a special problem. He naturally tries to improve on what may be a masterpiece, but can never be sure of succeeding or even producing anything which equals his first work, reminding us of the vast gap between Benjamin Constant's *Adolphe,* which was published in 1816, and his *Cécile,* which had to wait until 1951 for publication. There was a time when *Le Diable au corps* was treated as an extremely promising first novel or, as Cocteau put it in his preface to the second novel, a 'masterpiece of promise', with 'the promise fulfilled' in *Le Bal du comte d'Orgel.*

With the passing of time there has been a change of view. *Le Bal du comte d'Orgel* is a highly talented novel, in which Radiguet becomes the omniscient novelist instead of the autobiographical novelist, is much more sophisticated than *Le Diable au corps,* and there are even moments when we have the impression that it is more mature, but it has nothing like the same impact as the first novel. The feeling or, as one is tempted to call it, the illusion of greater maturity is easily explained. When he began his second novel Radiguet, who was a precocious child, was at least two years older, had mixed freely with literary society, had seen more of life and, as we shall find, chose very different protagonists from those of his first novel. The impact of *Le Diable au corps* is naturally the result not

simply of talent, but of the strongly personal element in the
story and the narrator's use of the first-person singular. Although the love story in *Le Bal du comte d'Orgel* reveals great
insight and is decidedly moving, it is much less personal and
has a detachment that reminds us of *La Princesse de Clèves*,
which was a major influence on the work.

A young man named François de Séryeuse meets the Comte
d'Orgel and his wife and becomes one of their friends. François
and Mahaut fall in love, but remain chaste, with the result
that Radiguet's 'scabrous' only applies to their feelings and not
to their behaviour. The couple are, indeed, profoundly disturbed to find themselves in love. They are careful never to
make a declaration to one another. The furthest that they go is
an occasional polite kiss on the cheeks. The first causes embarrassment because it is instigated by the husband, who con-
vinces himself for social reasons that the pair are cousins.

In spite of the differences, the two novels are clearly a pair.
The illicit love affair of the two adolescents belonging to the
bourgeoisie is matched by the chaste love affair of two people
who are older, more responsible and belong to a higher class of
society. We have seen the importance of the setting of the wartime period in *Le Diable au corps*. The setting of the postwar
period in *Le Bal du comte d'Orgel* is also important and in
some respects more far-reaching.

Although Radiguet deals like his great predecessor with high
society, he is no imitator. The skill is apparent from the way
in which he brings out the decline which has taken place since
the seventeenth-century. When we set Mme de La Fayette's portrait of M. de Nemours beside Radiguet's of the Comte d'Orgel,
we begin to see what has happened:

> Mais ce prince était un chef-d'oeuvre de la nature; ce qu'il avait
> de moins admirable, c'était d'être l'homme du monde le mieux
> fait et le plus beau. Ce qui le mettait au-dessus des autres était
> une valeur incomparable et un agrément dans son esprit, dans
> son visage et dans ses actions que l'on n'a jamais vu qu'à lui seul.

> Le Comte Anne d'Orgel était jeune; il venait d'avoir trente ans.
> On ne savait de quoi sa gloire, ou du moins son extraordinaire
> position était faite. Son nom n'y entrait pas pour grand'chose,
> tant, même chez ceux qu'hypnotise un nom, le talent prime tout.

Mais, il faut le reconnaître, ses qualités, n'étaient que celles de sa race, et un talent mondain.

[But this prince was a masterpiece of nature; what was least admirable was to to be a man of the world with the best figure and the handsomest face. What put him above everybody else was his incomparable gallantry and a charm of mind, face and action which nobody had ever seen except in him alone.]

[Comte Anne d'Orgel was young; he had just become thirty. No one knew what had gone to the making of his great reputation, or at least his extraordinary position. His name played no great part in it because talent comes first even among those who are hynotised by a name. But, as we must realise, his qualities were only those of race and his social talent.]

There is immense conviction behind Mme de La Fayette's 'chef-d'oeuvre de la nature' and 'valeur incomparable', which we do not find in the portrait of the count. Radiguet speaks of his 'gloire', using the popular seventeenth-century term, feels at once that it will not do, changes it to 'extraordinaire position', and concludes that it must be due to 'ses qualités [qui] n'étaient que celles de sa race' and 'talent mondain', which suggests nothing more than birth and the position that it gives him in smart society. The truth is that the old Europe has gone and that when applied to the count the famous seventeenth-century word reverberates hollowly in the void. A new word will be added which seems to echo it and at the same time undermines it. It is 'frivolités'.

Comte Anne d'Orgel is charming, but incorrigibly frivolous. His role is twofold. He is the husband in a triangular love affair, but he is also a symbolical figure. He is the usurper, the representative of the social class which has retained its privileges and its pride, but lost the functions which justified them. In this way he is the link between the personal and the social themes. The king and his court, which were the pivot of Mme de La Fayette's complicated hierarchy, have vanished. The royal tournaments and the court balls, where her characters distinguished themselves, have been replaced by the Médrano Circus, the *dancing* at Robinson, or the fancy-dress ball which is rehearsed but does not take place in the novel, in spite of its title.

The novel is constructed with the same skill as *Le Diable au corps*. It begins with something like a psychological portrait of Mahaut. It goes on to look at the history of her family, which will help to explain the peculiarities of her psychology and reminds us of Radiguet's treatment of the prewar period in the first novel. Mahaut married Anne d'Orgel when she was eighteen. We learn, significantly, that 'She fell madly in love with her husband who in return showed her great gratitude and the warmest friendship which he himself took for love'. We are then told something about his family.

The Orgels' meeting with François, which takes place in the first chapter, introduces us to some of the minor characters who contribute to the picture of post-war society, but are naturally much more individualist than the minor characters in *Le Diable au corps*.

The count's dead father is not without importance. Our glimpse of him is a perfect vignette of the crusty, old world French aristocrat. When his ancestral seat was occupied during the war by French military authorities, he replied to anyone asking for the password: 'I am M. d'Orgel'. He was incapable of distinguishing the different ranks and 'addressed every soldier who had a stripe as "Monsieur l'Officier", whether he happened to be a sergeant or a colonel'. He did better when French changed to German occupation. The Germans treated him with much more consideration for the snobbish reason that his name, which had German connections, took up more space than any others in their directories. The contrast here is between the father's pompousness and the son's 'frivolity'.

In the opening paragraph, we are told of Mahaut:

> Les mouvements d'un coeur comme celui de la comtesse d'Orgel sont-ils surannés? Un tel mélange du devoir et de la mollesse semblera peut-être de nos jours, incroyable, même chez une personne de race et une créole. Ne serait-ce plutôt que l'attention se détourne de la pureté sous prétexte qu'elle offre moins de saveur que le désordre?
>
> Mais les manoeuvres inconscientes d'une âme pure sont encore plus singulières que les combinaisons du vice. C'est ce que nous répondrons aux femmes, qui, les unes, trouveront Mme d'Orgel trop honnête, et les autres trop facile.

[Are the movements of a heart like the Comtesse d'Orgel's old-fashioned? Such a mixture of a sense of duty and weakness will perhaps appear in these days to be unbelievable, even in a person of breeding and a Creole. Might this not be rather because attention turns away from purity on the same pretext that it offers less savour than irregularity?

But the unconscious manoeuvres of a pure soul are still more unusual than combinations of vice. That will be our reply to women, some of whom will find Mme d'Orgel too virtuous and others too susceptible.]

'Surannés' is one of the focal words of the novel. The ambiguity is intentional. The novel sets out to explore certain feelings which to the present day appear old-fashioned, to analyse their composition and to see whether they are authentic. It is a characteristic of Radiguet's style that while the tone of the passage is necessarily ambiguous, the vocabulary is extremely precise. The precision is evident from the linking of the words 'devoir-mollesse', 'pureté-désordre', 'honnête-facile'. They are in no sense idle antitheses put in to give the passage pattern and balance. Radiguet's aim is to reveal a state of suspense which keeps the mind delicately poised between two sets of conflicting impulses. It is brought out by the word 'saveur', which suggests a peculiar form of dual weakness: weakness of the temptation and weakness of the methods of resistance which are reflected by 'trop honnête' and 'trop facile' in the last sentence.

There is a further set of words which calls for attention, the words suggesting motion: 'mouvements d'un coeur', 'manoeuvres inconscientes', 'combinaisons du vice'. The novel is not concerned merely with feeling, but with *movement* of feeling, with 'les manoeuvres inconscientes d'une âme pure' in order to avoid 'les combinaisons du vice'.

Altogether the two paragraphs form a plan in which the key-words and phrases show the direction in which the novel will move and the way in which feelings will be explored. It can, as we shall see, be summed up by a phrase which is used in a different context near the end of the novel: 'bizarreries du coeur'.

This takes us next to the analysis of François' attachment to Mahaut:

L'amour venait de s'installer en lui à une profondeur où lui-même ne pouvait descendre. François de Séryeuse, comme beaucoup d'êtres très jeunes, était ainsi machiné qu'il ne percevait que ses sensations les plus vives, c'est-à-dire les plus grossières. Un désir mauvais l'eût bien autrement remué que la naissance de cet amour.

C'est lorsqu'un mal entre en nous, que nous nous croyons en danger. Dès qu'il sera installé, nous pourrons faire bon ménage avec lui, voire même ne pas soupçonner sa présence. François ne pouvait se mentir plus longtemps, ni boucher ses oreilles à la rumeur qui montait. Il ne savait même pas s'il aimait Mme d'Orgel, et de quoi au juste il pouvait l'accuser; mais certes la responsable c'était elle, et personne d'autre.

[Love had taken root in him at a depth to which he himself could not penetrate. François de Séryeuse like many other very young men was so constituted that he was only aware of his most vivid, that is to say, his coarsest sensations. An evil desire would have affected him very differently from the birth of his love.

It is when an evil enters us that we imagine ourselves in danger, but as soon as it has taken root, we can settle down comfortably with it and without even suspecting its presence. François could not go on lying to himself any longer or close his ears to the rising sound. He did not even know whether he loved Mme d'Orgel, and of exactly what he could accuse her; but certainly she was the person responsible and nobody else.]

The interest of the passage lies in the skill with which the novelist shows us François' feelings functioning simultaneously at two different levels, described as 'une profondeur où lui-même ne pouvait descendre' and 'ses sensations . . . les plus grossières'. The most complex word is 'un désir mauvais'. The birth of his love for Mahaut is not 'evil' since he was not aware that he was in love, and we know that their 'purity' will always prevent them from becoming lovers in the practical sense. The feeling, however, is 'evil' in the sense that he has fallen in love with another man's wife. Although he still does not know whether he loves Mahaut, reminding us of the vacillations of the narrator in *Le Diable au corps,* he feels that something is wrong and that it is she alone who is responsible. There is no question of 'settling down comfortably'; we are told that he

'could not go on lying to himself', which means that he is on
the way to discovering his true feelings.

The passage only gains its fullest effect when it is seen in relation to the pronouncements about the count and his wife. It
does not occur to the count that there is anything unusual
about the speed with which François has become the best
friend of himself and his wife, and in spite of the effect on him,
he does not for a moment suspect that they are falling in love
with one another:

> Il n'analysait pas le motif de cette préférance. La raison en
> était d'ailleurs incroyable. Il eût haussé les épaules, comme qui-
> conque, si on la lui avait révélée. Orgel préférait François à tous
> parce que François aimait sa femme . . .
>
> Non seulement l'amour de François était la raison mystérieuse
> de la préférance du comte d'Orgel, mais encore cet amour décida
> son amour pour sa femme. Il commençait de l'aimer, comme s'il
> avait fallu une convoitise pour lui en apprendre le prix . . .
>
> Il avait toujours évité l'amour comme une chose trop exclusive.
> Pour aimer il faut du loisir, et les frivolités l'accaparaient.

> [He did not analyse the motives for his preference. As it hap-
> pened, the reason was incredible and the count would simply
> have shrugged his shoulders if anyone had revealed it to him.
> Orgel preferred François to all his friends because François was
> in love with his wife . . .
>
> François' love was not merely the mysterious explanation of the
> Comte d'Orgel's preference for him; it was this love that made the
> count fall in love with his own wife. He began to love her as
> though the desire of another had been necessary to make him
> appreciate her value . . .
>
> He had always avoided love as being something too exclusive.
> In order to love one must have leisure, and he had always been
> absorbed by frivolities.]

The passage illustrates the differences and the resemblances
between the characters. There is an inward and an outward
movement; a tendency for feelings to deepen and 'take root',
and a tendency to become superficial or surface feelings, to
cheapen and change into 'coarsest sensations' or 'frivolities'.
This brings out the differences between the count and the

couple. Their feelings deepen in spite of themselves and take what is for them the wrong turning. The whole of the count's career has been a flight from depth and reality, a gravitation towards 'frivolities'. The statement that 'he had always avoided love as being something too exclusive' is to a certain extent a condemnation because 'exclusive' stands for order and integration as opposed to dissipation, and the few superficial liaisons in which he has indulged. Yet in spite of his attempts to remain disengaged, we can see that what is described as 'the stratagem of the heart' has broken down in the same way for him as for François, that 'Passion [for his wife] has made its way into him with such skill that he could hardly take account of it'. It happened on a day on which he caught sight of the couple sitting down and talking to one another. Without the faintest suspicion of François' being in love with his wife, we are told that 'On that day, the husband coveted Mahaut as though she had not been his wife'.

The irony of the last sentence lies in the fact that while the couple are moving in spite of themselves in what for them is morally the wrong direction, the count is carried in the right direction by the wrong feeling—the feeling which led to his liaisons with other women.

There has been a comparatively early breakdown, or partial breakdown, in François' resistance. The breakdown in Mahaut's comes a good deal later, but is complete and much more disturbing than François':

> Les mots ont une grande puissance. Mme d'Orgel s'était cru d'attribuer à une prédilection pour François le sens qu'elle voulait. Ainsi avait-elle moins combattu un sentiment que la crainte de lui donner son véritable nom.
>
> Ayant jusqu'ici mené de front le devoir et l'amour, elle avait pu imaginer, dans sa pureté, que les sentiments interdits sont sans douceur. Elle avait donc mal interprété le sien envers François, car il lui était doux. Aujourd'hui ce sentiment, couvé, nourri, grandi dans l'ombre, venait de se faire reconnaître.
>
> Mauhaut dut s'avouer qu'elle aimait François.

> [Words have great power. Mme d'Orgel believed herself free to interpret her predilection for François in the way she wanted.

This meant that she struggled less against a feeling than the fear of giving it its true name.

Up to this point by matching duty and love, she had imagined in her purity that forbidden feelings are without sweetness. She had therefore misinterpreted her own feeling for François because of its sweetness. Today a feeling which had been hatched, nourished and had grown up in the dark compelled recognition.

Mahaut had to admit to herself that she was in love with François.]

It is another example of the complexity of the protagonists' minds, or what Radiguet calls in his first chapter 'the unconscious manoeuvring of a pure soul'. For Mahaut the confusion between word and thing, between 'feeling' and 'fear', leads us to the illusory balance of 'duty' and 'love', which is supported by a further misunderstanding. For it is Mahaut's own 'purity' which prevents her from interpreting her feelings correctly and it is only at this late stage that she comes to realise that 'forbidden feelings' are not necessarily disagreeable and gives them their 'true name'. What is clearly highly original is the way in which Radiguet shows the difference between real and imagined feelings.

'Mahaut', we are told, 'was one of those women who cannot regard agitation as their daily fare'. When she realises that she can no longer shut her eyes to her love for François, she is badly shaken and decides that she must find a remedy. She confesses her love in a letter to François' mother, mentions that she has followed her husband's example by becoming an unbeliever, and appeals for help. The move is prompted by her concern for 'calm' and, without realising it, by the hope that it will lead to François' discovery that she is in love with him. What happens of course is that the moment that Mme de Séryeuse comes to see Mahaut, she tells her that her son is in love with her. It produces a scene in which 'agitation' carries all before it:

> Mme d'Orgel gave a cry . . . Her face was lighted up for a second by a look of insane joy before Mme de Séryeuse was able to see the uprooted being shaken by suffering. If François had turned up at that moment, Mahaut would have been his. Nothing would have prevented her from falling into his arms, not even his mother's presence.

It is an admirable picture of the complexity and contradiction of her feelings.

The dinner party at which the Comte d'Orgel and his friends plan, or rather rehearse, the fancy-dress ball is the climax and illustrates all Radiguet's gifts as a novelist:

> Hester Wayne, with a notebook on her lap, drew a picture of shapeless costumes. Hortense d'Austerlitz went in for improvisation on herself. She ransacked the drawing-room, used a lampshade as a hat, tried out the endless masquerades which aroused in Anne the profoundest passion of men of his class throughout the centuries: the passion for disguise.

'Disguise' is the focal word of the passage and underlines the novel's principal theme. Its meaning is twofold, or perhaps we should say manifold. It stands for the protagonists' unsuccessful attempts to 'disguise' their real feelings from themselves, to make all feelings and all actions conform at least outwardly to the pattern imposed on the aristocratic society to which they belong. It is also an ironical reference to the opposite tendency which is found in some of the characters, including the count: the desire to escape temporarily from their official selves by putting on fancy dress and giving full rein to 'frivolity', which is what happens at the dinner party, with some disturbing results.

The decisive event is the unexpected arrival of Prince Naroumov, an old friend of the count's and a Russian refugee who has lost everything in the Revolution. His arrival causes an immediate feeling of gloom. In a moment of aberration, or extreme 'frivolity', the count puts on Naroumov's hat and does a few steps of a Russian dance:

> 'Excuse me', Naroumov said. 'That's my hat. It was given to me by some Austrian friends who had nothing else to offer.'
> A horrible chill paralysed the whole company. In the uproar they had forgotten the presence of Naroumov. He now assumed the aspect of a judge who was calling scoffers to order and reminding them of the respect due to misfortune.

Naroumov is another symbolic figure, a visitant from a country where an aristocratic society, which had lost its moral fibre and surrendered to 'frivolity', had been swept away. He is clearly intended as a foil to the count, as a warning voice calling, or attempting to call, a supposedly doomed society back to seriousness and reality. Although he is a righteous man who has been ruined by the Revolution, his attitude remains profoundly charitable. He feels no bitterness towards the revolutionaries and has no sympathy for Hester Wayne, the American guest, when she says to him: 'How you must loathe those Bolshevists'.

When he says to himself, 'War has made the whole world go mad', he is quietly pronouncing a verdict not merely on the society portrayed in the novel, but on the world to which they belong and reveals himself as a 'judge calling the scoffers to order'.

His exemplary behaviour compared with their 'frivolity' causes great embarrassment, but can naturally do nothing to cure it, which turns him into something like a prophet whose warnings go unheeded. The worst moment is reached when Mahaut follows her husband's example and goes one better by putting on an even more offensive turn with Naroumov's hat. She does it purely and simply in the hope of discrediting herself with François. This, too, is a failure. Although he is horrified by the way in which in his opinion the husband 'degrades' her, it does nothing to put an end to his love:

> If anything had been capable of weakening Séryeuse's love, Mahaut would have harvested the fruit of her sacrifice to the full. But she was unable to arouse anything in him except the sadness which increases love.

Radiguet keeps the wife's confession to her husband, which corresponds in a way to the Princesse de Clèves' *aveu* to her husband, for the last pages. The results are very different. The Prince de Clèves dies of a broken heart, but in spite of this the Princesse de Clèves refuses to marry M. de Nemours and retires to a convent. The count is shaken, but promptly begins to close his eyes to what he has heard:

'It's absurd . . . We must look for a way of putting everything right'.

His first move is paradoxical, but is characteristic of a man who has mysteriously been made to fall in love with his wife by another man's love for her before he comes to learn about it. He promptly says that François will be coming to the ball. He goes further and adds: 'François must be with us when we make our entry into the ball. You shall choose a costume for him'—a particular engaging suggestion for the reader!

Mahaut is in bed. Her husband is about to withdraw from her bedroom:

> Framed in the doorway, Anne was splendid. Was he not performing a superbly frivolous duty when, as he stepped back into the hall, he employed unconsciously, with a regal movement of his head, the phrase dear to hypnotists:
> 'And now, Mahaut, go to sleep! *Je le veux*'.

The lordly attitude, the contrast between a 'superbly frivolous duty' and a 'regal movement of his head' are a final comment on the world in which we have been living and make a perfect ending with our feeling of the curtain coming down.

It remains to add that though there has been no suggestion that *Le Bal du comte d'Orgel* is in any way an unfinished novel, we cannot help speculating out of curiosity about what the protagonists' future would have been. We know that the Comte d'Orgel has belatedly fallen in love with his wife and we know that François and Mahaut would never have committed adultery. The assumption is that the husband and wife would have continued to live together with increased pleasure on the husband's part and probably less on the wife's part, while at most the relations between her and François would have turned into something like an *amitié amoureuse* which might have continued if he had married somebody else. For only if the husband had died could the two chaste lovers have become husband and wife themselves.

It remains to add that there are other factors which invite comparisons with many other French novels. Although the protagonists' deep love for one another, their determination never to 'fall' and their confessions to a parent and a husband naturally have marked resemblances, as already suggested, with *La Princesse de Clèves*, there are marked contrasts with the behaviour of the protagonists, whether married or unmarried, in other novels, including most of those dealt with in the present work. In *Le Paysan parvenu*, as far as it goes, the married protagonist is only saved from adultery by the appearance of an apparent rival when he is visiting a woman who was on the verge of becoming his mistress, but there are falls by both married and unmarried in the novels of Crébillon *fils*, Rousseau, Flaubert and, in spite of the apparent concealment of the ultimate relations, between Meaulnes and Valentine, in Alain-Fournier's. The strongest contrast of all is naturally between Radiguet's two novels which paradoxically is the most important factor in making them into a pair.

I have already mentioned the importance of the expression 'bizarreries du coeur'. We know that it well describes the confusion of the feelings of François and Mahaut. Crébillon *fils*'s 'égarements du coeur et de l'esprit' is a stronger term, but it not only applies to the confusion that overtakes the protagonist of his most important novel; the two terms, even when they are not repeated, clearly apply to all the lovers, whether innocent or guilty, in the novels dealt with in this study, and reflect the fundamental resemblances between heart and mind of all lovers whatever the period and the conditions of the society in which they live.

When we look at Cocteau's contrast between 'roots' and 'flower' in Radiguet's two novels, we see that it is misleading. A careful reading shows that Radiguet's primary concern in both of them was with the 'roots' of being, which makes them a pair. A novel about a violent and illicit love affair ending in tragedy is naturally disturbing. A novel about chaste lovers who do not give in is stimulating or, one might even say, uplifting, considering that most French novelists deal with falls. Our impression that in *Le Bal du comte d'Orgel* we are looking at an elegant 'flower' is naturally strengthened when the chaste lovers are living in a society that, in spite of 'frivolities', is remarkable for its grace and an absence of anything like the 'tyrannical' impulses, which applies even more strongly to Radiguet's world than to Mme de La Fayette's. Our verdict must therefore be that the 'phenomenon' or, as I prefer to call him, the 'infant prodigy', was the author of two of the outstanding psychological novels of his day, and it is sad to think that he was taken away from us at the age of twenty.

BIBLIOGRAPHY

In the absence of a contrary indication, books in English are published in London and books in French in Paris.

The bibliographies of Stendhal and Flaubert are supplementary to those contained in *The Novel in France* and *The Art of French Fiction*.

GENERAL

Brooks, P., *The Novel of Worldliness*. (Crébillon, Marivaux, Laclos, Stendhal). Princetown University Press, 1969, 295 pp.

Charvet, P. E., *A Literary History of France:* Vol. IV, *The Nineteenth Century 1789–1870*. Vol. V, *The Nineteenth and Twentieth Centuries 1870–1940*. Ernest Benn, 1967, 395 and 315 pp.

Clouard, H., *Petite histoire de la littérature française*, Albin Michel, 1965, 332 pp.

Coulet, H., *Le Roman jusqu'à la Révolution*, Armand Colin, 1967–68, Vol. I, 560 pp.; Vol. II, 282 pp.
(Valuable guide.)

Deloffre, F., *La Nouvelle en France à l'âge classique*, Dedier, 1967, 130 pp.

Deloffre, F. (Editor), *Oeuvres complètes de Robert Chasles*, Société d'Édition, 'Les Belles Lettres', two volumes, 3rd ed., 1973, 613 pp.
(Introduction, pp. vii–lxv.)

Friedrich, H., *Drei Klassiker des Franzischen Romans*, Frankfurt am Main: Vittorio Klostermann, 3rd ed., 1960, 163 pp.
(Stendhal, pp. 37–85; Balzac, pp. 86–117; Flaubert, pp. 118–55.)

Goncourt, E., and J., *La Femme au dix-huitième siècle*, Nouvelle édition, Charpentier, 1901, 525 pp.

Levin, H., *The Gates of Horn*, 'A Study of Five French Realists', New York: Oxford University Press, 1963, 554 pp.
(Stendhal, pp. 84–149; Flaubert, pp. 214–304.)

MAURIAC, F., *Trois Grands Hommes devant Dieu,* Editions du Capitole, 1930, 185 pp.
(Rousseau, pp. 55–129; Flaubert, pp. 131–85.)

MAY, G., *Le Dilemme du roman au XVIIIᵉ siècle,* Études sur les rapports du roman et de la critique (1715–1761), New Haven: Yale University Press; Paris: Presses Universitaires de France, 1963, 294 pp.

MYLNE, V., *The Eighteenth-Century French Novel,* 'Techniques of Illusion', Manchester University Press, 1965, 280 pp.

RAIMOND, M., *Le Roman depuis la Révolution,* Armand Colin, 1967, 469 pp.

ROUSSEL, J., *Forme et signification,* José Corti, 2nd. ed., 1964, 200 pp.
(Studies of Marivaux, Rousseau, Flaubert.)
Narcisse romancier, José Corti, 1973, 159 pp.
(Studies of Marivaux, Chasles, Crébillon *fils*.)

MARIVAUX

ARLAND, M., *Marivaux,* Gallimard, 1950, 270 pp.

COULET, H., and GILOT, M., *Marivaux,* 'Un Humanisme expérimental', Librarie Larousse, 1973, 287 pp.

DELOFFRE, F., *Une Préciosité nouvelle: Marivaux et le Marivaudage,* Armand Colin, 2nd ed., 1967, 613 pp.

DESVIGNES-PARENT, L., *Marivaux et l'Angleterre,* Kleinsieck, 1970, 541 pp.

FALVEY, J., 'Psychological analysis and moral ambiguity in the narrative processes of Chasles, Prévost and Marivaux' in *Studies on Voltaire and the Eighteenth Century,* Vol. 94, 1972, pp. 141–58.

GAZAGNE, P., *Marivaux par lui-même* (Écrivains de Toujours, No. 26), Éditions du Seuil, 1954, 192 pp.

GREEN, E. J. H., *Marivaux,* University of Toronto Press, 1965, x + 541 pp.

HECKMAN, J., 'Marianne: The Making of an Author'. MLN, Vol. 86, No. 4, May, 1971, pp. 509–22.

JAMIESON, R. K., *Marivaux,* 'A Study in Sensibility', New York: King's Crown Press, 1941, 202 pp.

LAGRAVE, H., *Marivaux et sa fortune littéraire* (Collection 'Tels qu'en eux-mêmes'), Bordeaux: Saint-Médard-en-Jalles, 1970, 250 pp.

MUHLEMANN, S., *Ombres et lumière dans l'oeuvre de Pierre Carlet de Chamblain de Marivaux*, Berne: Herbert Lang et Cie, S.A., 1970, 116 pp.

ROY, C., *Lire Marivaux* (Collection des Cahiers du Rhône, No. 66), Éditions du Seuil, 1947, 152 pp.

SCHAAD, H., *Le Thême de l'être et du paraître dans l'oeuvre de Marivaux*, Zurich: Juris Druck Verlag, 1969, 164 pp.

SPITZER, L., *Romanische Literaturstudien 1936–1956*, Tübingen: Max Niemeyer Verlag, 1959, 944 pp.
   ('A Propos de la Vie de Marivaux, pp. 248–76.)

CRÉBILLON *FILS*

CHERPACK, C., *An Essay on Crébillon fils*, Durham, North Carolina: Duke University Press, 1962, xvi + 190 pp.

CONROY, P. V., *Crébillon fils: techniques of the novel*, ('Studies on Voltaire and the Eighteenth Century', Vol. XCIX), Banbury (Oxfordshire): The Voltaire Foundation, Thorpe and Manderville House, 1972, 235 pp.

DAY, D. A., 'Crébillon *fils*, ses exils et ses rapports avec l'Angleterre avec deux lettres inédites', *Revue de Littérature Comparée*, Avril–Juin, 1959, pp. 180–91.

ETIEMBLE (Editor), *Les Égarements du coeur et de l'esprit*, Armand Colin, 1961, 219 pp.
   (Excellent introduction, pp. vii–xxxi.)

HENRIOT, E., *Les Livres du second rayon*, Grasset, 1948, 399 pp.
   (Unfavourable view of Crébillon *fils*, pp. 177–201.)

PALACHE, J. G., *Four Novels of the Old Regime*, Jonathan Cape, 1926, xi + 271 pp.
   (Crébillon *fils*, pp. 21–51.)

STURM, E., *Crébillon fils et le libertinage au dix-huitième siècle*, Nizet, 1970, 153 pp.

ROUSSEAU

BOREL, J., *Génie et folie de Jeanne-Jacques Rousseau*, José Corti, 1966, 314 pp.

DEDEYAN, C., *J–J. Rousseau et la sensibilité littéraire*, Société d'Édition et d'Enseignement Supérieur, 1966, 429 pp.

GILSON, E., *Les Idées et les lettres*, Vrin, 1932, 298 pp.
('La Méthode de Wolmar', pp. 275–89.)

LECERTE, J–L., *Rousseau et l'art du roman*, Armand Colin, 1969, 481 pp.

MAY, G., *Rousseau par lui-même* ('Écrivains de Toujours', No. 53), Éditions de Seuil, 1961, 190 pp.

MORNET, D. (Editor), *La Nouvelle Héloïse*, 4 vols, Hachette, 1925.
(Vol. I, 396 pages are devoted to a full-length study of every aspect of Rousseau's novel.)

RAYMOND, M., *Jean-Jacques Rousseau la quête de soi et de la rêverie*, José Corti, 1962, 219 pp.

STAROBINSKI, J., *L'Oeil vivant*, Gallimard, 1961, 262 pp.
('Jean-Jacques Rousseau et le péril de la réflexion', pp. 93–190.)
Jean-Jacques Rousseau: La transparence et l'obstacle, suivi des sept essais sur Rousseau, Gallimard, 1971, 457 pp.

STENDHAL

ADAMS, R. M., *Stendhal: Notes on a Novelist*, The Merlin Press, 1959, 228 pp.

BARDECHE, M., *Stendhal romancier*, Éditions de la Table Ronde, 1947, 473 pp.

BILLY, A., *Ce Cher Stendhal: Récits de sa vie*, Flammarion, 1958, 282 pp.

BROMBERT, V., *Stendhal: Fiction and the Themes of Freedom*, New York: Random House, 1968, 209 pp.
(Excellent and very stimulating.)

BROMBERT, V. (Editor), *Stendhal: A Collection of Critical Essays*, Englewood Cliffs, N.J.: Prentice-Hall, Inc., 1962, xii + 171 pp.

FELMAN, S., *La 'Folie' dans l'oeuvre romanesque de Stendhal*, José Corti, 1971, 253 pp.
(Recommended.)

FRANCINE, M. A., *Stendhal* (Classiques du XIXᵉ siècle), Éditions Universitaires, 1959, 127 pp.

GIDE, A. (Editor), *Lamiel*, 'Roman de Stendhal précédé de En

relisant *Lamiel* par André Gide', (Les Classiques du XIXᵉ), Éditions du Livre Français, 283 pp.
(Introduction, pp. 9–36.)

HEMMINGS, F. W. J., *Stendhal: A Study of his Novels,* Clarendon Press, 1964, 232 pp.
(Recommended.)

IMBERT, H-F., *Les Métamorphoses de la liberté ou Stendhal devant la Restauration et le Risorgimento,* José Corti, 1967, 670 pp.
Stendhal et la tentation janséniste, Geneva: Librarie Droz, 1970, 202 pp.

RICHARDSON, J., *Stendhal,* 'A Biography', Victor Gollancz, 1974, 344, pp.

ROY, C., *Stendhal par lui-même* ('Écrivains de Toujours', No. 2), Éditions du Seuil, 1957, 191 pp.

STRICKLAND, G., *Stendhal: the Education of a Novelist,* Cambridge University Press, 1974, 302 pp.

TILLETT, M., *Stendhal,* 'The Background to the Novels', Oxford University Press, 1971, 157 pp.

TROUT, P., *La Vocation romanesque de Stendhal,* Éditions Universitaires, 1970, 367 pp.

WALTHER, M. S., *La Présence de Stendhal aux Etats-Unis 1818–1970* (Collection Stendhalienne No. 18), Switzerland: Aran, Éditions du Grand Chêne, 1974, 240 pp.

WEBER, J-P., *Stendhal: Les Structures thématiques de l'oeuvre et du destin,* Société d'Édition d'Enseignement Supérieur, 1969, 665 pp.

FLAUBERT

1. Novels

BART, B. F., *Flaubert,* Syracuse University Press, 1967, xiv + 791 pp.

BART, B. F. (Editor), *Madame Bovary and the Critics,* New York: University Press, 1966, 197 pp.

BOPP, L., *Commentaire sur Madame Bovary,* Neuchâtel: La Baconnière, 1951, 551 pp.

BROMBERT, V., *The Novels of Flaubert,* 'A Study of Themes and Techniques', Princetown University Press, 1966, 301 pp.
Flaubert par lui-même ('Écrivains de Toujours', No. 4),

Éditions du Seuil, 1971, 190 pp. (Replaces the earlier work of La Varende, 1951)

(Excellent studies like his work on Stendhal.)

BRUNEAU, J., *Les Débuts littéraires de Gustave Flaubert,* Armand Colin, 1962, 637 pp.

CULLER, J., *Flaubert,* 'The Uses of Uncertainty', Paul Elek, 1974, 264 pp.

DANE, I., *Die Symbolische Gestaltung in der Dichtung Flauberts,* Löningen-i-Oldburg: Friedrich von Schmücker, 1933, 118 pp.

DANGER, P., *Sensations et objets dans le roman de Flaubert,* Armand Colin, 1974, 363 pp.

DUQUETTE, J-P., *Flaubert ou l'architecture du vide,* Les Presses de l'Université de Montréal, 1972, 187 pp.

GOTHOT-MERSCHI, C., *La Genèse de Madame Bovary,* José Corti, 1961, 303 pp.

NADEAU, M., *Gustave Flaubert écrivain* ('Lettres Nouvelles'), Denoël, 1969, 335 pp.

RICHARD, J-P., *Littérature et sensation,* Éditions du Seuil, 1954, 287 pp.

('La Création de la forme chez Flaubert', pp. 117–219.)

SHERRINGTON, R. J., *Three Novels by Flaubert,* 'A Study of Techniques', Clarendon Press, 1970, 363 pp.

STARKIE, E., *Flaubert,* 'The Making of a Master', Weidenfeld and Nicolson, 1967, 403 pp.

Flaubert the Master, 'A Critical and Biographical Study, 1856–1880', Weidenfeld and Nicolson, 1971, 390 pp.

TILLETT, M. G., *On Reading Flaubert,* Oxford University Press, 1961, 136 pp.

2. Films

ARNHEIM, R., *Film as Art,* Faber and Faber, 1958, 194 pp.

BERGMAN, I., *Four Screen Plays of Ingmar Bergman,* Translated by Lars Malstrom & David Kushner, Secker and Warburg, 1960, xxii + 330 pp.

(Bergman discusses filmmaking in the introduction.)

BRESSON, R., *The Films of Robert Bresson* (A. Ayfré, R. Durgnat, D. Millar, L. Murray, C. Barr), Studio Vista, 1969, 128 pp.

COCTEAU, J., *Cocteau on the Film*. A conversation recorded by André Fraigneau. Eng. tr., Vera Traill, Dennis Dobson, 1954, 140 pp.

DICKINSON, T., *A Discovery of Cinema*, Oxford University Press, 1971, xi + 164 pp.

EISENSTEIN, S. M., *The Film Sense*, Edited and translated by Jay Leyda, Faber and Faber, 1943, 207 pp.
Film Form, Edited and translated by Jay Leyda, Dennis Dobson, 1951, 279 pp.
Notes of a Film Director, Translated by X. Danko, Lawrence and Wishart, 1959, 208 pp.

HOUSTON, P., *The Contemporary Cinema*, Pelican Books, 1963, 222 pp.

KRACAUER, S., *Nature of Film*, Dennis Dobson, 1961, xix + 364 pp.

LINDGREN, E., *The Art of the Film*, George Allen and Unwin, 4th impression, 1970, 258 pp.

PUDOVKIN, V. I., *Film Technique*, Translated by Ivor Montague, George Newnes, 1933, xviii + 204 pp.

ROBINSON, D., *World Cinema*, 'A Short History', Eyre Methuen, 1973, xi + 440 pp.

ROSENBAUM, J. (Editor), *Rivette Texts and Interviews*, British Film Institute, 1977, 101 pp.

STEPHENSON, R. and DEBRIX, J. R., *The Cinema as Art*, Penguin Books, 1965, 272 pp.

TAYLOR, J. R., *Cinema Eye, Cinema Ear*, 'Some key film-makers in the sixties', Methuen, 1964, 294 pp.

WAGNER, G., *The Novel and the Cinema*, London: The Tantivity Press, 1975, 394 pp.

WOLLEN, P., *Signs and Meaning of the Cinema*, Secker and Warburg, 1972, 176 pp.

ALAIN-FOURNIER

BASTAIRE, J., *Alain-Fournier ou la tentation de l'enfance* ('La Recherche de l'Absolu'), Plon, 1964, 193 pp.

CELLIER, L., *Le Grand Meaulnes ou l'intention manquée* (Étude de Critique et d'Histoire Littéraire, No. 51), Archive de Lettres Modernes, 1962, 45 pp.

DELETTREZ, J-M., *Alain-Fournier et Le Grand Meaulnes,* Émile-Paul, 1954; 1964, 288 pp.

GENUIST, P., *Alain-Fournier face à l'angoisse* (Collection 'Themes et Mythes', No. 9.), M. J. Minard Lettres Modernes, 1965, 184 pp.

GIBSON, R., *The Quest of Alain-Fournier,* Hamish Hamilton, 1953, 295 pp.
The Land Without a Name, 'Alain-Fournier and his World', Paul Elek, 1975, 328 pp.

GIBSON, R. (Editor), *Le Grand Meaulnes,* Harrap, 1968, cxxxvi + 197 pp.
(Important studies).)

GILLET, H., *Alain-Fournier,* Émile-Paul, 1948, 348 pp.

GUIOMAR, M., *Inconscient et imaginaire dans Le Grand Meaulnes,* José Corti, 1964, 255 pp.
(Recommended.)

JÖHR, W., *Alain-Fournier ou le Le Paysage d'une âme,* (Collection 'Les Cahiers du Rhône' No. 61, 'Série Blanche' No. 25), Neuchâtel, Éditions de la Baconnière, 1945, 218 pp.

LOIZE, J., *Alain-Fournier sa vie et Le Grand Meaulnes,* Hachette, 1968, 526 pp.

MACLEAN, M., *Le Jeu Suprême,* 'Structure et thèmes dans "Le Grand Meaulnes"', José Corti, 1973, 187 pp.

PENAULT, P-J., *Alain-Fournier et le pays des merveilles,* 'L'Amitié par le lion', Blainville-sur-Mer, 1965, 174 pp.

RIVIÈRE, I., *Images d'Alain-Fournier,* Émile-Paul, 1947, 341 pp.
Vie et passion d'Alain-Fournier, Monaco: Jaspard, Polus and Cie., 1963, 535 pp.
(Important.)

RIVIÈRE, J. (Editor), Alain-Fournier: *Miracles,* Gallimard, 1924, 220 pp.
(Important introduction by Jacques Rivière, pp. 11–89.)

RIVIÈRE, J. and ALAIN-FOURNIER, *Correspondance 1905–1914,* Gallimard, 18th ed. 1948, Vol. I, 441 pp. Vol. II, 459 pp.

SIMONE, *Sous de nouveaux soleils,* Gallimard, 1957, 300 pp.
(Account of her relations with Alain-Fournier in Part II, 'Histoire d'une amitié et d'un amour'.)

SONET, A., *Le Rêve d'Alain-Fournier,* Belgium: Gembloux, Éditions J. Duculot, S.A., 1965, 163 pp.

SUFFRAN, M., *Alain-Fournier ou Le Mystère limpide* (Collection 'Conversions Célèbres'), Westmael-Charlier, 1969, 247 pp.

ULLMANN, S., *The Images in the French Novel*, Cambridge University Press, 1960, 315 pp.
('The Symbol of the Sea in *Le Grand Meaulnes*', pp. 99–123. Helpful.)

VALLOTON, H., *Alain-Fournier ou La pureté retrouvée*, Nouvelles Éditions Debressé, 1957, 190 pp.

RADIGUET

BOILLAT, G., *Un Maître de 17 ans: Raymond Radiguet*, Neufchatel, Éditions de la Baconnière, 1973, 115 pp.

BORGAL, C., *Radiguet* ('Classiques du XXᵉ Siècle'), Éditions Universitaires, 1969, 125 pp.

COCTEAU, J., *La Difficulté d'Etre*, Paul Morihien 1947, 276 pp.
(Interesting comment on Radiguet, pp. 33–36.)
The Journals of Jean Cocteau, Edited and translated by Wallace Fowlie, Museum Press, 1957, 250 pp.
(Radiguet, pp. 85–88.)

CROSLAND, M., *Raymond Radiguet*, 'A Biographical Study with Selections from His Work', Peter Owen, 1976, 153 pp.

GOESCH, K., *Radiguet*, avec des textes inédits. Paris-Geneva: La Palatine, 1955, 196 pp.

MAURIAC, F., *Mes Grand hommes*, Monaca: Éditions du Rocher, 1949, 255 pp.
(Radiguet, pp. 237–244.)

NOAKES, D., *Raymond Radiguet* ('Poètes d'Aujourd'hui'), Seghers, 1952; 1968, 189 pp.

ODOUARD, N., *Les Années folles de Raymond Radiguet*, Seghers, 1973, 315 pp.
(Informative.)

SACHS, M., *Au Temps du Boeuf sur le Toit*, Nouvelle Revue Critique, 1939, 241 pp.
(Radiguet, pp. 166, 178–79, 183–74.)

SALMON, A., *Souvenirs sans fin*.
Deuxième époque (1908–1920) 1956, 348 pp.
(Radiguet, pp. 42, 43, 44, 45, 46, 47, 304.)
Troisième époque (1920–1940), Gallimard, 1961, 397 pp.
(Radiguet, pp. 67, 147, 201.)

INDEX